YOUNG'S
NIGHT THOUGHTS.

With Life, Critical Dissertation, and Explanatory Notes,

BY THE
REV. GEORGE GILFILLAN.

(A Timeless Classic)

.

ON THE LIFE AND POETIC GENIUS OF
EDWARD YOUNG.

BETWEEN the period of George Herbert, and that of Edward Young, some singular changes had taken place in British poetry as well as in British manners, politics, and religion. There had passed over the land the thunderstorm of the Puritanic Revolt, which had first clouded and then cleared, for a season, the intellectual and moral horizon. The effect of this on poetry was, for such fugitive though felicitous hymns as those of Herbert, to substitute the epic unities and grand choral harmonies of Milton. Then came the Restoration—the Apotheosis of falsehood; including in that term false principles, false politics, and false taste. Britain became the degraded slave of France, at once in laws and in literature. Dryden, indeed, maintained, in some measure, the character and the taste of his nation, but he stood almost alone. To him succeeded Addison and Pope, both gifted but both timid men, whose genius, great as it was, never, or rarely, ventured on original and daring flights, and who seemed always to be haunted by the fear of French criticism. Pope, especially, lent all his influence to confirm and seal the power of a foreign code of literary laws; and so general and so deep was the submission, that it is to us one of the strongest proofs of Edward Young's genius, that he ventured, in that polished but powerless era, to uplift a native voice of song, and not to uplift it in vain; for, if he did not absolutely make a revolution, or found a school, he yet established himself, and left his poetry as a glorious precedent to all who should afterwards be so hardy as to "go and do likewise."

Edward Young was born in June 1681 (according to some, two years earlier), in the village of Upham, Hampshire. His father was rector of the parish, and is represented as a man of great learning and abilities. He was the author of some volumes of sermons, and, on account of their merit, and through the patronage of Lord Bradford, he was appointed chaplain to King William, and Dean of Salisbury. He died in 1705, in the sixty-third year of his age, and Bishop Burnet, the Sunday after his decease, pronounced a glowing panegyric on his character, in a funeral sermon delivered in the Cathedral.

Edward was sent to Winchester School, and thence to Oxford, where he obtained a law fellowship in All-Souls College, and afterwards took successively the degrees of Bachelor and Doctor of Civil Law, besides obtaining a fellowship in 1706. When the Codrington Library was founded, he was appointed to deliver the Latin oration. It was published, but met with a frigid reception, being full of conceits and puerilities, and the author wisely omitted it from his collected works. Little else is known of his career at College. He is said to have blended fits of study with frequent dissipation. When he relaxed, it was in the company of the infamous Duke of Wharton, who patronised, corrupted, and laughed at him. When he studied, he would shut his windows, create around him an artificial night, and make it more hideous by piling up skulls, cross-bones, and instruments of death in his room. His talent was then as well known as his eccentricity. Tindal the

1

sceptic bore a striking testimony to this when he said, "The other boys I can always answer, because I always know where they have their arguments, which I have read a hundred times; but that fellow Young is continually pestering me with something of his own."

He seems to have been nearly thirty ere he began to tune that lyre which was afterwards to thrill with vibrations of song so powerful and melodious. His first choice of a subject was characteristic of the lofty and ambitious tone of his genius: it was, "The Last Day." This poem was written in 1710, although not given to the world till 1713. He had previously, in 1712, published an epistle to Lord Lansdown, which displayed little of his peculiar power, but was at once feeble and pretentious. Young became afterwards heartily ashamed of it. In the same year that "The Last Day" appeared, he prefixed to Addison's "Cato" a copy of verses of no great merit. Shortly after, he issued a poem entitled, "The Force of Religion; or, Vanquished Love:" it was founded on the story of Lady Jane Grey and her husband, and was ushered in by a flaming dedication to the Countess of Salisbury. On the death of the Queen, in 1714, he published a panegyric in verse on her memory, and inscribed it to Addison. In these days flattery to princes and nobles was a commodity almost essential to poetry—a tawdry court dress which every poet was obliged to put on for the nonce; and not even Dryden has excelled Young in the violent unlikeness and unsparing incense of his adulations. It is satisfactory to remember that, on cool reflection, he cancelled the most of those unworthy effusions; although he continued to the last very much of a courtier, as the dedications to the "Night Thoughts" sufficiently prove. He is supposed about the year 1717 to have visited Ireland in company with Wharton.

In 1719 his tragedy of "Busiris" appeared on the stage, and had considerable success. He sold the copyright afterwards to B. Lintot, for £84, which, for a first play by an author previously unknown, was thought a large sum. "Busiris" is a play of that solemnly pompous and intensely artificial school, the race of which has been long since gathered to its fathers. It is conceived and written in Ercles' vein; and Nat Lee himself, in his wild ranting plays, has scarcely surpassed the torrents of bombastic nonsense which issue from the lips of Myron. Immediately after "Busiris" he published his Paraphrase on part of the Book of Job, a production scarcely worthy either of Young or of the sublime original. The descriptions in that grandest of all poems, which are so rich and massive as to press almost on the sense, are more fairly represented in our common prose translation than in the poetical paraphrase of Young. We are far, however, from being opposed, with some critics, to the principle of paraphrasing Scripture. We admire to enthusiasm many of the Scottish paraphrases, some of Byron's and Moore's Hebrew Melodies, and Croly's *Scenes from Scripture*; and should like to see all the poetry of the Bible versified by some competent hand.

In 1721 appeared "The Revenge," by far the most powerful of his tragedies. Its great fault lies in its likeness to Othello: its great praise is, that, though it imitates and challenges comparison with that Shakspearean masterpiece, it has not been utterly sunk and eclipsed before it. As a play, we think it decidedly second-rate; the plot is not artistically managed, and the means by which jealousy is excited in the mind of Alonzo, are a very poor and shabby copy of those in Shakspeare. Zanga has been called a "vulgar caricature of Iago;" he is so in part, perhaps, but Young has abated the vulgarity of the imitation by endowing his hero with a wild and native vein of poetry. Iago is a subtler, colder fiend than Zanga, and indulges more in sneers and in smut than in declamation. Zanga's speeches exhaust the rhetoric of revenge. Iago has nothing but intellect, wit, and malignity. Zanga has an imagination worthy of the hot and lion-peopled land of his birth. Iago, after his detection, sinks into obstinate silence; he stiffens into the statue of a demon. Zanga dies, using lofty imagery.

Indeed, "The Revenge" owes all its interest to the flames of poetic genius which burst out at every pore of its otherwise coarse and copied structure. It was dedicated to Wharton, with whom Young continued to be intimate; whom he taught to speak good Latin *in the space of six weeks*; and who lent him money to reimburse him for the expenses of an unsuccessful attempt to get into Parliament. This was in 1721; the place was Cirencester. The election, however, was contested, and fortunately, perhaps, both for Young and the world, he was unsuccessful. Had he gained the seat, he had very probably,

> "Though born for the universe, narrow'd his mind,
> And to party given up what was meant for mankind;"

and what comparison between a series of eloquent, forgotten speeches, and the starry, ever-burning splendours of the "Night Thoughts"?

His disappointment in this attempt, coupled, probably, with remorse for the follies and vices of a misspent youth, seems to have soured Young, and ripened him to the point when satire becomes the unavoidable expression of the irritated yet unsubdued spirit. In 1725 appeared the first part of his "Universal Passion;" the rest came out in successive satires between that and 1728, when they were collected and published, along with a somewhat querulous preface, in which he hints that he had not found poetry very favourable to preferment. He gained, however, £3000 by these poems, of which, according to Spence, £2000 was contributed by the Duke of Grafton, who did not, however, regret the price. His inscriptions of the several satires were, as usual at the time, stuffed with fulsome praise of such men as Dorset, Dodington, Campton, and Sir Robert Walpole, all of whom appreciated and rewarded the compliments. We reserve our criticism on these remarkable productions till afterwards, noticing only at present, that they were published *before* the satires of Pope, and that they became instantly popular.

As if to propitiate the Nemesis, who always stands behind the chariot of the popular writer, Young next issued two of the poorest of all his unequal productions. The first of these, entitled "The Instalment," was addressed to Sir Robert Walpole, and is, perhaps, although the word be a wide one, the

3

most nonsensical and trashy *lie in verse* ever addressed to a prime minister. The second is an "Ode to Ocean," a compound of doggrel and stilted dulness—which, indeed, any sailor of education might have composed, if "half-seas-over."

At length, sick of dissipation, of the stage, of bad odes, and good satires, Young determined to become wise, and enter into orders. An irresistible current had long been carrying him on, with many a convulsive recalcitration on his part, to this determination. That great intellect and heart, over which, already, the shadow of the "Night Thoughts" was beginning to gather, could not be satisfied with the society of "peers, poets," and demireps; with the applause of sweltering crowds collected in theatres; or with the ebullitions of its own giant spleen, in the shape of epigrammatic satires. The world, which once seemed to his eye so fresh and fair, had withered gradually to a skeleton, with sockets for eyes, with eternal baldness for hair, with a "stench instead of a sweet savour, and burning instead of beauty." He resolved to proclaim the particulars of this painful yet blessed disenchantment to the ends of the earth, and to all classes of mankind. And for this purpose, he first of all mounted the pulpit, and then began to wield what was even then the mightier engine of the press. He was no novice when he entered the ministry. Would that we had more who, like Young, do not go up by a mechanical ladder, and the mere force of custom, to the pulpit, but who come down upon it from long and vain wanderings elsewhere, and with a conviction, as the result of mature experience, that God there still desires to dwell, and that it constitutes even yet a pinnacle of prospect, and power, and promise! Thus came Herbert, and Chalmers, and Foster, to their real work as ministers of the gospel. It is not a boy, but a Boanerges-ministry that introduces the Word with most effect to a gainsaying world. Young was full forty-seven—mature in years, in acquirements, in experience, and in reputation—when he began to publish the "News that it is well." Like the eminent men we have just mentioned, and like others whom we might mention, his motives in entering the Church have been calumniated. He has been compared to a lady disappointed in love, taking the veil; and, rather inconsistently with this figure, to a sated sensualist becoming an anchorite. How can both be true? If Young was disappointed, how could he be sated? and if sated, how could he be chagrined by the want of satisfaction? The fact is, that such men as Young, Chalmers, Herbert, and Foster, are altogether superior to common standards of judgment, and must be tried by their peers. All had their own share of the disgusts and dissatisfactions connected with life, and all felt them keenly. But all had a deeper reason still—a reason, we grant, probably stirred by circumstances into action, for renouncing the empty arena of this world's honours and wealth, and devoting themselves to a higher and nobler purpose. They all saw into the hollowness of society, into the misery of the human heart; and felt that the gospel alone could fill that aching void, and satisfy those dreary cravings. Hence, Herbert quitted the pleasures of a court; Chalmers dropped his air-pump and his telescope; Foster resigned his philosophic speculations; and Young shook off the blandishments of peers, and forgot the claps of multitudes, to proclaim the glad tidings to perishing sinners; and verily all, in different measures, had their reward.

In April 1728 he was appointed chaplain to George II. His tragedy, "The Brothers," which had been in rehearsal, was prudently withdrawn. It is a play superior to "Busiris," but very much inferior to "The Revenge." Full of passion and poetry, of startling scenes, and vivid images, its subject is unpleasing, and the various perplexities of the plot are not skilfully disentangled.

In the same year he published "A True Estimate of Human Life," written with force and ingenuity; and a long and very loyal sermon, preached before the House of Commons, on the Martyrdom of Charles I. It was entitled, "An Apology for Princes; or, the Reverence due to Governments."

Hitherto Young had lived on the proceeds of his fellowship, and on presents from Wharton, who, at his death, too, left him a pension. He became now, however, very naturally anxious for promotion in that new sphere on which he had entered, and was compelled, *proh pudor*! to lay his case before Mrs Howard, the favourite mistress of George II.—that identical "good Howard," who figures so curiously in the famous scene between Jeanie Deans and Queen Caroline. The fact of the application, as well as the terms of the letter he wrote her, renders this the most humiliating incident in all Young's history. In 1730, he published "Imperium Pelagi," another naval lyric, as bad and much longer than his "Ode to Ocean." In the same year he wrote an epistle to Pope, which resembles a coarser and more careless production of the little man of Twickenham.

In July 1730, Young was presented by his college to the rectory of Welwyn in Hertfordshire. We refer our readers, for various delightful speculations and anecdotes about his residence and labours there, to Bulwer's *Student*. He was a powerful preacher. His sermons seem to have been striking in thought, rich in image, intensely practical in tendency, and were delivered with great animation and effect. It is told, that on one occasion, while preaching at St James's before the Court and His Majesty, on some subject of transcendent importance, and not being able to command the attention or awaken the feelings of his audience, he at length threw himself back into the pulpit, and burst into tears. That was itself a sermon! The figure of this weeping Titan, who could have rent rocks and severed mountains, but who had failed in breaking the hearts of any of his courtly hearers, is one of the most affecting in the annals of pulpit oratory. Alas! what preacher who has ever aimed at Young's object, has not been at times tempted to assume Young's attitude, and to shed Young's bitter and burning tears? "Who hath believed our report, and to whom is the arm of the Lord revealed?"

In 1731, Young, at the mature age of fifty, married the Lady Elizabeth Lee, daughter of the Earl of Lichfield, and widow of Colonel Lee. This marriage sprung out of his father's acquaintance with Lady Ann Wharton, who was co-heiress of Sir Henry Lee of Ditchley in Oxfordshire, and seems to have been very happy. He next published another of those stupid odes by which he seemed predestined to disgrace his genius, entitled "A Sea Piece." It was as though Milton had tried to write Anacreontics. A few years afterwards appeared "The Foreign Address, or the Best Argument for Peace," occasioned by the posture of affairs in which the British fleet was then placed, and written in the character of a sailor. It is a mere tissue of sounding verbiage—or, as Hamlet hath it, "Words, words, words." About this time Young met with Voltaire, who, according to the story, was ridiculing Milton's allegory of "Death and Sin," when our hero struck in with the extempore epigram:—

> "Thou art so witty, profligate, and thin,
> That thou thyself art Milton, Death, and Sin."

We cannot see very much wit in this epigram, even in that best shape which we have now given it; but it was not inappropriate to the lean denier, who sought to empty everything of the important element—its God; to leave the universe, like himself, a grinning skeleton, and to smile in ghastly sympathy over the completed ruin. We fancy we see the two gifted men, the one the representative of the scepticism of France, the other, of the belief of England, meeting and conversing together. Voltaire is not much in advance of thirty; Young is fifty, and more. Voltaire's face is worn with premature thought and inordinate laughter; Young's, though older, bears a warmer and more sanguine flush. Voltaire has the insincerest of smiles playing constantly over his face like the light of an aurora borealis; Young's countenance is grave, settled, open, and serene, as the radiance of an autumn sunset. In Voltaire's eye you see the future "Candide" laughing down in its depths, while on Young's brow lies the dim and magnificent promise of the "Night Thoughts." After meeting, talking, bowing, wondering, and recoiling, they part for ever; Voltaire sighing through smiles as he thinks of the "misled giant of Religion;" and Young smiling through sighs as he thinks of the "wondrous and well-nigh human ape of Infidelity."

By his wife Young had one son, Frederick. He does not seem to have been a particularly well-behaved youth; indeed, his father for some time before his death refused to see him, although he ultimately sent him his forgiveness, and made him his heir. But no son of illustrious father has ever had harder measure dealt him. It has been generally supposed that he was the Lorenzo of the "Night Thoughts," a poem published when Frederick was only eight years of age, and when he could scarcely have even thought of committing those crimes of scepticism and reckless self-gratification with which Young charges his imaginary or half-real hero.

The Poet's life, during the first ten years of his rectorship at Welwyn, flowed on in an even tenor. He was regular in his conduct, happy in his family, diligent in his pastoral duties, and easy in his fortune. His preaching was popular and useful. His studies were principally connected with his own profession, and yielded him a growing satisfaction. An anonymous writer in the *Gentleman's Magazine* for 1782, who seems to have been intimate with him, thus describes him:—"The dignity of a great and good mind appeared in all his actions, and in all his words. He conversed on religious subjects with the cheerfulness of virtue; his piety was undebased by gloom or enthusiasm; he was regular in the performance of all its duties, both in public and in private. In his domestic character he was amiable as he was venerable in the Christian. His politeness was such as I never saw equalled: it was invariable to his superiors in rank; to his equals and to his inferiors it differed only in degrees of elegance. I never heard him speak with roughness to the meanest servant. In conversation upon lively subjects he had a brilliancy of wit which was peculiar to himself; I know not how to describe it but by saying that it was both heightened and softened by the amiable qualities of his soul. I have seen him ill and in pain, yet the serenity of his mind remained unruffled. I never heard a peevish expression fall from his lips." Few of his brilliancies are preserved, since, unfortunately, he had no Boswell attached to his heels. But one or two of the sayings that have floated down to us are singularly characteristic. On one very stormy night Young went out to his garden, and remained some time. When he returned, one expressed wonder why he had stayed so long in such an evening. "Oh," he replied, "it is a very fine night; *the Lord is abroad*." He was very fond of a garden, and inscribed on the wall of his summer-house the words, *Ambulantes in horto audiebant vocem Dei* (Walking in the garden, they heard the voice of God). He had also erected a dial with the inscription, *Eheu fugaces!* which, he said with a smile to Mr Langton, "was sadly verified, for by the next morning my dial had been carried off." Though sometimes melancholy, he was disposed to encourage mirth in others, and established an assembly and bowling-green in his parish.

And had this been all—had Young continued to pursue such an even, equable course—he had been by this time well-nigh forgotten; for we do not think that either his satires or plays would of themselves have preserved his name. But it was decreed that grief should co-operate with disappointment in unfolding the full riches of his mind. Antæus was strongest when he touched the ground. Job was never so eloquent till he was prostrated on his dunghill. And, in order to be able to write the "Night Thoughts," Young must be plunged in the deepest gloom of affliction— "Thrice flew the shaft, and thrice his peace was slain." In 1736, a daughter of his wife, by a former husband, died. This was Mrs Temple—the Narcissa of his great poem. Her disease was a lingering one. Young accompanied her to Lyons, where she died, and where her remains were brutally denied sepulture, as the dust of a Protestant. Her husband, Mr Temple, or Philander, died four years later; and in 1741, Young's wife, or Lucia, also expired. He now felt himself alone, and blasted in his solitude. But his grief did not sink into sullen inactivity. He made it oracular, and distilled his tears into song. The "Night Thoughts" were immediately commenced, and published between 1742 and 1744. This marvellous poem was all composed either at night, or when riding on horseback—an exercise, by the way, which gives a sense of mastery and confidence, stirs the blood, elevates the animal spirits, and has been felt by many to be eminently favourable to thought and mental composition. It inspired, we know, such men as Burns, Byron, Shelley, and Delta. We love to think of Young riding through the green lanes of his parish, and cooing out to himself his plaintive minstrelsies. We love better still to watch his lonely lamp shining at midnight, like a star, through the darkness, and seeming to answer the far signal of those mightier luminaries which are burning above in the Great Bear and Orion—the poet the while now dipping his pen to indite his ardent immortalities—now leaning his head on his widowed arm, and surrendering himself to paroxysms of uncontrollable anguish—and now looking out upon the Night as the "Lord is abroad" on the wings of the tempest, or as He is silently shining out his name in suns and galaxies—those unwearied "Watchers" and unbaptized "Holy Ones."

In 1745, Young wrote "Reflections on the Public Situation of the Kingdom"—a production which made no impression at the time, and is now entirely forgotten. He did not include it in the collection of his works. In 1753, the tragedy of "The Brothers," which had lain past for thirty years, was produced on the stage. Young gave the profits of the play, and several hundreds from his own pocket, amounting to a thousand pounds in all, to the Society for the Propagation of the Gospel—an act which surely balances the stories usually told of his love of money and thirst for preferment.

His next work was, "The Centaur not Fabulous, in Six Letters to a Friend." Its subjects were, the infidelity and licentiousness of that age. It is a pity that this book has fallen into oblivion, as it is a very rich and powerful piece of writing. It is full of clear, sharp, sententious truth. Its style palpitates with energy, and glitters with poetic image. We wish we saw it reprinted in a cheap form; for, although infidelity and pleasure have both materially changed their phases, there is much in Young's little work that has an imperishable application, and that would be even yet eminently useful. The character of Altamont is supposed to represent Lord Euston—a nobleman notorious for his vices. The age in which Young's lot was cast was characterised by a low, sneering scepticism, and his earnest and awful letters were treated with ridicule. Many pronounced him mad, others whispered about dotage. *Now*, the book seems replete with wisdom, and burning almost with prophetic fire.

Young, in fact, was not generally appreciated during his lifetime. Tried by the Boileau and Pope standard, his writings were pronounced turgid, strained, and extravagant. Even Warburton, who should have known better, passed a severe judgment on the "Night Thoughts." He had, however, his warm admirers, prominent among whom was the amiable and learned Joseph Warton. He dedicated to Young his "Essay on Pope"—an essay containing the first sober and discriminating estimate of that most artificial of true poets, and with the opinions expressed in which Young is supposed to have coincided; for, although he admired, and too often imitated, Pope's brilliant point and antithesis, he was aware of far higher models, and found Homer, Milton, and Job far more congenial companions in his studious midnights. In 1758, he published a short and in nowise remarkable sermon, preached before the King at Kensington.

Richardson, the novelist, was one of Young's greatest friends. Their views on moral and religious subjects were identical; and in gravity of tone, and severity of genius, they resembled each other—Richardson being a duller Young, and Young a more elastic and brilliant Richardson. Although both lived in a most depraved age, neither catered to its tastes. To Richardson, Young addressed, in 1759, a letter on Original Composition, which betrays no symptoms of senility, but is full of vigorous and striking remark. In 1762, when upwards of eighty, he wrote his last and worst poem. It is entitled "Resignation," and requires, on the part of the reader, considerable exercise of that grace. It has very little of Young's peculiar power, and is chiefly filled with weak and toothless abuse of his old acquaintance Voltaire. It was written, it appears, at the instance of Mrs Boscawen—the widow of the Admiral—who, having found consolation from the "Night Thoughts," visited Young, and was still more captivated by his conversation.

During the latter years of his life, he is said to have fallen too much under the dominion of his housekeeper, Mrs Hallowes, the widow of a clergyman, who is reported to have ruled him with a rod of iron. Ere his death he revised his printed works, and gave charges in his will that all his MSS. should be burned. He applied, when past eighty, to Archbishop Secker for promotion, and was appointed Clerk of the Closet to the Princess-Dowager of Wales. In April 1765, at the age of eighty-four, he breathed his last. He had been previously unable to perform duty for three or four years, but retained his faculties to the last. He left his property principally to his son, who was found by Johnson and Boswell, in 1781, residing at Welwyn, and cherishing the memory of his father.

Young was unquestionably a neglected man. Out of all sight the greatest genius then connected with the ministry of the Church of England, he never mounted one step higher than the rectorship his own college had conferred on him. Many reasons have been assigned for this. Some say that it was because he had attached himself to the side of Frederick, Prince of Wales, and had preached an obnoxious sermon at St James's; others, that it was because he had received a pension through Sir Robert Walpole. We think that the real cause lay in the vulgar and senseless prejudice which prevailed then, and in some measure prevails still, against a literary divine, as if he were a hybrid, or "centaur, not fabulous." Let us not blame that age so long as we remember the burning shame reflected on ours by the fact that the gifted and high-charactered author of *Salathiel*, and *Paris* in 1815, is still only the rector of St Stephen's, Walbrook, while many younger men, who in comparison with him are of little mark, have reached the episcopal bench. Probably Young felt himself consoled for his bad success, by the knowledge that his name and great poem had travelled to foreign lands, and that Madame Klopstock was wondering—good, simple soul!—that her husband's idol and her own, had not been made Archbishop of Canterbury.

Very little beyond what we have mentioned has been left on record about his private habits and manners. It was his custom, when well pleased with a passage in the course of his reading, to double down the leaf—when particularly gratified, to mark it by two folds; and some favourite works, such as *The Rambler*, had so many of these marks of approbation that they would not shut. On one occasion, in replying to Tonson and Lintot, who were both candidates for printing one of his works, he misdirected the letters; and when Lintot opened his, he found it begun—"Bernard Lintot is so great a scoundrel," &c. Young was proverbial for absence of mind, and sometimes forgot whether he had dined or not. Yet in Welwyn his mode of life was rather systematic. He rose early, made his domestics join him in morning prayer, read little, ate and drank moderately, walked much in his churchyard, and, in general, retired to rest punctually at eight evening. His son told Dr Johnson that he was cheerful in company, but gloomy when alone, and that he never fully recovered his spirits after his wife's death. Mr Jones, his curate, has confirmed this statement, although the gossiping and heartless tone of his letters about such a man cannot be too strongly condemned. Young was subject to fits of inspiration, which stupid people confounded with madness. At times his poetry rushed upon him like a whirlwind, and caught him up

"Like swift Ezekiel, by his lock of hair"—

and when he came down he seemed weak, panting, and powerless. Mrs Boscawen and others describe his conversation as still more remarkable than his writings, although occasionally disfigured by conceits and bad puns.

We come now to speak of his genius, especially as manifested in the "Night Thoughts." The subject of this wonderful strain was one which, in its novelty, dignity, and depth, challenged the very highest exercise of the very highest faculties; and had Young risen to the full height of his great argument, he had become the greatest of all poets. This we by no means affirm he did; but we do assert, that many of the aspects of his magnificent theme have been fully and eloquently expressed by him, and that some of his passages are unsurpassed in the language of men.

The poem demands a brief critical consideration as to its *season*, its *argument*, its *imagery*, its *style*, its *versification*, its *comparative place* and *merit*, and, lastly, the *genius* of its author. First, of its *season*—the Night—and the use to which he turns it. Night had never before found a worthy laureate. Its profound silence, as if it were listening to catch the accents of some supernal voice—the shadowy grandeur and mysterious newness it gives to objects on the earth—the divine hues into which its moon discolours all things—the deep sleep which then falleth upon men, and changes the world into one hushed grave—the supernatural shapes and mystic sounds which have been supposed to walk in its darkness, or to echo through its depths—the voices scarce less solemn, which often break its silence, of howling winds, and wailing rivers, and shrieking tempests, and groaning thunders, and the wild cries of human misery and despair—and last and highest, its withdrawal of the bright mist and mantle of day from the starry universe, and the pomp with which it unrols and exhibits its "great map" of suns and systems—its silvery satellites—its meek planets, each shining in its own degree of reflected splendour—its oceans of original and ever-burning fire called suns—its comets, those serpents of the sky, trailing their vast volumes of deadly glory through the shuddering system—its fantastic and magnificent shapes and collocations of stars, the constellations—its firmaments rising above firmaments, like rounds in a ladder, at the top of which is the throne of God—and those two awful arms into which its Milky Way diverges, and which seem uplifted to heaven in silent prayer, or in some deep and dread protest,—all these elements of interest and grandeur had existed from the beginning of the world in Night, and yet had never, till Young arose, awakened any consecutive and lofty strain of poetic adoration. Many beautiful and many sublime sentiments had been uttered by poets about particular features of Night, but there had been no attempt to represent it as a whole. There were many single thoughts, but no large and sounding Hymn. The views of the Pagan poets about astronomy were, of course, warped by the absurd systems of their day; and this served to damp their fire, and to render their poetic tributes rather fantastic than truly powerful. Even Dante and Milton are somewhat embarrassed by the Ptolemaic system, although it proves the strength of their genius that they have extracted so much poetry from it. But before Young arose,

> "Nature and nature's laws lay hid in night;
> God said, Let Newton be, and all was light;"

and he has set the Newtonian system to his own martial music.

We are far from contending that Young has exhausted the poetry of the theme. Since his time the telescopes of Herschell and Lord Rosse have been turned to the skies, and have greatly extended the size and splendour of that vast midnight Apparition—the starry scheme. Our recent poets have availed themselves of these discoveries, as witness the eloquent rhapsodies about the stars by Bailey, A. Smith, and Bigg. And there is even yet room for another great poem on the subject, entitled "Night," were the author come. But Young deserves praise for the following things:—

1st, He has nobly sung the magnitude and unutterable glory of the starry hosts. His soul kindles, triumphs, exults under the midnight canopy. As the Tartar horse when led forth from his stable to the free steppes and free firmament of the desert, bounds, prances, and caracoles for joy, so does Young, in the last part of his poem. Escaped from dark and mournful contemplations on Man, Death, Infidelity, and Earth's "melancholy map," he sees the stars like bright milestones on the way to heaven, and his spirit is glad within him, and tumultuous is the grandeur, and fierce and rapid the torrent, of his song.

2dly, He has brought out, better than any other poet, the religion of the stars. "Night," says Isaac Taylor, "has three daughters, Atheism, Superstition, and Religion." Following out this fine thought, we see Atheism looking up with impudent eye, brazen brow, and naked figure, to the midnight sky, as if it were only a huge toy-shop of glittering gew-gaws; Superstition shrouding herself in a black mantle, and falling down prostrate and trembling before these innumerable fires, as if they were the eyes of an infinite enemy; while Religion turns aloft her humble, yet fearless form, her tear-trembling yet radiant visage, and murmurs, "My Father made them all." Young, we need scarcely say, finds in the nocturnal heavens lessons neither of Atheism nor of Superstition, but of Religion, and reads in the face of Old Night her divine origin, the witness she bears to the existence of God, her dependence upon her Author, and her subordination to His purposes. He had magnified, as Newton himself could not so eloquently have done, the extent of the universe; and yet his loyalty to Scripture compels him to intimate that this system, so far from being God, or infinite, or, strictly speaking, Divine, is to perish and pass away. One look from the angry Judge, one uplifting of His rod, and its voluminous waves of glory, like another Red Sea, are to be dried up, that the people of God may pass through and enter on the land of the real Immortality, the "inheritance incorruptible, undefiled, and that shall never fade away." We refer our readers to that most eloquent picture, near the beginning of the Ninth Night, of the Last Day. We once heard a lecturer on chemistry close a superb description of the material universe, with the words, "And it is to shine on forever." We thought of the words of Peter, "All these things shall be dissolved." And then we fancied an invisible animalcule inhabiting one of the mountain peaks of a furnace, looking abroad from one of its surging spires, and saying, "This wondrous blaze is to burn for ever," and yet, ere a few hours have passed, the flame is sunk in ashes, and the animalcule is gone. So the Heavens shall pass away with a great noise. They shall perish, but Thou God remainest; nay, thou Man, too, art destined to survive this splendid nursery, and to enter on new Heavens and a new Earth!

The argument of the "Night Thoughts" may be stated in general to be as follows:—It is to shew the vanity of man as mortal; to inculcate the lowness, misery, and madness of the sensual life; to prove the superiority of the Christian to the man of the world, both in life and in death, and the worthlessness of merely human friendship; to argue, from nature and reason, the truth of man's immortality; to shew the reasonableness of religion, and to inculcate the necessity of a divine revelation, and of a propitiatory sacrifice. That this argument is always steadily pursued, or logically pled, we do not pretend. It has its flaws;—we particularly demur to many of its proofs of the immortality of the soul, which seem to us very feeble and unsatisfactory; but, taking it as a whole, it is unanswerable and overwhelming. Its links are of red-hot iron; its appeals to the conscience are irresistible; and he who can read it with indifference, or rise from it unimpressed and unawed, must be either something worse or something less than man. It needs not to be surrounded by panegyrics. Convinced, purified, elevated, saved Souls, are the gems in its crown. We are inclined to believe that, in this aspect, the "Night Thoughts" has effected more practical good than the "Paradise Lost." The latter is a splendid picture; the former a searching, powerful sermon. Now, although pictures with a strong moral contained in them have often done much good, they want the point, emphasis, and effect of great sermons. You may gaze long enough at Milton with no feeling besides admiration of his genius; but in every page Young is grappling with your conscience, and saying, "Don't look at me, but look to yourself." Foster, one of the greatest of our practical reasoners on religion, has been much indebted to Young, whom he resembled also in the sombre grandeur of his genius.

Young's imagery is distinguished by its richness, originality, and exceeding boldness. It was verily a new thing in that timid and conventional age. Like the imagery of all highest poets, it is selected alike from low and from lofty objects, from the gay and the gloomy, from stars and dunghills. His mind moves along through the poem like a great wheel, now descending and now ascending, easy to criticise, but impossible to resist. You may question the taste of many of his figures, such as that of the Sun—

"Rude drunkard, rising rosy from the main;"

or when he speaks of God as the "Great Philanthropist;" or calls the moon "the Portland of the skies;" but you always feel yourself in contact with a new, native, overflowing mind—with a mind which has read nature through man, and man through nature. There is to Young's genius nothing common or unclean in the material universe. *All* points up to God, and looks round significantly to man. His imagination has no limits, and, when he is thoroughly roused, like the war-horse of Job, the "glory of his nostrils is terrible;" it is the fury of power, the revel of conscious wealth, the "prancing of a mighty one;" not the dance of mere fancy, but the earnestness and energy of one treading a winepress alone. In proof of this, we appeal to his splendid passages on the miserable state of Man, on Dreams, on Procrastination, to one half of his defence of Immortality, and to the whole of his descant on the Stars. This everyone feels is power—barbarous power, if you will—savage, mismanaged power, if you please to call it so; but power that moves, agitates, overwhelms, hurries you away like an infant on the stream of a cataract.

His diction is, on the whole, a worthy medium to his thought. It has been somewhat spoiled by intimacy with Pope's writings, and is often vitiated with antithesis, an excess in which was the mode of the day. Now and then, too, he is coarse and violent, to vulgarity, in his expressions. But whenever he forgets Pope, and remembers Milton—or, still more, when he becomes swallowed up in the magnitude of his theme—his language is easy, powerful, and magnificent. It never, as Mitford asserts, is unsupported by a "corresponding grandeur of thought." There is more thought in Young's poem—more sharp, clear, original reflection—more of that matter which leaves stings behind it—more moral sublimity—than in any poem which has appeared since in Britain. Mitford says, that "every image is amplified to the utmost." Some images unquestionably are; but amplification is not a prevailing vice of Young's style—it is, indeed, inconsistent with that pointed intensity which is his general manner; and how comes it, if he be a diffuse and wordy writer, that his pages literally sparkle with maxims, and that, next perhaps to Shakspeare, no poet has been so often quoted? What the same writer means by Young "fatiguing the reader's mind," we can understand; since it is fatiguing to look long at the sun, or to follow the grand parabola of the eagle's flight; but how he should "dissatisfy" the mind of any intelligent and candid reader, is to us extraordinary. It is not true that the work has "a uniformity of subject." Its tone is rather uniform, but its subjects are as varied as they are important. They are—Man—the World—Ambition—Pleasure—Infidelity—Immortality—Death—Judgment—Heaven—Hell—the Stars—Eternity. Mr Mitford compares Young to Seneca; as if a cold collector of stiff maxims, and a poet whose wisdom was set in enthusiasm as in a ring of fire, were proper subjects of comparison. And it is strange how he should introduce the name of Cicero, as if he were not that very master of amplification, and of over-copiousness of expression, which Mitford *imagines* Young to be! "No selection—no discreet and graceful reservation—no experienced taste!"—in other words, he was not Pope or Campbell, but Edward Young—not a middle-sized, neat, and well-dressed citizen, but a hirsute giant—not an elegant *parterre*, but an American forest, bowing only to the old Tempests, and offering up a holocaust of native wealth and glory, not to Man, but to God.

His versification is a more vulnerable point. We grant at once that it is, as a whole, rugged and imperfect, and that, while his single lines are often exceedingly melodious, he rarely reaches, any more than Pope or Johnson, those long and linked swells of sound—

> "Floating, mingling, interweaving,
> Rising, sinking, and receiving
> Each from each, while each is giving
> On to each, and each relieving
> Each, the pails of gold, the living
> Current through the air is heaving"—

which Goëthe has so beautifully, although unintentionally, described in these words, applied by him to the elements of Nature; and which he and Milton, and Spenser, and Coleridge, and Shelley, have so admirably exemplified in their verse. Young's style is too broken and sententious to permit the miracles of melody which are found in some of our poets. Yet he has a few passages which approach even to this high standard. Take the following:—

> "Look nature through, 'tis revolution all;
> All change, no death. Day follows night, and night
> The dying day; stars rise and set and rise;
> Earth takes th' example. See the summer gay,
> With her green chaplet, and ambrosial flowers,
> Droops into pallid autumn; winter gray,
> Horrid with frost, and turbulent with storm,

> Blows autumn, and his golden fruits away;
> Then melts into the spring. Soft spring, with breath
> Favonian, from warm chambers of the south,
> Recalls the first."

Or take the well-known burst which closes the First Night:—

> "The sprightly lark's shrill matin wakes the morn;
> Grief's sharpest thorn hard pressing on my breast,
> I strive, with wakeful melody, to cheer
> The sullen gloom, sweet Philomel! like thee,
> And call the stars to listen: every star
> Is deaf to mine, enamour'd of thy lay.
> Yet be not vain; there are, who thine excel,
> And charm through distant ages: wrapt in shade,
> Prisoner of darkness! to the silent hours
> How often I repeat their rage divine,
> To lull my griefs, and steal my heart from woe!
> I roll their raptures, but not catch their fire,
> Dark, though not blind, like thee, Mæonides!
> Or his, who made Mæonides our own.
> Man, too, he sung; immortal man I sing;
> Oft bursts my song beyond the bounds of life;
> What, now, but immortality, can please?
> O had he press'd his theme, pursued the track
> Which opens out of darkness into day!
> O had he, mounted on his wing of fire,
> Soar'd where I sink, and sung immortal man!
> How had it bless'd mankind, and rescued me!"

The reader will notice how, in this noble passage, the individual sentences and points are all subordinated to the main purpose of the poet, and being subjected to the general stress of the strain, do not detract from, but add to, its musical unity.

The comparative place of the poem, and the genius of the writer, are two subjects which are closely connected, and indeed slide into each other. The "Night Thoughts" must not be named, in interest, finish, sustained sublimity, and artistic completeness, with the "Iliad," the "Divina Commedia," or the "Paradise Lost." It ranks, however, at the top of such a high class of poems as Cowper's Poems, Thomson's "Seasons," Byron's Poems, Blair's "Grave," Pollock's "Course of Time," and a few others not very often criticised now-a-days. Young, however, seems to us to have been capable of even higher things than he has effected in his works. He was one of those prolific, fiery, inexhaustible souls, who never seem nearing a limit, or dreaming of a shallow in their genius; who, often stumbling over precipices or precipitated into pools, rise stronger, and rush on faster, from their misadventures; who, sometimes stopping too long to moralise on fungi and ant-hillocks, are all the better breathed to career through endless forests, and to take Alps and Andes at a flying leap; and who are

> "Ne'er so sure our pleasure to create,
> As when they tread the brink of all we hate."

15

His taste was not equal certainly to his other faculties, and he was guilty of occasional extravagances, and stumbled not unfrequently over the brink of the bathos; but his genius possessed the following qualities:—It was original. He had read much, but he copies little, and never slavishly. His mind looks at everything—at skulls and stars—through a medium of its own. It was subtle as well as native and strong, and in its movements it is broadly based on a vigorous intellect. It was progressive and prophetic in its spirit, and many of our recent speculations or semi-speculations on the relations of man and nature, are to be found in Young—ay, in the mere spray his mind threw off on its way to an ulterior result. Think of this, for instance, and then remember a similar expression in Carlyle:—

> "Man's grief is but his grandeur in disguise;
> And discontent is immortality."

Finally, his genius, with all its compass and daring, was reverent and religious. He gloried in the universe; he swam, as it were, and circled like a strong swimmer, in that starry sea; but he bent before the Cross, and, instead of looking up, looked down, and cried out, "God be merciful to me a sinner."

We commend his masterpiece to readers, partly, indeed, for its power,—a power that has hitherto rather been felt than acknowledged, rather admired in silence than analysed; but principally because, like "The Temple" of Herbert, it is holy ground. The author, amid his elaborate ingenuities, and wilful though minor perversities, never ceases to love and to honour truth; in pursuit of renown, he is never afraid to glory in the Cross of our Lord Jesus Christ; and if his flights of fancy be at times too wild, and if his thoughts be often set to the tune of the tempest, it is a tempest on whose wings, to use his own simple but immortal words, "The Lord is abroad."

THE COMPLAINT:

OR,

NIGHT THOUGHTS.

PREFACE.

As the occasion of this Poem was real, not fictitious; so the method pursued in it was rather imposed by what spontaneously arose in the Author's mind on that occasion, than meditated or designed. Which will appear very probable from the nature of it. For it differs from the common mode of poetry, which is, from long narrations to draw short morals. Here, on the contrary, the narrative is short, and the morality arising from it makes the bulk of the Poem. The reason of it is, that the facts mentioned did naturally pour these moral reflections on the thought of the Writer.

NIGHT FIRST.

ON
LIFE, DEATH, AND IMMORTALITY.

TO THE RIGHT HONOURABLE

ARTHUR ONSLOW, ESQ.,
SPEAKER OF THE HOUSE OF COMMONS.

TIRED Nature's sweet restorer, balmy Sleep!
He, like the world, his ready visit pays
Where Fortune smiles; the wretched he forsakes;
Swift on his downy pinion flies from woe,
And lights on lids unsullied with a tear.
    From short (as usual) and disturb'd repose,
I wake: how happy they, who wake no more!
Yet that were vain, if dreams infest the grave.
I wake, emerging from a sea of dreams
Tumultuous; where my wreck'd desponding thought   10
From wave to wave of fancied misery
At random drove, her helm of reason lost.
Though now restored, 'tis only change of pain,
(A bitter change!) severer for severe:
The day too short for my distress; and night,   15
Even in the zenith of her dark domain,
Is sunshine to the colour of my fate.
    Night, sable goddess! from her ebon throne,
In rayless majesty, now stretches forth
Her leaden sceptre o'er a slumbering world.
Silence, how dead! and darkness, how profound!
Nor eye, nor listening ear, an object finds;
Creation sleeps. 'Tis as the general pulse   23
Of life stood still, and nature made a pause;
An awful pause! prophetic of her end.
And let her prophecy be soon fulfill'd;
Fate! drop the curtain; I can lose no more.
    Silence and darkness: solemn sisters! twins
From ancient Night, who nurse the tender thought
To reason, and on reason build resolve   30
(That column of true majesty in man),
Assist me: I will thank you in the grave;
The grave, your kingdom: there this frame shall fall

A victim sacred to your dreary shrine.
But what are ye?—
    Thou, who didst put to flight
Primeval Silence, when the morning stars,
Exulting, shouted o'er the rising ball;
O Thou, whose word from solid darkness struck
That spark, the sun; strike wisdom from my soul;   40
My soul, which flies to thee, her trust, her treasure,
As misers to their gold, while others rest.
Through this opaque of nature, and of soul,
This double night, transmit one pitying ray,
To lighten, and to cheer. O lead my mind,
(A mind that fain would wander from its woe),
Lead it through various scenes of life and death;
And from each scene the noblest truths inspire.
Nor less inspire my conduct, than my song;   49
Teach my best reason, reason; my best will
Teach rectitude; and fix my firm resolve
Wisdom to wed, and pay her long arrear:
Nor let the phial of thy vengeance, pour'd
On this devoted head, be pour'd in vain.
    The bell strikes one. We take no note of time
But from its loss. To give it then a tongue
Is wise in man. As if an angel spoke,
I feel the solemn sound. If heard aright,
It is the knell of my departed hours:
Where are they? With the years beyond the flood.   60
It is the signal that demands despatch:
How much is to be done? My hopes and fears
Start up alarm'd, and o'er life's narrow verge
Look down—on what? a fathomless abyss;
A dread eternity! how surely mine!
And can eternity belong to me,
Poor pensioner on the bounties of an hour?
    How poor, how rich, how abject, how august,
How complicate, how wonderful, is man!
How passing wonder He who made him such!   70
Who centred in our make such strange extremes!
From different natures marvellously mix'd,
Connexion exquisite of distant worlds!
Distinguish'd link in being's endless chain!
Midway from nothing to the Deity!
A beam ethereal, sullied and absorb'd!
Though sullied and dishonour'd, still divine!
Dim miniature of greatness absolute!
An heir of glory! a frail child of dust!

Helpless immortal! insect infinite! 80
A worm! a god!—I tremble at myself,
And in myself am lost! At home a stranger,
Thought wanders up and down, surprised, aghast, 83
And wondering at her own: how reason reels!
O what a miracle to man is man,
Triumphantly distress'd! what joy, what dread!
Alternately transported and alarm'd!
What can preserve my life, or what destroy?
An angel's arm can't snatch me from the grave;
Legions of angels can't confine me there. 90
    'Tis past conjecture; all things rise in proof:
While o'er my limbs sleep's soft dominion spread,
What though my soul fantastic measures trod
O'er fairy fields; or mourn'd along the gloom
Of pathless woods; or down the craggy steep
Hurl'd headlong, swam with pain the mantled pool;
Or scaled the cliff; or danced on hollow winds,
With antic shapes, wild natives of the brain?
Her ceaseless flight, though devious, speaks her nature
Of subtler essence than the trodden clod; 100
Active, aërial, towering, unconfined,
Unfetter'd with her gross companion's fall.
Even silent night proclaims my soul immortal:
Even silent night proclaims eternal day.
For human weal, Heaven husbands all events;
Dull sleep instructs, nor sport vain dreams in vain.
    Why then their loss deplore that are not lost?
Why wanders wretched thought their tombs around,
In infidel distress? Are angels there?
Slumbers, raked up in dust, ethereal fire? 110
    They live! they greatly live a life on earth
Unkindled, unconceived; and from an eye
Of tenderness let heavenly pity fall
On me, more justly number'd with the dead.
This is the desert, this the solitude:
How populous, how vital, is the grave!
This is creation's melancholy vault, 117
The vale funereal, the sad cypress gloom;
The land of apparitions, empty shades!
All, all on earth, is shadow, all beyond
Is substance; the reverse is Folly's creed:
How solid all, where change shall be no more!
    This is the bud of being, the dim dawn, 123
The twilight of our day, the vestibule;
Life's theatre as yet is shut, and death,

Strong death, alone can heave the massy bar,
This gross impediment of clay remove,
And make us embryos of existence free.
From real life, but little more remote
Is he, not yet a candidate for light,   130
The future embryo, slumbering in his sire.
Embryos we must be, till we burst the shell,
Yon ambient azure shell, and spring to life,
The life of gods, O transport! and of man.
      Yet man, fool man! here buries all his thoughts;
Inters celestial hopes without one sigh.
Prisoner of earth, and pent beneath the moon,
Here pinions all his wishes; wing'd by heaven
To fly at infinite; and reach it there,
Where seraphs gather immortality,   140
On life's fair tree, fast by the throne of God.
What golden joys ambrosial clustering glow
In His full beam, and ripen for the just,
Where momentary ages are no more!
Where time, and pain, and chance, and death, expire!
And is it in the flight of threescore years
To push eternity from human thought,
And smother souls immortal in the dust?
A soul immortal, spending all her fires,
Wasting her strength in strenuous idleness   150
Thrown into tumult, raptured, or alarm'd,   151
At aught this scene can threaten or indulge,
Resembles ocean into tempest wrought,
To waft a feather, or to drown a fly.
      Where falls this censure? It o'erwhelms myself;
How was my heart encrusted by the world!
O how self-fetter'd was my grovelling soul!
How, like a worm, was I wrapt round and round
In silken thought, which reptile fancy spun,
Till darken'd reason lay quite clouded o'er   160
With soft conceit of endless comfort here,
Nor yet put forth her wings to reach the skies!
      Night-visions may befriend (as sung above):
Our waking dreams are fatal. How I dream'd
Of things impossible! (could sleep do more?)
Of joys perpetual in perpetual change!
Of stable pleasures on the tossing wave!
Eternal sunshine in the storms of life!
How richly were my noontide trances hung
With gorgeous tapestries of pictured joys!   170
Joy behind joy, in endless perspective!

Till at death's toll, whose restless iron tongue
Calls daily for his millions at a meal,
Starting I woke, and found myself undone.
Where now my phrensy's pompous furniture?
The cobwebb'd cottage, with its ragged wall
Of mouldering mud, is royalty to me!
The spider's most attenuated thread
Is cord, is cable, to man's tender tie
On earthly bliss; it breaks at every breeze.   180
    O ye blest scenes of permanent delight!
Full above measure! lasting beyond bound!
A perpetuity of bliss is bliss.
Could you, so rich in rapture, fear an end,
That ghastly thought would drink up all your joy,   185
And quite unparadise the realms of light.
Safe are you lodged above these rolling spheres;
The baleful influence of whose giddy dance
Sheds sad vicissitude on all beneath.
Here teems with revolutions every hour;
And rarely for the better; or the best,
More mortal than the common births of fate.
Each moment has its sickle, emulous   193
Of Time's enormous scythe, whose ample sweep
Strikes empires from the root; each moment plays
His little weapon in the narrower sphere
Of sweet domestic comfort, and cuts down
The fairest bloom of sublunary bliss.
    Bliss! sublunary bliss!—proud words, and vain!
Implicit treason to divine decree!   200
A bold invasion of the rights of Heaven!
I clasp'd the phantoms, and I found them air.
Oh! had I weigh'd it ere my fond embrace,
What darts of agony had miss'd my heart!
    Death! great proprietor of all! 'tis thine
To tread out empire, and to quench the stars.
The sun himself by thy permission shines;
And, one day, thou shalt pluck him from his sphere.
Amid such mighty plunder, why exhaust
Thy partial quiver on a mark so mean?   210
Why thy peculiar rancour wreak'd on me?
Insatiate archer! could not one suffice?
Thy shaft flew thrice;[1] and thrice my peace was slain;
And thrice, ere thrice yon moon had fill'd her horn.

---

[1] 'Thrice:' alluding to the death of his wife, his daughter Mrs Temple, and Mr
Temple.—See *Life*.

O Cynthia! why so pale? dost thou lament
Thy wretched neighbour? grieve to see thy wheel
Of ceaseless change outwhirl'd in human life?   217
How wanes my borrow'd bliss! from fortune's smile,
Precarious courtesy! not virtue's sure,
Self-given, solar ray of sound delight.
  In every varied posture, place, and hour,
How widow'd every thought of every joy!
Thought, busy thought! too busy for my peace!
Through the dark postern of time long lapsed,   224
Led softly, by the stillness of the night,
Led, like a murderer, (and such it proves!)
Strays (wretched rover!) o'er the pleasing past;
In quest of wretchedness perversely strays;
And finds all desert now; and meets the ghosts
Of my departed joys; a numerous train!   230
I rue the riches of my former fate;
Sweet comfort's blasted clusters I lament;
I tremble at the blessings once so dear;
And every pleasure pains me to the heart.
  Yet why complain? or why complain for one?
Hangs out the sun his lustre but for me,
The single man? Are angels all beside?
I mourn for millions: 'tis the common lot;
In this shape, or in that, has fate entail'd
The mother's throes on all of woman born,   240
Not more the children, than sure heirs, of pain.
  War, famine, pest, volcano, storm, and fire,
Intestine broils, oppression, with her heart
Wrapt up in triple brass, besiege mankind.
God's image disinherited of day,
Here, plunged in mines, forgets a sun was made.
There, beings deathless as their haughty lord,
Are hammer'd to the galling oar for life;
And plough the winter's wave, and reap despair.
Some, for hard masters, broken under arms,   250
In battle lopp'd away, with half their limbs,   251
Beg bitter bread through realms their valour saved,
If so the tyrant, or his minion, doom.
Want and incurable disease (fell pair!)
On hopeless multitudes remorseless seize
At once; and make a refuge of the grave.
How groaning hospitals eject their dead!
What numbers groan for sad admission there!
What numbers, once in fortune's lap high-fed,
Solicit the cold hand of charity!   260

To shock us more, solicit it in vain!
Ye silken sons of pleasure! since in pains
Ye rue more modish visits, visit here,
And breathe from your debauch: give, and reduce
Surfeit's dominion o'er you: but so great
Your impudence, you blush at what is right.
Happy, did sorrow seize on such alone!
Not prudence can defend, or virtue save;
Disease invades the chastest temperance;
And punishment the guiltless; and alarm,   270
Through thickest shades pursues the fond of peace.
Man's caution often into danger turns,
And his guard falling, crushes him to death.
Not happiness itself makes good her name!
Our very wishes give us not our wish.
How distant oft the thing we doat on most,
From that for which we doat, felicity!
The smoothest course of nature has its pains;
And truest friends, through error, wound our rest.
Without misfortune, what calamities!   280
And what hostilities, without a foe!
Nor are foes wanting to the best on earth.
But endless is the list of human ills,
And sighs might sooner fail, than cause to sigh.
     A part how small of the terraqueous globe   285
Is tenanted by man! the rest a waste,
Rocks, deserts, frozen seas, and burning sands:
Wild haunts of monsters, poisons, stings, and death.
Such is earth's melancholy map! But, far
More sad! this earth is a true map of man.
So bounded are its haughty lord's delights
To woe's wide empire; where deep troubles toss,
Loud sorrows howl, envenom'd passions bite,   293
Ravenous calamities our vitals seize,
And threatening fate wide opens to devour.
     What then am I, who sorrow for myself?
In age, in infancy, from others' aid
Is all our hope; to teach us to be kind.
That, nature's first, last lesson to mankind;
The selfish heart deserves the pain it feels;   300
More generous sorrow, while it sinks, exalts;
And conscious virtue mitigates the pang.
Nor virtue, more than prudence, bids me give
Swoln thought a second channel; who divide,
They weaken, too, the torrent of their grief.
Take then, O world! thy much-indebted tear:

How sad a sight is human happiness,
To those whose thought can pierce beyond an hour!
O thou! whate'er thou art, whose heart exults!
Would'st thou I should congratulate thy fate? 310
I know thou would'st; thy pride demands it from me.
Let thy pride pardon, what thy nature needs,
The salutary censure of a friend.
Thou happy wretch! by blindness thou art blest;
By dotage dandled to perpetual smiles.
Know, smiler! at thy peril art thou pleased;
Thy pleasure is the promise of thy pain.
Misfortune, like a creditor severe,
But rises in demand for her delay; 319
She makes a scourge of past prosperity,
To sting thee more, and double thy distress.
    Lorenzo, Fortune makes her court to thee,
Thy fond heart dances, while the syren sings.
Dear is thy welfare; think me not unkind;
I would not damp, but to secure thy joys.
Think not that fear is sacred to the storm:
Stand on thy guard against the smiles of fate.
Is Heaven tremendous in its frowns? Most sure;
And in its favours formidable too:
Its favours here are trials, not rewards; 330
A call to duty, not discharge from care;
And should alarm us, full as much as woes;
Awake us to their cause, and consequence;
O'er our scann'd conduct give a jealous eye,
And make us tremble, weigh'd with our desert;
Awe nature's tumult, and chastise her joys,
Lest, while we clasp, we kill them; nay, invert
To worse than simple misery, their charms.
Revolted joys, like foes in civil war,
Like bosom friendships to resentment sour'd, 340
With rage envenom'd rise against our peace.
Beware what earth calls happiness; beware
All joys, but joys that never can expire.
Who builds on less than an immortal base,
Fond as he seems, condemns his joys to death.
    Mine died with thee, Philander![1] thy last sigh
Dissolved the charm; the disenchanted earth
Lost all her lustre. Where her glittering towers?
Her golden mountains, where? all darken'd down
To naked waste; a dreary vale of tears: 350

---

[1] 'Philander:' Mr Temple, his son-in-law.

The great magician's dead! Thou poor, pale piece
Of outcast earth, in darkness! what a change 352
From yesterday! Thy darling hope so near
(Long-labour'd prize!), O how ambition flush'd
Thy glowing cheek! ambition truly great,
Of virtuous praise. Death's subtle seed within
(Sly, treacherous miner!), working in the dark,
Smiled at thy well-concerted scheme, and beckon'd
The worm to riot on that rose so red,
Unfaded ere it fell; one moment's prey! 360
    Man's foresight is conditionally wise;
Lorenzo![1] wisdom into folly turns
Oft, the first instant, its idea fair
To labouring thought is born. How dim our eye!
The present moment terminates our sight;
Clouds thick as those on doomsday, drown the next;
We penetrate, we prophesy in vain.
Time is dealt out by particles; and each,
Ere mingled with the streaming sands of life,
By fate's inviolable oath is sworn 370
Deep silence, "where eternity begins."
    By nature's law, what may be, may be now;
There's no prerogative in human hours.
In human hearts what bolder thought can rise,
Than man's presumption on to-morrow's dawn!
Where is to-morrow? In another world.
For numbers this is certain; the reverse
Is sure to none; and yet on this perhaps,
This peradventure, infamous for lies,
As on a rock of adamant, we build 380
Our mountain hopes; spin out eternal schemes,
As we the fatal sisters could out-spin,
And, big with life's futurities, expire.
    Not even Philander had bespoke his shroud;
Nor had he cause; a warning was denied. 385
How many fall as sudden, not as safe!
As sudden, though for years admonish'd home.
Of human ills the last extreme beware,
Beware, Lorenzo! a slow sudden death.
How dreadful that deliberate surprise!
Be wise to-day; 'tis madness to defer;
Next day the fatal precedent will plead; 392
Thus on, till wisdom is push'd out of life.
Procrastination is the thief of time;

[1] 'Lorenzo:' not Young's son, but probably the Earl of Wharton.

Year after year it steals, till all are fled,
And to the mercies of a moment leaves
The vast concerns of an eternal scene.
If not so frequent, would not this be strange?
That 'tis so frequent, this is stranger still.
 Of man's miraculous mistakes, this bears   400
The palm, "That all men are about to live,"
For ever on the brink of being born.
All pay themselves the compliment to think
They one day shall not drivel: and their pride
On this reversion takes up ready praise;
At least, their own; their future selves applaud;
How excellent that life they ne'er will lead!
Time lodged in their own hands is folly's vails;
That lodged in fate's, to wisdom they consign;
The thing they can't but purpose, they postpone;   410
'Tis not in folly, not to scorn a fool;
And scarce in human wisdom to do more.
All promise is poor dilatory man,
And that through every stage: when young, indeed,
In full content we, sometimes, nobly rest,
Unanxious for ourselves; and only wish,
As duteous sons, our fathers were more wise.
At thirty, man suspects himself a fool;
Knows it at forty, and reforms his plan;   419
At fifty, chides his infamous delay,
Pushes his prudent purpose to resolve;
In all the magnanimity of thought
Resolves; and re-resolves; then dies the same.
 And why? Because he thinks himself immortal.
All men think all men mortal, but themselves:
Themselves, when some alarming shock of fate
Strikes through their wounded hearts the sudden dread;
But their hearts wounded, like the wounded air,
Soon close; where pass'd the shaft, no trace is found.
As from the wing no scar the sky retains;   430
The parted wave no furrow from the keel;
So dies in human hearts the thought of death.
Even with the tender tear which nature sheds
O'er those we love, we drop it in their grave.
Can I forget Philander? That were strange!
O my full heart!——But should I give it vent,
The longest night, though longer far, would fail,
And the lark listen to my midnight song.
 The sprightly lark's shrill matin wakes the morn;
Grief's sharpest thorn hard pressing on my breast, 440

27

I strive, with wakeful melody, to cheer
The sullen gloom, sweet Philomel! like thee,
And call the stars to listen: every star
Is deaf to mine, enamour'd of thy lay.
Yet be not vain; there are, who thine excel,
And charm through distant ages: wrapt in shade,
Prisoner of darkness! to the silent hours,
How often I repeat their rage divine,
To lull my griefs, and steal my heart from woe!
I roll their raptures, but not catch their fire.   450
Dark, though not blind, like thee, Mæonides![1]
Or, Milton! thee; ah, could I reach your strain!   452
Or his, who made Mæonides our own.[2]
Man too he sung: immortal man I sing;
Oft bursts my song beyond the bounds of life;
What, now, but immortality, can please?
O had he press'd his theme, pursued the track,
Which opens out of darkness into day!
O had he, mounted on his wing of fire,
Soar'd where I sink, and sung immortal man!   460
How had it bless'd mankind, and rescued me!

[1] 'Mæonides:' Homer.
[2] 'His, who made:' Pope.

NIGHT SECOND.

ON
TIME, DEATH, AND FRIENDSHIP.

TO THE RIGHT HONOURABLE
THE EARL OF WILMINGTON.

"WHEN the cock crew, he wept"—smote by that eye
Which looks on me, on all: that Power, who bids
This midnight sentinel, with clarion shrill
(Emblem of that which shall awake the dead),
Rouse souls from slumber, into thoughts of heaven.
Shall I too weep? Where then is fortitude?
And, fortitude abandon'd, where is man?
I know the terms on which he sees the light;
He that is born, is listed; life is war;
Eternal war with woe. Who bears it best,   10
Deserves it least.—On other themes I'll dwell.
Lorenzo! let me turn my thoughts on thee,
And thine, on themes may profit; profit there,
Where most thy need; themes, too, the genuine growth
Of dear Philander's dust. He thus, though dead,
May still befriend—what themes? Time's wondrous price,
Death, friendship, and Philander's final scene.
So could I touch these themes, as might obtain
Thine ear, nor leave thy heart quite disengaged,
The good deed would delight me; half impress   20
On my dark cloud an Iris; and from grief
Call glory.—Dost thou mourn Philander's fate?
I know thou say'st it: says thy life the same?
He mourns the dead, who lives as they desire.
Where is that thrift, that avarice of time,
(O glorious avarice!) thought of death inspires,
As rumour'd robberies endear our gold?
O time! than gold more sacred; more a load
Than lead to fools; and fools reputed wise.
What moment granted man without account?   30
What years are squander'd, wisdom's debt unpaid!
Our wealth in days, all due to that discharge.
Haste, haste, he lies in wait, he's at the door,
Insidious Death! should his strong hand arrest,

No composition sets the prisoner free.
Eternity's inexorable chain
Fast binds; and vengeance claims the full arrear.
How late I shudder'd on the brink! how late
Life call'd for her last refuge in despair!
That time is mine, O Mead! to thee I owe;   40
Fain would I pay thee with eternity.
But ill my genius answers my desire;
My sickly song is mortal, past thy cure.
Accept the will;—that dies not with my strain.
For what calls thy disease, Lorenzo? not
For Esculapian, but for moral aid.
Thou think'st it folly to be wise too soon.
Youth is not rich in time, it may be poor;
Part with it as with money, sparing; pay
No moment, but in purchase of its worth;   50
And what its worth, ask death-beds; they can tell.
Part with it as with life, reluctant; big
With holy hope of nobler time to come;
Time higher aim'd, still nearer the great mark   54
Of men and angels; virtue more divine.
Is this our duty, wisdom, glory, gain?
(These Heaven benign in vital union binds)
And sport we like the natives of the bough,
When vernal suns inspire? Amusement reigns
Man's great demand: to trifle, is to live:
And is it then a trifle, too, to die?
Thou say'st I preach, Lorenzo! 'tis confess'd.   62
What, if for once, I preach thee quite awake?
Who wants amusement in the flame of battle?
Is it not treason to the soul immortal,
Her foes in arms, eternity the prize?
Will toys amuse, when medicines cannot cure?
When spirits ebb, when life's enchanting scenes
Their lustre lose, and lessen in our sight,
As lands, and cities with their glittering spires,   70
To the poor shatter'd bark, by sudden storm
Thrown off to sea, and soon to perish there?
Will toys amuse? No: thrones will then be toys,
And earth and skies seem dust upon the scale.
Redeem we time?—its loss we dearly buy.
What pleads Lorenzo for his high-prized sports?
He pleads time's numerous blanks; he loudly pleads
The straw-like trifles on life's common stream.
From whom those blanks and trifles, but from thee?
No blank, no trifle, nature made, or meant.   80

Virtue, or purposed virtue, still be thine;
This cancels thy complaint at once, this leaves
In act no trifle, and no blank in time.
This greatens, fills, immortalizes all;
This, the bless'd art of turning all to gold;
This, the good heart's prerogative to raise
A royal tribute from the poorest hours;
Immense revenue! every moment pays.   88
If nothing more than purpose in thy power;
Thy purpose firm, is equal to the deed:
Who does the best his circumstance allows,
Does well, acts nobly; angels could no more.
Our outward act, indeed, admits restraint;
'Tis not in things o'er thought to domineer;
Guard well thy thought; our thoughts are heard in heaven.
        On all-important time, through every age,
Though much, and warm, the wise have urged; the man
Is yet unborn, who duly weighs an hour.
"I've lost a day"—the prince who nobly cried
Had been an emperor without his crown;   100
Of Rome? say, rather, lord of human race:
He spoke, as if deputed by mankind.
So should all speak; so reason speaks in all:
From the soft whispers of that God in man,
Why fly to folly, why to phrensy fly,
For rescue from the blessing we possess?
Time the supreme!—Time is eternity;
Pregnant with all eternity can give;
Pregnant with all that makes archangels smile.
Who murders time, he crushes in the birth   110
A power ethereal, only not adored.
        Ah! how unjust to Nature, and himself,
Is thoughtless, thankless, inconsistent man!
Like children babbling nonsense in their sports,
We censure Nature for a span too short;
That span too short, we tax as tedious too;
Torture invention, all expedients tire,
To lash the lingering moments into speed,
And whirl us (happy riddance!) from ourselves.
Art, brainless Art! our furious charioteer   120
(For Nature's voice unstifled would recall),
Drives headlong towards the precipice of death;   122
Death, most our dread; death thus more dreadful made:
Oh, what a riddle of absurdity!
Leisure is pain; takes off our chariot wheels;
How heavily we drag the load of life!

Blest leisure is our curse; like that of Cain,
It makes us wander; wander earth around,
To fly that tyrant, thought. As Atlas groan'd
The world beneath, we groan beneath an hour.   130
We cry for mercy to the next amusement;
The next amusement mortgages our fields;
Slight inconvenience! prisons hardly frown,
From hateful time if prisons set us free.
Yet when Death kindly tenders us relief,
We call him cruel; years to moments shrink,
Ages to years. The telescope is turn'd.
To man's false optics (from his folly false),
Time, in advance, behind him hides his wings,
And seems to creep, decrepit with his age;   140
Behold him, when pass'd by; what then is seen,
But his broad pinions swifter than the winds?
And all mankind, in contradiction strong,
Rueful, aghast! cry out on his career.
      Leave to thy foes these errors and these ills;
To Nature just, their cause and cure explore.
Not short Heaven's bounty, boundless our expence;
No niggard, Nature; men are prodigals.
We waste, not use our time; we breathe, not live.
Time wasted is existence, used is life.   150
And bare existence, man, to live ordain'd,
Wrings, and oppresses with enormous weight.
And why? since time was given for use, not waste,
Enjoin'd to fly; with tempest, tide, and stars,
To keep his speed, nor ever wait for man;
Time's use was doom'd a pleasure: waste, a pain;   156
That man might feel his error, if unseen:
And, feeling, fly to labour for his cure;
Not, blundering, split on idleness for ease.
Life's cares are comforts; such by Heaven design'd;
He that has none, must make them, or be wretched.
Cares are employments; and without employ
The soul is on a rack; the rack of rest,   163
To souls most adverse; action all their joy.
      Here then, the riddle, mark'd above, unfolds;
Then time turns torment, when man turns a fool.
We rave, we wrestle, with great Nature's plan;
We thwart the Deity; and 'tis decreed,
Who thwart his will shall contradict their own.
Hence our unnatural quarrels with ourselves;   170
Our thoughts at enmity; our bosom-broils;
We push Time from us, and we wish him back;

Lavish of lustrums, and yet fond of life;
Life we think long, and short; death seek, and shun;
Body and soul, like peevish man and wife,
United jar, and yet are loth to part.
      Oh the dark days of vanity! while here,
How tasteless! and how terrible, when gone!
Gone! they ne'er go; when past, they haunt us still;
The spirit walks of every day deceased;   180
And smiles an angel, or a fury frowns.
Nor death, nor life delight us. If time past,
And time possess'd, both pain us, what can please?
That which the Deity to please ordain'd,
Time used. The man who consecrates his hours
By vigorous effort, and an honest aim,
At once he draws the sting of life and death;
He walks with Nature; and her paths are peace.
      Our error's cause and cure are seen: see next
Time's nature, origin, importance, speed;   190
And thy great gain from urging his career.—
All-sensual man, because untouch'd, unseen,
He looks on time as nothing. Nothing else
Is truly man's; 'tis fortune's.—Time's a god.
Hast thou ne'er heard of Time's omnipotence?
For, or against, what wonders he can do,
And will? To stand blank neuter he disdains.
Not on those terms was Time (Heaven's stranger!) sent
On his important embassy to man.
Lorenzo! no: on the long-destined hour,   200
From everlasting ages growing ripe,
That memorable hour of wondrous birth,
When the Dread Sire, on emanation bent,
And big with Nature, rising in his might,
Call'd forth creation (for then Time was born),
By Godhead streaming through a thousand worlds;
Not on those terms, from the great days of heaven,
From old Eternity's mysterious orb,
Was Time cut off, and cast beneath the skies;
The skies, which watch him in his new abode,   210
Measuring his motions by revolving spheres;
That horologe machinery divine.
Hours, days, and months, and years, his children play,
Like numerous wings around him, as he flies:
Or, rather, as unequal plumes, they shape
His ample pinions, swift as darted flame,
To gain his goal, to reach his ancient rest,
And join anew Eternity his sire;

In his immutability to nest,
When worlds, that count his circles now, unhinged   220
(Fate the loud signal sounding), headlong rush
To timeless night and chaos, whence they rose.
        Why spur the speedy? why with levities
New wing thy short, short day's too rapid flight?   224
Know'st thou, or what thou dost, or what is done?
Man flies from time, and time from man; too soon
In sad divorce this double flight must end:
And then where are we? where, Lorenzo! then
Thy sports? thy pomps?—I grant thee, in a state
Not unambitious; in the ruffled shroud,
Thy Parian tomb's triumphant arch beneath.
Has Death his fopperies? Then well may life   232
Put on her plume, and in her rainbow shine.
Ye well-array'd! ye lilies of our land!
Ye lilies male! who neither toil nor spin
(As sister lilies might), if not so wise
As Solomon, more sumptuous to the sight!
Ye delicate! who nothing can support,
Yourselves most insupportable! for whom
The winter rose must blow, the sun put on   240
A brighter beam in Leo; silky-soft
Favonius breathe still softer, or be chid;
And other worlds send odours, sauce, and song,
And robes, and notions, framed in foreign looms!
O ye Lorenzos of our age! who deem
One moment unamused, a misery
Not made for feeble man! who call aloud
For every bauble drivell'd o'er by sense;
For rattles, and conceits of every cast,
For change of follies, and relays of joy,   250
To drag your patient through the tedious length
Of a short winter's day—say, sages! say,
Wit's oracles! say, dreamers of gay dreams!
How will you weather an eternal night,
Where such expedients fail?
        O treacherous Conscience! while she seems to sleep
On rose and myrtle, lull'd with syren song;
While she seems, nodding o'er her charge, to drop   258
On headlong appetite the slacken'd rein,
And give us up to licence, unrecall'd,
Unmark'd;—see, from behind her secret stand,
The sly informer minutes every fault,
And her dread diary with horror fills.
Not the gross act alone employs her pen;

She reconnoitres fancy's airy band,
A watchful foe! the formidable spy,
Listening, o'erhears the whispers of our camp:
Our dawning purposes of heart explores,
And steals our embryos of iniquity.
As all-rapacious usurers conceal   270
Their doomsday-book from all-consuming heirs;
Thus, with indulgence most severe, she treats
Us spendthrifts of inestimable time;
Unnoted, notes each moment misapplied;
In leaves more durable than leaves of brass,
Writes our whole history; which Death shall read
In every pale delinquent's private ear;
And Judgment publish; publish to more worlds
Than this; and endless age in groans resound.
Lorenzo, such that sleeper in thy breast!   280
Such is her slumber; and her vengeance such
For slighted counsel; such thy future peace!
And think'st thou still thou canst be wise too soon?
      But why on Time so lavish is my song?
On this great theme kind Nature keeps a school,
To teach her sons herself. Each night we die,
Each morn are born anew: each day, a life!
And shall we kill each day? If trifling kills;
Sure vice must butcher. Oh, what heaps of slain
Cry out for vengeance on us! Time destroy'd   290
Is suicide, where more than blood is spilt.
Time flies, Death urges, knells call, Heaven invites, 292
Hell threatens: all exerts; in effort, all;
More than creation labours!—labours more?
And is there in creation what, amidst
This tumult universal, wing'd despatch,
And ardent energy, supinely yawns?—
Man sleeps; and man alone; and man, whose fate,
Fate irreversible, entire, extreme,
Endless, hair-hung, breeze-shaken, o'er the gulf   300
A moment trembles; drops! and man, for whom
All else is in alarm! man, the sole cause
Of this surrounding storm! and yet he sleeps,
As the storm rock'd to rest.—Throw years away?
Throw empires, and be blameless. Moments seize;
Heaven's on their wing: a moment we may wish,
When worlds want wealth to buy. Bid Day stand still,
Bid him drive back his car, and re-import
The period past, re-give the given hour.
Lorenzo, more than miracles we want;   310

Lorenzo—O for yesterdays to come!
    Such is the language of the man awake;
His ardour such, for what oppresses thee.
And is his ardour vain, Lorenzo? No;
That more than miracle the gods indulge;
To-day is yesterday return'd; return'd
Full power'd to cancel, expiate, raise, adorn,
And reinstate us on the rock of peace.
Let it not share its predecessor's fate;
Nor, like its elder sisters, die a fool.   320
Shall it evaporate in fume? fly off
Fuliginous, and stain us deeper still?
Shall we be poorer for the plenty pour'd?
More wretched for the clemencies of Heaven?
    Where shall I find him? Angels! tell me where.
You know him: he is near you: point him out: 326
Shall I see glories beaming from his brow?
Or trace his footsteps by the rising flowers?
Your golden wings, now hovering o'er him, shed
Protection; now, are waving in applause
To that bless'd son of foresight! lord of fate!
That awful independent on to-morrow!
Whose work is done; who triumphs in the past;   333
Whose yesterdays look backwards with a smile;
Nor, like the Parthian, wound him as they fly;
That common but opprobrious lot! past hours,
If not by guilt, yet wound us by their flight,
If folly bounds our prospect by the grave,
All feeling of futurity benumb'd;
All god-like passion for eternals quench'd;   340
All relish of realities expired;
Renounced all correspondence with the skies;
Our freedom chain'd; quite wingless our desire;
In sense dark-prison'd all that ought to soar;
Prone to the centre; crawling in the dust;
Dismounted every great and glorious aim;
Embruted every faculty divine;
Heart-buried in the rubbish of the world.
The world, that gulf of souls, immortal souls,
Souls elevate, angelic, wing'd with fire   350
To reach the distant skies, and triumph there
On thrones, which shall not mourn their masters changed,
Though we from earth; ethereal, they that fell.
Such veneration due, O man, to man.
    Who venerate themselves, the world despise.
For what, gay friend! is this escutcheon'd world,

Which hangs out death in one eternal night?
A night, that glooms us in the noontide ray,
And wraps our thought, at banquets, in the shroud.
Life's little stage is a small eminence,   360
Inch-high the grave above; that home of man,
Where dwells the multitude: we gaze around;
We read their monuments; we sigh; and while
We sigh, we sink; and are what we deplored;
Lamenting, or lamented, all our lot!
    Is Death at distance? No: he has been on thee;
And given sure earnest of his final blow.
These hours that lately smiled, where are they now?
Pallid to thought, and ghastly! drown'd, all drown'd
In that great deep, which nothing disembogues!   370
And, dying, they bequeathed thee small renown.
The rest are on the wing: how fleet their flight!
Already has the fatal train took fire;
A moment, and the world's blown up to thee;
The sun is darkness, and the stars are dust.
    'Tis greatly wise to talk with our past hours;
And ask them, what report they bore to heaven;
And how they might have borne more welcome news.
Their answers form what men experience call;
If Wisdom's friend, her best; if not, worst foe.   380
"Oh, reconcile them!" kind Experience cries;
"There's nothing here, but what as nothing weighs;
The more our joy, the more we know it vain;
And by success are tutor'd to despair."
Nor is it only thus, but must be so.
Who knows not this, though grey, is still a child.
Loose then from earth the grasp of fond desire,
Weigh anchor, and some happier clime explore.
    Art thou so moor'd thou canst not disengage,
Nor give thy thoughts a ply to future scenes?   390
Since, by life's passing breath, blown up from earth,
Light as the summer's dust, we take in air
A moment's giddy flight, and fall again;
Join the dull mass, increase the trodden soil,   394
And sleep, till earth herself shall be no more;
Since then (as emmets, their small world o'erthrown)
We, sore-amazed, from out earth's ruins crawl,
And rise to fate extreme of foul or fair,
As man's own choice (controller of the skies!)
As man's despotic will, perhaps one hour
(O how omnipotent is time!) decrees;
Should not each warning give a strong alarm?

Warning, far less than that of bosom torn   403
From bosom, bleeding o'er the sacred dead!
Should not each dial strike us as we pass,
Portentous, as the written wall, which struck,
O'er midnight bowls, the proud Assyrian pale,
Erewhile high-flush'd, with insolence, and wine?
Like that, the dial speaks; and points to thee,
Lorenzo! loth to break thy banquet up: 410
"O man, thy kingdom is departing from thee;
And, while it lasts, is emptier than my shade."
Its silent language such: nor need'st thou call
Thy Magi, to decipher what it means.
Know, like the Median, fate is in thy walls:
Dost ask, How? Whence? Belshazzar-like, amazed?
Man's make encloses the sure seeds of death;
Life feeds the murderer: ingrate! he thrives
On her own meal, and then his nurse devours.

But, here, Lorenzo, the delusion lies;   420
That solar shadow, as it measures life,
It life resembles too: life speeds away
From point to point, though seeming to stand still.
The cunning fugitive is swift by stealth:
Too subtle is the movement to be seen;
Yet soon man's hour is up, and we are gone.
Warnings point out our danger; gnomons, time:
As these are useless when the sun is set: 423
So those, but when more glorious reason shines.
Reason should judge in all; in reason's eye,
That sedentary shadow travels hard.
But such our gravitation to the wrong,
So prone our hearts to whisper what we wish,
'Tis later with the wise than he's aware:
A Wilmington goes slower than the sun:
And all mankind mistake their time of day;
Even age itself. Fresh hopes are hourly sown
In furrow'd brows. To gentle life's descent
We shut our eyes, and think it is a plain.
We take fair days in winter, for the spring;   440
And turn our blessings into bane. Since oft
Man must compute that age he cannot feel,
He scarce believes he's older for his years.
Thus, at life's latest eve, we keep in store
One disappointment sure, to crown the rest;
The disappointment of a promised hour.

On this, or similar, Philander! thou,
Whose mind was moral, as the preacher's tongue;

And strong, to wield all science, worth the name;
How often we talk'd down the summer's sun,   450
And cool'd our passions by the breezy stream!
How often thaw'd and shorten'd winter's eve,
By conflict kind, that struck out latent truth,
Best found, so sought; to the recluse more coy!
Thoughts disentangle passing o'er the lip;
Clean runs the thread; if not, 'tis thrown away,
Or kept to tie up nonsense for a song;
Song, fashionably fruitless; such as stains
The fancy, and unhallow'd passion fires;
Chiming her saints to Cytherea's[1] fane.   460
    Know'st thou, Lorenzo! what a friend contains?   461
As bees mix'd nectar draw from fragrant flowers,
So men from friendship, wisdom and delight;
Twins tied by Nature, if they part, they die.
Hast thou no friend to set thy mind abroach?
Good sense will stagnate. Thoughts shut up, want air,
And spoil, like bales unopen'd to the sun.
Had thought been all, sweet speech had been denied;
Speech, thought's canal! speech, thought's criterion too!
Thought in the mine, may come forth gold, or dross;
When coin'd in words, we know its real worth.   471
If sterling, store it for thy future use;
'Twill buy thee benefit; perhaps, renown.
Thought, too, deliver'd, is the more possess'd;
Teaching, we learn; and, giving, we retain
The births of intellect; when dumb, forgot.
Speech ventilates our intellectual fire;
Speech burnishes our mental magazine;
Brightens, for ornament; and whets, for use.
What numbers, sheathed in erudition, lie,   480
Plunged to the hilts in venerable tomes,
And rusted in; who might have borne an edge,
And play'd a sprightly beam, if born to speech;
If born bless'd heirs of half their mother's tongue!
'Tis thought's exchange, which, like th' alternate push
Of waves conflicting, breaks the learned scum,
And defecates the student's standing pool.
    In contemplation is his proud resource?
'Tis poor, as proud, by converse unsustain'd.
Rude thought runs wild in contemplation's field;   490
Converse, the menage, breaks it to the bit

---

[1] 'Cytherea:' Venus, from Cythera, one of the Ionian Islands, where she was worshipped.

Of due restraint; and emulation's spur
Gives graceful energy, by rivals awed.
'Tis converse qualifies for solitude;
As exercise, for salutary rest.   495
By that untutor'd, contemplation raves;
And Nature's fool, by wisdom is undone.
    Wisdom, though richer than Peruvian mines,
And sweeter than the sweet ambrosial hive,
What is she, but the means of happiness?
That unobtain'd, than folly more a fool;
A melancholy fool, without her bells.
Friendship, the means of wisdom, richly gives   503
The precious end, which makes our wisdom wise.
Nature, in zeal for human amity,
Denies, or damps, an undivided joy.
Joy is an import; joy is an exchange;
Joy flies monopolists: it calls for two;
Rich fruit! heaven-planted! never pluck'd by one.
Needful auxiliars are our friends, to give   510
To social man true relish of himself.
Full on ourselves, descending in a line,
Pleasure's bright beam is feeble in delight:
Delight intense, is taken by rebound;
Reverberated pleasures fire the breast.
    Celestial happiness, whene'er she stoops
To visit earth, one shrine the goddess finds,
And one alone, to make her sweet amends
For absent heaven—the bosom of a friend;
Where heart meets heart, reciprocally soft,   520
Each other's pillow to repose divine.
Beware the counterfeit: in passion's flame
Hearts melt, but melt like ice, soon harder froze.
True love strikes root in reason; passion's foe:
Virtue alone entenders us for life:
I wrong her much—entenders us for ever:
Of friendship's fairest fruits, the fruit most fair
Is virtue kindling at a rival fire,
And, emulously, rapid in her race.   529
O the soft enmity! endearing strife!
This carries friendship to her noontide point,
And gives the rivet of eternity.
From friendship, which outlives my former themes,
Glorious survivor of old time and death;
    From friendship, thus, that flower of heavenly seed,
The wise extract earth's most Hyblean bliss,
Superior wisdom, crown'd with smiling joy.

But for whom blossoms this Elysian flower?
Abroad they find, who cherish it at home.
Lorenzo! pardon what my love extorts,   540
An honest love, and not afraid to frown.
Though choice of follies fasten on the great,
None clings more obstinate, than fancy, fond
That sacred friendship is their easy prey;
Caught by the wafture of a golden lure,
Or fascination of a high-born smile.
Their smiles, the great, and the coquette, throw out
For others' hearts, tenacious of their own;
And we no less of ours, when such the bait.
Ye fortune's cofferers! ye powers of wealth!   550
Can gold gain friendship? Impudence of hope!
As well mere man an angel might beget.
Love, and love only, is the loan for love.
Lorenzo! pride repress; nor hope to find
A friend, but what has found a friend in thee.
All like the purchase; few the price will pay;
And this makes friends such miracles below.
    What if (since daring on so nice a theme)
I show thee friendship delicate, as dear,
Of tender violations apt to die?   560
Reserve will wound it; and distrust, destroy.
Deliberate on all things with thy friend.
But since friends grow not thick on every bough,   563
Nor every friend unrotten at the core;
First, on thy friend, deliberate with thyself;
Pause, ponder, sift; not eager in the choice,
Nor jealous of the chosen; fixing, fix;
Judge before friendship, then confide till death.
Well, for thy friend; but nobler far for thee;
How gallant danger for earth's highest prize!   570
A friend is worth all hazards we can run.
"Poor is the friendless master of a world:
A world in purchase for a friend is gain."
    So sung he (angels hear that angel sing!
Angels from friendship gather half their joy),
So sung Philander, as his friend went round
In the rich ichor, in the generous blood
Of Bacchus, purple god of joyous wit,
A brow solute, and ever-laughing eye.
He drank long health, and virtue, to his friend;   580
His friend, who warm'd him more, who more inspired.
Friendship's the wine of life; but friendship new
(Not such was his) is neither strong, nor pure.

O for the bright complexion, cordial warmth,
And elevating spirit, of a friend,
For twenty summers ripening by my side;
All feculence of falsehood long thrown down;
All social virtues rising in his soul;
As crystal clear; and smiling, as they rise!
Here nectar flows; it sparkles in our sight;   590
Rich to the taste, and genuine from the heart.
High-flavour'd bliss for gods! on earth how rare!
On earth how lost!—Philander is no more.
    Think'st thou the theme intoxicates my song?
Am I too warm?—Too warm I cannot be.
I loved him much; but now I love him more.
Like birds, whose beauties languish, half-conceal'd,   597
Till, mounted on the wing, their glossy plumes
Expanded shine with azure, green, and gold;
How blessings brighten as they take their flight!
His flight Philander took; his upward flight,
If ever soul ascended. Had he dropp'd
(That eagle genius!), oh! had he let fall
One feather as he flew; I, then, had wrote,   604
What friends might flatter; prudent foes forbear;
Rivals scarce damn; and Zoilus reprieve.
Yet what I can, I must: it were profane
To quench a glory lighted at the skies,
And cast in shadows his illustrious close.
Strange! the theme most affecting, most sublime,   610
Momentous most to man, should sleep unsung!
And yet it sleeps, by genius unawaked,
Paynim or Christian; to the blush of wit.
Man's highest triumph! man's profoundest fall!
The death-bed of the just! is yet undrawn
By mortal hand; it merits a divine:
Angels should paint it, angels ever there;
There, on a post of honour, and of joy.
    Dare I presume, then? But Philander bids;
And glory tempts, and inclination calls—   620
Yet am I struck; as struck the soul, beneath
Aërial groves' impenetrable gloom;
Or, in some mighty ruin's solemn shade;
Or, gazing by pale lamps on high-born dust,
In vaults; thin courts of poor unflatter'd kings;
Or, at the midnight altar's hallow'd flame.
Is it religion to proceed? I pause—
And enter, awed, the temple of my theme.
Is it his death-bed? No: it is his shrine:

Behold him, there, just rising to a god.   630
    The chamber where the good man meets his fate,   631
Is privileged beyond the common walk
Of virtuous life, quite in the verge of heaven.
Fly, ye profane! if not, draw near with awe,
Receive the blessing, and adore the chance,
That threw in this Bethesda your disease;
If unrestored by this, despair your cure.
For here, resistless demonstration dwells;
A death-bed's a detector of the heart.
Here tired Dissimulation drops her mask,   640
Through life's grimace, that mistress of the scene!
Here real and apparent are the same.
You see the man; you see his hold on heaven;
If sound his virtue; as Philander's, sound.
Heaven waits not the last moment; owns her friends
On this side death; and points them out to men,
A lecture, silent, but of sovereign power!
To vice, confusion; and to virtue, peace.
    Whatever farce the boastful hero plays,
Virtue alone has majesty in death;   650
And greater still, the more the tyrant frowns.
Philander! he severely frown'd on thee.
"No warning given! Unceremonious fate!
A sudden rush from life's meridian joy!
A wrench from all we love! from all we are!
A restless bed of pain! a plunge opaque
Beyond conjecture! feeble Nature's dread!
Strong reason's shudder at the dark unknown!
A sun extinguish'd! a just opening grave!
And, oh! the last, last, what? (can words express?   660
Thought reach it?)—the last—silence of a friend!"
Where are those horrors, that amazement, where,
This hideous group of ills, which singly shock,
Demand from man?—I thought him man till now.
    Through nature's wreck, through vanquish'd agonies
(Like the stars struggling through this midnight gloom),
What gleams of joy! what more than human peace!
Where, the frail mortal? the poor abject worm?
No, not in death, the mortal to be found.
His conduct is a legacy for all;   670
Richer than Mammon's for his single heir.
His comforters he comforts; great in ruin,
With unreluctant grandeur, gives, not yields,
His soul sublime; and closes with his fate.
    How our hearts burn'd within us at the scene!

Whence this brave bound o'er limits fix'd to man?
His God sustains him in his final hour!
His final hour brings glory to his God!
Man's glory Heaven vouchsafes to call her own.
We gaze, we weep; mix'd tears of grief and joy!   680
Amazement strikes! devotion bursts to flame!
Christians adore! and infidels believe!
    As some tall tower,[1] or lofty mountain's brow,
Detains the sun, illustrious, from its height;
While rising vapours, and descending shades,
With damps, and darkness, drown the spacious vale;
Undamp'd by doubt, undarken'd by despair,
Philander, thus, augustly rears his head,
At that black hour, which general horror sheds
On the low level of th' inglorious throng: 690
Sweet peace, and heavenly hope, and humble joy,
Divinely beam on his exalted soul;
Destruction gild, and crown him for the skies,
With incommunicable lustre, bright.

---

[1] 'As some tall tower:' Goldsmith has borrowed this fine image in his description of the good pastor's death, in the 'Deserted Village.'

NIGHT THIRD.

NARCISSA.

TO HER GRACE
THE DUCHESS OF P———.[1]

Ignoscenda quidem, scirent si ignoscere manes.—VIRG.

FROM dreams, where thought in fancy's maze runs mad,
To reason, that heaven-lighted lamp in man,
Once more I wake; and at the destined hour,
Punctual as lovers to the moment sworn,
I keep my assignation with my woe.
    Oh! lost to virtue, lost to manly thought,
Lost to the noble sallies of the soul!
Who think it solitude to be alone.
Communion sweet! communion large and high!
Our reason, guardian angel, and our God!   10
Then nearest these, when others most remote;
And all, ere long, shall be remote, but these.
How dreadful, then, to meet them all alone,
A stranger! unacknowledged, unapproved!
Now woo them, wed them, bind them to thy breast;
To win thy wish, creation has no more.
Or if we wish a fourth, it is a friend—
But friends, how mortal! dangerous the desire.
    Take Phœbus to yourselves, ye basking bards!   19
Inebriate at fair fortune's fountain-head;
And reeling through the wilderness of joy;
Where sense runs savage, broke from reason's chain,
And sings false peace, till smother'd by the pall.
My fortune is unlike; unlike my song;
Unlike the deity my song invokes.
I to Day's soft-eyed sister pay my court
(Endymion's rival!), and her aid implore;
Now first implored in succour to the Muse.
    Thou, who didst lately borrow[2] Cynthia's form,

----

[1] 'P———:' Portland.
[2] 'Didst lately borrow:' at the Duke of Norfolk's masquerade.

And modestly forego thine own! O thou, 30
Who didst thyself at midnight hours inspire!
Say, why not Cynthia patroness of song?
As thou her crescent, she thy character
Assumes; still more a goddess by the change.

    Are there demurring wits, who dare dispute
This revolution in the world inspired?
Ye train Pierian! to the lunar sphere,
In silent hour address your ardent call
For aid immortal; less her brother's right.
She, with the spheres harmonious, nightly leads 40
The mazy dance, and hears their matchless strain;
A strain for gods, denied to mortal ear.
Transmit it heard, thou silver Queen of Heaven!
What title, or what name, endears thee most?
Cynthia! Cyllene! Phœbe!—or dost hear
With higher gust, fair P——d of the skies?
Is that the soft enchantment calls thee down,
More powerful than of old Circean charm?
Come; but from heavenly banquets with thee bring
The soul of song, and whisper in my ear 50
The theft divine; or in propitious dreams
(For dreams are thine) transfuse it through the breast 52
Of thy first votary—but not thy last;
If, like thy namesake, thou art ever kind.

    And kind thou wilt be; kind on such a theme;
A theme so like thee, a quite lunar theme,
Soft, modest, melancholy, female, fair!
A theme that rose all pale, and told my soul,
'Twas Night; on her fond hopes perpetual night;
A night which struck a damp, a deadlier damp, 60
Than that which smote me from Philander's tomb.
Narcissa[1] follows, ere his tomb is closed.
Woes cluster; rare are solitary woes;
They love a train, they tread each other's heel;
Her death invades his mournful right, and claims
The grief that started from my lids for him:
Seizes the faithless, alienated tear,
Or shares it, ere it falls. So frequent Death,
Sorrow he more than causes, he confounds;
For human sighs his rival strokes contend, 70
And make distress, distraction. Oh, Philander!
What was thy fate? A double fate to me;
Portent, and pain! a menace, and a blow!

---

[1] 'Narcissa:' Mrs Temple.

Like the black raven hovering o'er my peace,
Not less a bird of omen, than of prey.
It call'd Narcissa long before her hour;
It call'd her tender soul, by break of bliss,
From the first blossom, from the buds of joy;
Those few our noxious fate unblasted leaves
In this inclement clime of human life.   80
    Sweet harmonist! and beautiful as sweet!
And young as beautiful! and soft as young!
And gay as soft! and innocent as gay!
And happy (if aught happy here) as good!
For fortune fond had built her nest on high.   85
Like birds quite exquisite of note and plume,
Transfix'd by fate (who loves a lofty mark),
How from the summit of the grove she fell,
And left it unharmonious! all its charms
Extinguish'd in the wonders of her song!
Her song still vibrates in my ravish'd ear,
Still melting there, and with voluptuous pain
(O to forget her!) thrilling through my heart!   93
    Song, beauty, youth, love, virtue, joy! this group
Of bright ideas, flowers of paradise,
As yet unforfeit! in one blaze we bind,
Kneel, and present it to the skies; as all
We guess of heaven: and these were all her own.
And she was mine; and I was—was!—most blest!—
Gay title of the deepest misery!   100
As bodies grow more ponderous, robb'd of life;
Good lost weighs more in grief, than gain'd, in joy.
Like blossom'd trees o'erturn'd by vernal storm,
Lovely in death the beauteous ruin lay;
And if in death still lovely, lovelier there;
Far lovelier! pity swells the tide of love.
And will not the severe excuse a sigh?
Scorn the proud man that is ashamed to weep;
Our tears indulged, indeed deserve our shame.
Ye that e'er lost an angel! pity me.   110
Soon as the lustre languish'd in her eye,
Dawning a dimmer day on human sight;
And on her cheek, the residence of spring,
Pale omen sat; and scatter'd fears around
On all that saw; (and who would cease to gaze,
That once had seen?) with haste, parental haste,
I flew, I snatch'd her from the rigid north,
Her native bed, on which bleak Boreas blew,

And bore her nearer to the sun;[1] the sun 119
(As if the sun could envy) check'd his beam,
Denied his wonted succour; nor with more
Regret beheld her drooping, than the bells
Of lilies; fairest lilies, not so fair!
    Queen lilies! and ye painted populace!
Who dwell in fields, and lead ambrosial lives;
In morn and evening dew your beauties bathe,
And drink the sun; which gives your cheeks to glow,
And out-blush (mine excepted) every fair;
You gladlier grew, ambitious of her hand,
Which often cropp'd your odours, incense meet 130
To thought so pure! Ye lovely fugitives!
Coeval race with man! for man you smile;
Why not smile at him too? You share indeed
His sudden pass; but not his constant pain.
    So man is made, nought ministers delight,
By what his glowing passions can engage;
And glowing passions, bent on aught below,
Must, soon or late, with anguish turn the scale;
And anguish, after rapture, how severe!
Rapture? Bold man! who tempts the wrath divine, 140
By plucking fruit denied to mortal taste,
While here, presuming on the rights of heaven.
For transport dost thou call on every hour,
Lorenzo? At thy friend's expense be wise;
Lean not on earth; 'twill pierce thee to the heart;
A broken reed, at best; but, oft, a spear;
On its sharp point peace bleeds, and hope expires.
    Turn, hopeless thought! turn from her:—thought repell'd
Resenting rallies, and wakes every woe.
Snatch'd ere thy prime! and in thy bridal hour! 150
And when kind fortune, with thy lover, smiled! 151
And when high flavour'd thy fresh opening joys!
And when blind man pronounced thy bliss complete!
And on a foreign shore; where strangers wept!
Strangers to thee; and, more surprising still,
Strangers to kindness, wept: their eyes let fall
Inhuman tears: strange tears! that trickled down
From marble hearts! obdurate tenderness!
A tenderness that call'd them more severe;
In spite of nature's soft persuasion, steel'd; 160
While nature melted, superstition raved;

---

[1] 'Nearer to the sun:' Mrs Temple died at Lyons, on her way to Nice, accompanied by her father.

That mourn'd the dead; and this denied a grave.
    Their sighs incensed; sighs foreign to the will!
Their will the tiger suck'd, outraged the storm.
For oh! the cursed ungodliness of zeal!
While sinful flesh relented, spirit nursed
In blind infallibility's embrace,
The sainted spirit petrified the breast;
Denied the charity of dust, to spread
O'er dust! a charity their dogs enjoy.   170
What could I do? what succour? what resource?
With pious sacrilege, a grave I stole;
With impious piety, that grave I wrong'd;
Short in my duty; coward in my grief!
More like her murderer, than friend, I crept,
With soft-suspended step, and muffled deep
In midnight darkness, whisper'd my last sigh.
I whisper'd what should echo through their realms;
Nor writ her name, whose tomb should pierce the skies.
Presumptuous fear! How durst I dread her foes,   180
While nature's loudest dictates I obey'd?
Pardon necessity, bless'd shade! of grief
And indignation rival bursts I pour'd;
Half execration mingled with my prayer;
Kindled at man, while I his God adored;   185
Sore grudged the savage land her sacred dust;
Stamp'd the cursed soil; and with humanity
(Denied Narcissa) wish'd them all a grave.
    Glows my resentment into guilt? What guilt
Can equal violations of the dead?
The dead how sacred! Sacred is the dust
Of this heaven-labour'd form, erect, divine!   192
This heaven-assumed majestic robe of earth,
He deign'd to wear, who hung the vast expanse
With azure bright, and clothed the sun in gold.
When every passion sleeps that can offend;
When strikes us every motive that can melt;
When man can wreak his rancour uncontroll'd,
That strongest curb on insult and ill-will;
Then, spleen to dust? the dust of innocence?   200
An angel's dust?—This Lucifer transcends;
When he contended for the patriarch's bones,
'Twas not the strife of malice, but of pride;
The strife of pontiff pride, not pontiff gall.
    Far less than this is shocking in a race
Most wretched, but from streams of mutual love;
And uncreated, but for love divine;

And, but for love divine, this moment, lost,
By fate resorb'd, and sunk in endless night.
Man hard of heart to man! of horrid things   210
Most horrid! 'mid stupendous, highly strange!
Yet oft his courtesies are smoother wrongs;
Pride brandishes the favours He confers,
And contumelious his humanity:
What then his vengeance? Hear it not, ye stars!
And thou, pale moon! turn paler at the sound;
Man is to man the sorest, surest ill.
A previous blast foretells the rising storm;
O'erwhelming turrets threaten ere they fall;   219
Volcanos bellow ere they disembogue;
Earth trembles ere her yawning jaws devour;
And smoke betrays the wide-consuming fire:
Ruin from man is most conceal'd when near,
And sends the dreadful tidings in the blow.
Is this the flight of fancy? Would it were!
Heaven's Sovereign saves all beings, but himself,
That hideous sight, a naked human heart.

    Fired is the Muse? And let the Muse be fired:
Who not inflamed, when what he speaks, he feels,
And in the nerve most tender, in his friends?   230
Shame to mankind! Philander had his foes;
He felt the truths I sing, and I in him.
But he, nor I, feel more: past ills, Narcissa!
Are sunk in thee, thou recent wound of heart!
Which bleeds with other cares, with other pangs;
Pangs numerous, as the numerous ills that swarm'd
O'er thy distinguish'd fate, and, clustering there
Thick as the locusts on the land of Nile,
Made death more deadly, and more dark the grave.
Reflect (if not forgot my touching tale)   240
How was each circumstance with aspics arm'd?
An aspic, each! and all, a hydra woe:
What strong Herculean virtue could suffice?—
Or is it virtue to be conquer'd here?
This hoary cheek a train of tears bedews;
And each tear mourns its own distinct distress;
And each distress, distinctly mourn'd, demands
Of grief still more, as heighten'd by the whole.
A grief like this proprietors excludes:
Not friends alone such obsequies deplore;   250
They make mankind the mourner; carry sighs
Far as the fatal fame can wing her way;
And turn the gayest thought of gayest age,   253

Down their right channel, through the vale of death.
　　The vale of death! that hush'd Cimmerian vale,
Where darkness, brooding o'er unfinish'd fates
With raven wing incumbent, waits the day
(Dread day!) that interdicts all future change!
That subterranean world, that land of ruin!
Fit walk, Lorenzo, for proud human thought!
There let my thought expatiate, and explore　　　　　　　261
Balsamic truths, and healing sentiments,
Of all most wanted, and most welcome, here.
For gay Lorenzo's sake, and for thy own,
My soul! "the fruits of dying friends survey;
Expose the vain of life; weigh life and death;
Give death his eulogy; thy fear subdue;
And labour that first palm of noble minds,
A manly scorn of terror from the tomb."
　　This harvest reap from thy Narcissa's grave.　　　　　270
As poets feign'd from Ajax' streaming blood
Arose, with grief inscribed, a mournful flower;
Let wisdom blossom from my mortal wound.
And first, of dying friends; what fruit from these?
It brings us more than triple aid; an aid
To chase our thoughtlessness, fear, pride, and guilt.
　　Our dying friends come o'er us like a cloud,
To damp our brainless ardours; and abate
That glare of life, which often blinds the wise.
Our dying friends are pioneers, to smooth　　　　　　　280
Our rugged pass to death; to break those bars
Of terror, and abhorrence, nature throws
Cross our obstructed way; and, thus to make
Welcome, as safe, our port from every storm.
Each friend by fate snatch'd from us, is a plume
Pluck'd from the wing of human vanity,
Which makes us stoop from our aërial heights,　　　　　287
And, damp'd with omen of our own decease,
On drooping pinions of ambition lower'd,
Just skim earth's surface, ere we break it up,
O'er putrid earth to scratch a little dust,
And save the world a nuisance. Smitten friends
Are angels sent on errands full of love;
For us they languish, and for us they die:
And shall they languish, shall they die, in vain?
Ungrateful, shall we grieve their hovering shades,
Which wait the revolution in our hearts?
Shall we disdain their silent soft address;
Their posthumous advice, and pious prayer?

Senseless, as herds that graze their hallow'd graves,   300
Tread under foot their agonies and groans;
Frustrate their anguish, and destroy their deaths?
    Lorenzo! no; the thought of death indulge;
Give it its wholesome empire! let it reign,
That kind chastiser of thy soul in joy!
Its reign will spread thy glorious conquests far,
And still the tumults of thy ruffled breast:
Auspicious era! golden days, begin!
The thought of death shall, like a god, inspire.
And why not think on death? Is life the theme   310
Of every thought? and wish of every hour?
And song of every joy? Surprising truth!
The beaten spaniel's fondness not so strange.
To wave the numerous ills that seize on life
As their own property, their lawful prey;
Ere man has measured half his weary stage,
His luxuries have left him no reserve,
No maiden relishes, unbroach'd delights;
On cold served repetitions he subsists,
And in the tasteless present chews the past;   320
Disgusted chews, and scarce can swallow down.   321
Like lavish ancestors, his earlier years
Have disinherited his future hours,
Which starve on orts, and glean their former field.
    Live ever here, Lorenzo?—shocking thought!
So shocking, they who wish, disown it too;
Disown from shame what they from folly crave.
Live ever in the womb, nor see the light?
For what live ever here?—With labouring step
To tread our former footsteps? pace the round   330
Eternal? to climb life's worn, heavy wheel,
Which draws up nothing new? to beat, and beat
The beaten track? to bid each wretched day
The former mock? to surfeit on the same,
And yawn our joys? or thank a misery
For change, though sad? to see what we have seen?
Hear, till unheard, the same old slabber'd tale?
To taste the tasted, and at each return
Less tasteful? o'er our palates to decant
Another vintage? strain a flatter year,   340
Through loaded vessels, and a laxer tone?
Crazy machines to grind earth's wasted fruits!
Ill-ground, and worse concocted! load, not life!
The rational foul kennels of excess!
Still-streaming thoroughfares of dull debauch!

Trembling each gulp, lest death should snatch the bowl.
    Such of our fine ones is the wish refined!
So would they have it: elegant desire!
Why not invite the bellowing stalls, and wilds?
But such examples might their riot awe.   350
Through want of virtue, that is, want of thought
(Though on bright thought they father all their flights),
To what are they reduced? To love, and hate,
The same vain world; to censure, and espouse,
This painted shrew of life, who calls them fool   355
Each moment of each day; to flatter bad
Through dread of worse; to cling to this rude rock,
Barren, to them, of good, and sharp with ills,
And hourly blacken'd with impending storms,
And infamous for wrecks of human hope—
Scared at the gloomy gulf, that yawns beneath,
Such are their triumphs! such their pangs of joy!   362
    'Tis time, high time, to shift this dismal scene.
This hugg'd, this hideous state, what art can cure?
One only; but that one, what all may reach;
Virtue—she, wonder-working goddess! charms
That rock to bloom; and tames the painted shrew;
And what will more surprise, Lorenzo! gives
To life's sick, nauseous iteration, change;
And straightens nature's circle to a line.   370
Believest thou this, Lorenzo? lend an ear,
A patient ear, thou'lt blush to disbelieve.
    A languid, leaden iteration reigns,
And ever must, o'er those, whose joys are joys
Of sight, smell, taste: the cuckoo-seasons sing
The same dull note to such as nothing prize,
But what those seasons, from the teeming earth,
To doating sense indulge. But nobler minds,
Which relish fruits unripen'd by the sun,
Make their days various; various as the dyes   380
On the dove's neck, which wanton in his rays.
On minds of dove-like innocence possess'd,
On lighten'd minds, that bask in virtue's beams,
Nothing hangs tedious, nothing old revolves
In that for which they long, for which they live.
Their glorious efforts, wing'd with heavenly hope,
Each rising morning sees still higher rise;
Each bounteous dawn its novelty presents
    To worth maturing, new strength, lustre, fame;   389
While nature's circle, like a chariot-wheel
Rolling beneath their elevated aims,

Makes their fair prospect fairer every hour;
Advancing virtue, in a line to bliss;
Virtue, which Christian motives best inspire!
And bliss, which Christian schemes alone ensure!
And shall we then, for virtue's sake, commence
Apostates, and turn infidels for joy?
A truth it is, few doubt, but fewer trust,
"He sins against this life, who slights the next."
What is this life? How few their favourite know!   400
Fond in the dark, and blind in our embrace,
By passionately loving life, we make
Loved life unlovely; hugging her to death.
We give to time eternity's regard;
And, dreaming, take our passage for our port.
Life has no value as an end, but means;
An end deplorable! a means divine!
When 'tis our all, 'tis nothing; worse than nought;
A nest of pains: when held as nothing, much:
Like some fair humorists, life is most enjoy'd,   410
When courted least; most worth, when disesteem'd;
Then 'tis the seat of comfort, rich in peace;
In prospect richer far; important! awful!
Not to be mention'd, but with shouts of praise!
Not to be thought on, but with tides of joy!
The mighty basis of eternal bliss!
Where now the barren rock? the painted shrew?
Where now, Lorenzo! life's eternal round?
Have I not made my triple promise good?
Vain is the world; but only to the vain.   420
To what compare we then this varying scene,
Whose worth ambiguous rises, and declines?
Waxes, and wanes? (In all propitious, night   423
Assists me here) compare it to the moon;
Dark in herself, and indigent; but rich
In borrow'd lustre from a higher sphere.
When gross guilt interposes, labouring earth,
O'ershadow'd, mourns a deep eclipse of joy;
Her joys, at brightest, pallid, to that font
Of full effulgent glory, whence they flow.   430
    Nor is that glory distant: Oh, Lorenzo!
A good man, and an angel! these between
How thin the barrier! What divides their fate?
Perhaps a moment, or perhaps a year:
Or, if an age, it is a moment still;
A moment, or eternity's forgot.
Then be, what once they were, who now are gods;

Be what Philander was, and claim the skies.
Starts timid nature at the gloomy pass?
The soft transition call it; and be cheer'd: 440
Such it is often, and why not to thee?
To hope the best, is pious, brave, and wise;
And may itself procure, what it presumes.
Life is much flatter'd, death is much traduced;
Compare the rivals, and the kinder crown.
"Strange competition!"—True, Lorenzo! strange!
So little life can cast into the scale.
    Life makes the soul dependent on the dust;
Death gives her wings to mount above the spheres.
Through chinks, styled organs, dim life peeps at light;
Death bursts th' involving cloud, and all is day;   451
All eye, all ear, the disembodied power.
Death has feign'd evils, nature shall not feel;
Life, ills substantial, wisdom cannot shun.
Is not the mighty mind, that son of heaven!
By tyrant life dethroned, imprison'd, pain'd?
By death enlarged, ennobled, deified?   457
Death but entombs the body; life the soul.
"Is Death then guiltless? How he marks his way
With dreadful waste of what deserves to shine!
Art, genius, fortune, elevated power!
With various lustres these light up the world,
Which Death puts out, and darkens human race."   463
I grant, Lorenzo! this indictment just:
The sage, peer, potentate, king, conqueror!
Death humbles these; more barbarous life, the man.
Life is the triumph of our mouldering clay;
Death, of the spirit infinite! divine!
Death has no dread, but what frail life imparts;
Nor life true joy, but what kind death improves.   470
No bliss has life to boast, till death can give
Far greater; life's a debtor to the grave,
Dark lattice! letting in eternal day.
    Lorenzo! blush at fondness for a life,
Which sends celestial souls on errands vile,
To cater for the sense; and serve at boards,
Where every ranger of the wilds, perhaps
Each reptile, justly claims our upper hand.
Luxurious feast! a soul, a soul immortal,
In all the dainties of a brute bemired!   480
Lorenzo! blush at terror for a death,
Which gives thee to repose in festive bowers,
Where nectars sparkle, angels minister,

And more than angels share, and raise, and crown,
And eternize, the birth, bloom, bursts of bliss.
What need I more? O Death, the palm is thine.
     Then welcome, Death! thy dreaded harbingers,
Age and disease; disease, though long my guest;
That plucks my nerves, those tender strings of life;
Which, pluck'd a little more, will toll the bell,   490
That calls my few friends to my funeral;   491
Where feeble nature drops, perhaps, a tear,
While reason and religion, better taught,
Congratulate the dead, and crown his tomb
With wreath triumphant. Death is victory;
It binds in chains the raging ills of life:
Lust and ambition, wrath and avarice,
Dragg'd at his chariot-wheel, applaud his power.
That ills corrosive, cares importunate,
Are not immortal too, O Death! is thine.   500
Our day of dissolution!—name it right;
'Tis our great pay-day; 'tis our harvest, rich
And ripe: what though the sickle, sometimes keen,
Just scars us as we reap the golden grain?
More than thy balm, O Gilead! heals the wound.
Birth's feeble cry, and death's deep dismal groan,
Are slender tributes low-tax'd nature pays
For mighty gain: the gain of each, a life!
But O! the last the former so transcends,
Life dies, compared; life lives beyond the grave.   510
     And feel I, Death! no joy from thought of thee?
Death, the great counsellor, who man inspires
With every nobler thought, and fairer deed!
Death, the deliverer, who rescues man!
Death, the rewarder, who the rescued crowns!
Death, that absolves my birth; a curse without it!
Rich death, that realises all my cares,
Toils, virtues, hopes; without it a chimera!
Death, of all pain the period, not of joy;
Joy's source, and subject, still subsist unhurt;   520
One, in my soul; and one, in her great Sire;
Though the four winds were warring for my dust.
Yes, and from winds, and waves, and central night,
Though prison'd there, my dust too I reclaim
(To dust when drop proud nature's proudest spheres),
And live entire. Death is the crown of life: 526
Were death denied, poor man would live in vain;
Were death denied, to live would not be life;
Were death denied, even fools would wish to die.

Death wounds to cure: we fall; we rise; we reign!
Spring from our fetters; fasten in the skies;
Where blooming Eden withers in our sight:
Death gives us more than was in Eden lost.
This king of terrors is the prince of peace.
When shall I die to vanity, pain, death?
When shall I die?—When shall I live for ever? 536

NIGHT FOURTH.

THE

CHRISTIAN TRIUMPH.

CONTAINING OUR

ONLY CURE FOR THE FEAR OF DEATH; AND PROPER SENTIMENTS OF
HEART ON THAT INESTIMABLE BLESSING.

TO THE

HONOURABLE MR YORKE.

A MUCH-INDEBTED MUSE, O Yorke! intrudes.
Amid the smiles of fortune, and of youth,
Thine ear is patient of a serious song.
How deep implanted in the breast of man
The dread of death! I sing its sovereign cure.
    Why start at Death? Where is he? Death arrived,
Is past; not come, or gone, he's never here.
Ere hope, sensation fails; black-boding man
Receives, not suffers, Death's tremendous blow.
The knell, the shroud, the mattock, and the grave;   10
The deep damp vault, the darkness, and the worm;
These are the bugbears of a winter's eve,
The terrors of the living, not the dead.
Imagination's fool, and error's wretch,
Man makes a death, which nature never made;
Then on the point of his own fancy falls;
And feels a thousand deaths, in fearing one.
    But were death frightful, what has age to fear?
If prudent, age should meet the friendly foe,
And shelter in his hospitable gloom.   20
I scarce can meet a monument, but holds
My younger; every date cries—"Come away."
And what recalls me? Look the world around,
And tell me what: the wisest cannot tell.
Should any born of woman give his thought
Full range, on just dislike's unbounded field;
Of things, the vanity; of men, the flaws;
Flaws in the best; the many, flaw all o'er;
As leopards, spotted, or, as Ethiops, dark;
Vivacious ill; good dying immature;   30
(How immature, Narcissa's marble tells!)

And at his death bequeathing endless pain;
His heart, though bold, would sicken at the sight,
And spend itself in sighs, for future scenes.
    But grant to life (and just it is to grant
To lucky life) some perquisites of joy;
A time there is, when, like a thrice-told tale,
Long-rifled life of sweet can yield no more,
But from our comment on the comedy,
Pleasing reflections on parts well sustain'd,   40
Or purposed emendations where we fail'd,
Or hopes of plaudits from our candid Judge,
When, on their exit, souls are bid unrobe,
Toss fortune back her tinsel, and her plume,
And drop this mask of flesh behind the scene.
    With me, that time is come; my world is dead;
A new world rises, and new manners reign:
Foreign comedians, a spruce band! arrive,
To push me from the scene, or hiss me there.
What a pert race starts up! the strangers gaze,   50
And I at them; my neighbour is unknown;
Nor that the worst: ah me! the dire effect
Of loitering here, of Death defrauded long;
Of old so gracious (and let that suffice),   54
My very master knows me not.—
    Shall I dare say, peculiar is the fate?
I've been so long remember'd, I'm forgot.
An object ever pressing dims the sight,
And hides behind its ardour to be seen.
When in his courtiers' ears I pour my plaint,   60
They drink it as the nectar of the great;
And squeeze my hand, and beg me come to-morrow.
Refusal! canst thou wear a smoother form?
    Indulge me, nor conceive I drop my theme:
Who cheapens life, abates the fear of death:
Twice told the period spent on stubborn Troy,
Court favour, yet untaken, I besiege;
Ambition's ill-judged effort to be rich.
Alas! ambition makes my little less;
Embittering the possess'd: Why wish for more?   70
Wishing, of all employments, is the worst;
Philosophy's reverse; and health's decay!
Were I as plump as stall'd theology,
Wishing would waste me to this shade again.
Were I as wealthy as a South Sea dream,
Wishing is an expedient to be poor.
Wishing, that constant hectic of a fool;

Caught at a court; purged off by purer air,
And simpler diet; gifts of rural life!
  Bless'd be that hand divine, which gently laid   80
My heart at rest, beneath this humble shed.
The world's a stately bark, on dangerous seas,
With pleasure seen, but boarded at our peril;
Here, on a single plank, thrown safe ashore,
I hear the tumult of the distant throng,
As that of seas remote, or dying storms:
And meditate on scenes, more silent still;
Pursue my theme, and fight the fear of death.   88
Here, like a shepherd gazing from his hut,
Touching his reed, or leaning on his staff,
Eager ambition's fiery chace I see;
I see the circling hunt, of noisy men,
Burst law's enclosure, leap the mounds of right,
Pursuing, and pursued, each other's prey;
As wolves, for rapine; as the fox, for wiles;
Till Death, that mighty hunter, earths them all.
  Why all this toil for triumphs of an hour?
What though we wade in wealth, or soar in fame?
Earth's highest station ends in "Here he lies:"
And "Dust to dust" concludes her noblest song.   100
If this song lives, posterity shall know
One, though in Britain born, with courtiers bred,
Who thought even gold might come a day too late;
Nor on his subtle death-bed plann'd his scheme
For future vacancies in Church or State;
Some avocation deeming it—to die,
Unbit by rage canine of dying rich;
Guilt's blunder! and the loudest laugh of hell.
  O my coevals! remnants of yourselves!
Poor human ruins, tottering o'er the grave!   110
Shall we, shall aged men, like aged trees,
Strike deeper their vile root, and closer cling,
Still more enamour'd of this wretched soil?
Shall our pale, wither'd hands, be still stretch'd out,
Trembling, at once, with eagerness and age?
With avarice, and convulsions, grasping hard?
Grasping at air! for what has earth beside?
Man wants but little; nor that little, long;
How soon must he resign his very dust,
Which frugal nature lent him for an hour!   120
Years unexperienced rush on numerous ills;
And soon as man, expert from time, has found   122
The key of life, it opes the gates of death.

When in this vale of years I backward look,
And miss such numbers, numbers too of such,
Firmer in health, and greener in their age,
And stricter on their guard, and fitter far
To play life's subtle game, I scarce believe
I still survive: and am I fond of life,
Who scarce can think it possible, I live? 130
Alive by miracle! or, what is next,
Alive by Mead! if I am still alive,
Who long have buried what gives life to live,
Firmness of nerve, and energy of thought.
Life's lee is not more shallow, than impure,
And vapid; sense and reason show the door,
Call for my bier, and point me to the dust.
    O thou great arbiter of life and death!
Nature's immortal, immaterial Sun!
Whose all-prolific beam late call'd me forth 140
From darkness, teeming darkness, where I lay
The worm's inferior, and, in rank, beneath
The dust I tread on, high to bear my brow,
To drink the spirit of the golden day,
And triumph in existence; and could know
No motive, but my bliss; and hast ordain'd
A rise in blessing! with the patriarch's joy,
Thy call I follow to the land unknown;
I trust in thee, and know in whom I trust;
Or life, or death, is equal; neither weighs: 150
All weight in this—O let me live to thee!
    Though nature's terrors thus may be repress'd;
Still frowns grim Death; guilt points the tyrant's spear.
And whence all human guilt? From death forgot.
Ah me! too long I set at nought the swarm
Of friendly warnings, which around me flew; 156
And smiled, unsmitten: small my cause to smile!
Death's admonitions, like shafts upwards shot,
More dreadful by delay, the longer ere
They strike our hearts, the deeper is their wound;
O think how deep, Lorenzo! here it stings:
Who can appease its anguish? How it burns! 162
What hand the barb'd, envenom'd thought can draw?
What healing hand can pour the balm of peace?
And turn my sight undaunted on the tomb?
    With joy,—with grief, that healing hand I see;
Ah! too conspicuous! it is fix'd on high.
On high?—What means my phrensy? I blaspheme;
Alas! how low! how far beneath the skies!

The skies it form'd; and now it bleeds for me—   170
But bleeds the balm I want—yet still it bleeds;
Draw the dire steel—ah, no! the dreadful blessing
What heart or can sustain, or dares forego?
There hangs all human hope: that nail supports
The falling universe: that gone, we drop;
Horror receives us, and the dismal wish
Creation had been smother'd in her birth—
Darkness his curtain, and his bed the dust;
When stars and sun are dust beneath his throne!
In heaven itself can such indulgence dwell?   180
Oh, what a groan was there! a groan not his.
He seized our dreadful right; the load sustained;
And heaved the mountain from a guilty world.
A thousand worlds, so bought, were bought too dear;
Sensations new in angels' bosoms rise;
Suspend their song; and make a pause in bliss.
        O for their song, to reach my lofty theme!
Inspire me, Night! with all thy tuneful spheres;
Whilst I with seraphs share seraphic themes,
And show to men the dignity of man;   190
Lest I blaspheme my subject with my song.
Shall Pagan pages glow celestial flame,
And Christian languish? On our hearts, not heads,
Falls the foul infamy: my heart! awake.
What can awake thee, unawaked by this,
"Expended deity on human weal?"
Feel the great truths, which burst the tenfold night
Of heathen error, with a golden flood
Of endless day: to feel, is to be fired;
And to believe, Lorenzo! is to feel.   200
        Thou most indulgent, most tremendous Power!
Still more tremendous, for thy wondrous love!
That arms, with awe more awful, thy commands;
And foul transgression dips in sevenfold night;
How our hearts tremble at thy love immense!
In love immense, inviolably just!
Thou, rather than thy justice should be stain'd,
Didst stain the cross; and work of wonders far
The greatest, that thy dearest far might bleed.
        Bold thought! shall I dare speak it, or repress?   210
Should man more execrate, or boast, the guilt
Which roused such vengeance? which such love inflamed?
O'er guilt (how mountainous!), with outstretch'd arms,
Stern justice, and soft-smiling love embrace,
Supporting, in full majesty, thy throne,

When seem'd its majesty to need support,
Or that, or man, inevitably lost:
What, but the fathomless of thought divine,
Could labour such expedient from despair,
And rescue both? Both rescue! both exalt!   220
Oh, how are both exalted by the deed!
The wondrous deed! or shall I call it more?
A wonder in omnipotence itself!   223
A mystery no less to gods than men!
  Not, thus, our infidels th' Eternal draw,
A God all o'er, consummate, absolute,
Full-orb'd, in his whole round of rays complete:
They set at odds Heaven's jarring attributes;
And, with one excellence, another wound;
Maim Heaven's perfection, break its equal beams,
Bid mercy triumph over—God himself,   231
Undeified by their opprobrious praise:
A God all mercy, is a God unjust.
  Ye brainless wits! ye baptized infidels!
Ye worse for mending! wash'd to fouler stains!
The ransom was paid down; the fund of heaven,
Heaven's inexhaustible, exhausted fund,
Amazing, and amazed, pour'd forth the price,
All price beyond: though curious to compute,
Archangels fail'd to cast the mighty sum: 240
Its value vast, ungrasp'd by minds create,
For ever hides, and glows, in the Supreme.
  And was the ransom paid? It was: and paid
(What can exalt the bounty more?) for you.
The sun beheld it—No! the shocking scene,
Drove back his chariot: midnight veil'd his face;
Not such as this; not such as nature makes;
A midnight nature shudder'd to behold;
A midnight new! a dread eclipse (without
Opposing spheres) from her Creator's frown!   250
Sun! didst thou fly thy Maker's pain? or start
At that enormous load of human guilt,
Which bow'd His blessed head; o'erwhelm'd His cross;
Made groan the centre; burst earth's marble womb,
With pangs, strange pangs! deliver'd of her dead?
Hell howl'd; and heaven that hour let fall a tear;
Heaven wept, that men might smile! Heaven bled, that man
Might never die!——
  And is devotion virtue? 'Tis compell'd.   259
What heart of stone but glows at thoughts like these?
Such contemplations mount us; and should mount

The mind still higher; nor ever glance on man,
Unraptured, uninflamed.—Where roll my thoughts
To rest from wonders? Other wonders rise;
And strike where'er they roll: my soul is caught:
Heaven's sovereign blessings, clustering from the cross,
Rush on her, in a throng, and close her round,
The prisoner of amaze!—In his bless'd life,
I see the path, and, in his death, the price,
And in his great ascent, the proof supreme   270
Of immortality.—And did he rise?
Hear, O ye nations! hear it, O ye dead!
He rose! he rose! he burst the bars of death.
Lift up your heads, ye everlasting gates!
And give the King of glory to come in.
Who is the King of glory? He who left
His throne of glory, for the pang of death:
Lift up your heads, ye everlasting gates!
And give the King of glory to come in.
Who is the King of glory? He who slew   280
The ravenous foe, that gorged all human race!
The King of glory, he whose glory fill'd
Heaven with amazement at his love to man;
And with divine complacency beheld
Powers most illumined, wilder'd in the theme.

        The theme, the joy, how then shall man sustain?
O the burst gates! crush'd sting! demolish'd throne!
Last gasp of vanquish'd Death! Shout earth and heaven!
This sum of good to man. Whose nature then
Took wing, and mounted with him from the tomb!   290
Then, then, I rose; then first humanity   291
Triumphant pass'd the crystal ports of light
(Stupendous guest!), and seized eternal youth,
Seized in our name. E'er since, 'tis blasphemous
To call man mortal. Man's mortality
Was then transferr'd to death; and heaven's duration
Unalienably seal'd to this frail frame,
This child of dust—Man, all-immortal! hail;
Hail, Heaven! all lavish of strange gifts to man!
Thine all the glory; man's the boundless bliss.   300
        Where am I rapt by this triumphant theme?
On Christian joy's exulting wing, above
Th' Aonian mount?—Alas! small cause for joy!
What if to pain immortal? if extent
Of being, to preclude a close of woe?
Where, then, my boast of immortality?
I boast it still, though cover'd o'er with guilt;

For guilt, not innocence, his life he pour'd;
'Tis guilt alone can justify his death;
Nor that, unless his death can justify   310
Relenting guilt in Heaven's indulgent sight.
If, sick of folly, I relent; he writes
My name in heaven with that inverted spear
(A spear deep-dipp'd in blood!) which pierced his side,
And open'd there a font for all mankind,
Who strive, who combat crimes, to drink, and live:
This, only this, subdues the fear of death.
        And what is this?—Survey the wondrous cure:
And at each step, let higher wonder rise!
"Pardon for infinite offence! and pardon   320
Through means that speak its value infinite!
A pardon bought with blood! with blood divine!
With blood divine of Him I made my foe!
Persisted to provoke! though woo'd and awed,
Bless'd and chastised, a flagrant rebel still!   325
A rebel, 'midst the thunders of his throne!
Nor I alone! a rebel universe!
My species up in arms! not one exempt!
Yet for the foulest of the foul, he dies,
Most joy'd, for the redeem'd from deepest guilt!
As if our race were held of highest rank;
And Godhead dearer, as more kind to man!"   332
        Bound, every heart! and every bosom, burn!
O what a scale of miracles is here!
Its lowest round, high planted on the skies;
Its towering summit lost beyond the thought
Of man or angel! O that I could climb
The wonderful ascent, with equal praise!
Praise! flow for ever (if astonishment
Will give thee leave) my praise! for ever flow;   340
Praise ardent, cordial, constant, to high Heaven
More fragrant, than Arabia sacrificed,
And all her spicy mountains in a flame.
        So dear, so due to Heaven, shall praise descend,
With her soft plume (from plausive angel's wing
First pluck'd by man) to tickle mortal ears,
Thus diving in the pockets of the great?
Is praise the perquisite of every paw,
Though black as hell, that grapples well for gold?
O love of gold! thou meanest of amours!   350
Shall praise her odours waste on Virtue's dead,
Embalm the base, perfume the stench of guilt,
Earn dirty bread by washing Æthiops fair,

Removing filth, or sinking it from sight,
A scavenger in scenes, where vacant posts,
Like gibbets yet untenanted, expect
Their future ornaments? From courts and thrones,
Return, apostate praise! thou vagabond!
Thou prostitute! to thy first love return,   395
Thy first, thy greatest, once unrivall'd theme.
        There flow redundant; like Meander flow,
Back to thy fountain; to that parent Power,
Who gives the tongue to sound, the thought to soar,
The soul to be. Men homage pay to men,
Thoughtless beneath whose dreadful eye they bow
In mutual awe profound, of clay to clay,
Of guilt to guilt; and turn their back on thee,
Great Sire! whom thrones celestial ceaseless sing;
To prostrate angels, an amazing scene!
O the presumption of man's awe for man!—   370
Man's author! end! restorer! law! and judge!
Thine, all; day thine, and thine this gloom of night,
With all her wealth, with all her radiant worlds:
What, night eternal, but a frown from thee?
What, heaven's meridian glory, but thy smile?
And shall not praise be thine? not human praise?
While heaven's high host on hallelujahs live?
        O may I breathe no longer, than I breathe
My soul in praise to Him, who gave my soul,
And all her infinite of prospect fair,   380
Cut through the shades of hell great Love! by thee
O most adorable! most unadored!
Where shall that praise begin, which ne'er should end?
Where'er I turn, what claim on all applause!
How is night's sable mantle labour'd o'er,
How richly wrought with attributes divine!
What wisdom shines! what love! This midnight pomp,
This gorgeous arch, with golden worlds inlaid!
Built with divine ambition! nought to thee;
For others this profusion: Thou, apart,   390
Above! beyond! O tell me, mighty Mind!
Where art thou? Shall I dive into the deep,
Call to the sun, or ask the roaring winds,   393
For their Creator? Shall I question loud
The thunder, if in that th' Almighty dwells?
Or holds He furious storms in straiten'd reins,
And bids fierce whirlwinds wheel his rapid car?
        What mean these questions?—Trembling I retract;
My prostrate soul adores the present God:

Praise I a distant deity? He tunes   400
My voice (if tuned); the nerve, that writes, sustains:
Wrapp'd in his being, I resound his praise:
But though past all diffused, without a shore,
His essence; local is his throne (as meet),
To gather the dispersed (as standards call
The listed from afar): to fix a point,
A central point, collective of his sons,
Since finite every nature but his own.
     The nameless He, whose nod is nature's birth;
And nature's shield, the shadow of his hand;   410
Her dissolution, his suspended smile!
The great First-Last! pavilion'd high he sits,
In darkness from excessive splendour borne,
By gods unseen, unless through lustre lost.
His glory, to created glory, bright,
As that to central horrors; he looks down
On all that soars; and spans immensity.
     Though night unnumber'd worlds unfolds to view,
Boundless creation! what art thou? A beam,
A mere effluvium of his majesty: 420
And shall an atom of this atom-world
Mutter, in dust and sin, the theme of heaven?
Down to the centre should I send my thought
Through beds of glittering ore, and glowing gems,
Their beggar'd blaze wants lustre for my lay;
Goes out in darkness: if, on towering wing,
I send it through the boundless vault of stars!   427
The stars, though rich, what dross their gold to thee,
Great, good, wise, wonderful, eternal King!
If to those conscious stars thy throne around,
Praise ever-pouring, and imbibing bliss;
And ask their strain; they want it, more they want,
Poor their abundance, humble their sublime,   433
Languid their energy, their ardour cold,
Indebted still, their highest rapture burns;
Short of its mark, defective, though divine.
     Still more—this theme is man's, and man's alone;
Their vast appointments reach it not: they see
On earth a bounty not indulged on high;
And downward look for heaven's superior praise!   440
First-born of ether! high in fields of light!
View man, to see the glory of your God!
Could angels envy, they had envied here;
And some did envy; and the rest, though gods,
Yet still gods unredeem'd (their triumphs man,

Tempted to weigh the dust against the skies),
They less would feel, though more adorn, my theme.
They sung creation (for in that they shared);
How rose in melody, that child of love!
Creation's great superior, man! is thine;   450
Thine is redemption; they just gave the key:
'Tis thine to raise, and eternize, the song;
Though human, yet divine; for should not this
Raise man o'er man, and kindle seraphs here?
Redemption! 'twas creation more sublime;
Redemption! 'twas the labour of the skies;
Far more than labour—it was death in heaven.
A truth so strange! 'twere bold to think it true;
If not far bolder still to disbelieve.   459
        Here pause, and ponder—Was there death in heaven?
What then on earth? on earth, which struck the blow?
Who struck it? Who?—O how is man enlarged,   462
Seen through this medium! How the pigmy towers!
How counterpoised his origin from dust!
How counterpoised to dust his sad return!
How voided his vast distance from the skies!
How near he presses on the seraph's wing!
Which is the seraph? Which the born of clay?
How this demonstrates, through the thickest cloud
Of guilt, and clay condensed, the son of heaven!   470
The double son; the made, and the re-made!
And shall heaven's double property be lost?
Man's double madness only can destroy.
To man the bleeding cross has promised all;
The bleeding cross has sworn eternal grace;
Who gave his life, what grace shall he deny?
O ye who, from this Rock of Ages, leap,
Apostates, plunging headlong in the deep!
What cordial joy, what consolation strong,
Whatever winds arise, or billows roll,   480
Our interest in the Master of the storm!
Cling there, and in wreck'd nature's ruins smile;
While vile apostates tremble in a calm.
        Man! know thyself. All wisdom centres there;
To none man seems ignoble, but to man;
Angels that grandeur, men o'erlook, admire:
How long shall human nature be their book,
Degenerate mortal! and unread by thee?
The beam dim reason sheds shows wonders there;
What high contents! illustrious faculties!   490
But the grand comment, which displays at full

Our human height, scarce sever'd from divine,
By heaven composed, was publish'd on the Cross.
      Who looks on that, and sees not in himself
An awful stranger, a terrestrial god?   495
A glorious partner with the Deity
In that high attribute, immortal life?
If a god bleeds, he bleeds not for a worm:
I gaze, and, as I gaze, my mounting soul
Catches strange fire, eternity! at thee;
And drops the world—or rather, more enjoys:
How changed the face of nature! how improved!   502
What seem'd a chaos, shines a glorious world,
Or, what a world, an Eden; heighten'd all!
It is another scene! another self!
And still another, as time rolls along;
And that a self far more illustrious still.
Beyond long ages, yet roll'd up in shades
Unpierced by bold conjecture's keenest ray,
What evolutions of surprising fate!   510
How nature opens, and receives my soul
In boundless walks of raptured thought! where gods
Encounter and embrace me! What new births
Of strange adventure, foreign to the sun,
Where what now charms, perhaps, whate'er exists,
Old time, and fair creation, are forgot!
      Is this extravagant? Of man we form
Extravagant conception, to be just:
Conception unconfined wants wings to reach him:
Beyond its reach, the Godhead only, more.   520
He, the great Father! kindled at one flame
The world of rationals; one spirit pour'd
From spirit's awful fountain; pour'd himself
Through all their souls; but not in equal stream,
Profuse, or frugal, of th' inspiring God,
As his wise plan demanded; and when past
Their various trials, in their various spheres,
If they continue rational, as made,
Resorbs them all into himself again;   529
His throne their centre, and his smile their crown.
      Why doubt we, then, the glorious truth to sing,
Though yet unsung, as deem'd, perhaps, too bold?
Angels are men of a superior kind;
Angels are men in lighter habit clad,
High o'er celestial mountains wing'd in flight;
And men are angels, loaded for an hour,
Who wade this miry vale, and climb with pain,

And slippery step, the bottom of the steep.
Angels their failings, mortals have their praise;
While here, of corps ethereal, such enroll'd,   540
And summon'd to the glorious standard soon,
Which flames eternal crimson through the skies.
Nor are our brothers thoughtless of their kin,
Yet absent; but not absent from their love.
Michael has fought our battles; Raphael sung
Our triumphs; Gabriel on our errands flown,
Sent by the Sovereign: and are these, O Man!
Thy friends, thy warm allies? and thou (shame burn
The cheek to cinder!) rival to the brute?
    Religion's all. Descending from the skies   550
To wretched man, the goddess, in her left,
Holds out this world, and, in her right, the next;
Religion! the sole voucher man is man;
Supporter sole of man above himself;
Even in this night of frailty, change, and death,
She gives the soul a soul that acts a god.
Religion! Providence! an After-state!
Here is firm footing; here is solid rock!
This can support us; all is sea besides;
Sinks under us; bestorms, and then devours.   560
His hand the good man fastens on the skies,
And bids earth roll, nor feels her idle whirl.
    As when a wretch, from thick polluted air,   563
Darkness, and stench, and suffocating damps,
And dungeon horrors, by kind fate, discharged,
Climbs some fair eminence, where ether pure
Surrounds him, and Elysian prospects rise,
His heart exults, his spirits cast their load;
As if new-born, he triumphs in the change;
So joys the soul, when, from inglorious aims,
And sordid sweets, from feculence and froth   571
Of ties terrestrial, set at large, she mounts
To reason's region, her own element,
Breathes hopes immortal, and affects the skies.
    Religion! thou the soul of happiness;
And, groaning Calvary, of thee! there shine
The noblest truths; there strongest motives sting;
There sacred violence assaults the soul;
There, nothing but compulsion is forborne.
Can love allure us? or can terror awe?   580
He weeps!—the falling drop puts out the sun;
He sighs—the sigh earth's deep foundation shakes.
If in his love so terrible, what then

His wrath inflamed? his tenderness on fire?
Like soft, smooth oil, outblazing other fires?
Can prayer, can praise avert it?—Thou, my all!
My theme! my inspiration! and my crown!
My strength in age! my rise in low estate!
My soul's ambition, pleasure, wealth!—my world!
My light in darkness! and my life in death!   590
My boast through time! bliss through eternity!
Eternity, too short to speak thy praise!
Or fathom thy profound of love to man!
To man of men the meanest, even to me;
My sacrifice! my God!—what things are these!
    What then art Thou? by what name shall I call thee?—
Knew I the name devout archangels use,   597
Devout archangels should the name enjoy,
By me unrivall'd; thousands more sublime,
None half so dear as that which, though unspoke,
Still glows at heart: O how omnipotence
Is lost in love! Thou great Philanthropist!
Father of angels! but the friend of man!   603
Like Jacob, fondest of the younger born!
Thou, who didst save him, snatch the smoking brand
From out the flames, and quench it in thy blood!
How art thou pleased, by bounty to distress!
To make us groan beneath our gratitude,
Too big for birth! to favour, and confound;
To challenge, and to distance all return!   610
Of lavish love stupendous heights to soar,
And leave praise panting in the distant vale!
Thy right, too great, defrauds thee of thy due;
And sacrilegious our sublimest song.
But since the naked will obtains thy smile,
Beneath this monument of praise unpaid,
And future life symphonious to my strain,
(That noblest hymn to heaven!) for ever lie
Entomb'd my fear of death! and every fear,
The dread of every evil, but thy frown.   620
    Whom see I yonder, so demurely smile?
Laughter a labour, and might break their rest.
Ye quietists, in homage to the skies!
Serene! of soft address! who mildly make
An unobtrusive tender of your hearts,
Abhorring violence! who halt indeed;
But, for the blessing, wrestle not with Heaven!
Think you my song too turbulent? too warm?
Are passions, then, the Pagans of the soul?

Reason alone baptized? alone ordain'd   630
To touch things sacred? Oh for warmer still!   631
Guilt chills my zeal, and age benumbs my powers;
Oh for an humbler heart, and prouder song!
Thou, my much-injured theme! with that soft eye,
Which melted o'er doom'd Salem, deign to look
Compassion to the coldness of my breast;
And pardon to the winter in my strain.
        O ye cold-hearted, frozen, formalists!
On such a theme, 'tis impious to be calm;
Passion is reason, transport temper, here.   640
Shall Heaven, which gave us ardour, and has shown
Her own for man so strongly, not disdain
What smooth emollients in theology,
Recumbent virtue's downy doctors preach,
That prose of piety, a lukewarm praise?
Rise odours sweet from incense uninflamed?
Devotion, when lukewarm, is undevout;
But when it glows, its heat is struck to heaven;
To human hearts her golden harps are strung;
High heaven's orchestra chants amen to man.   650
        Hear I, or dream I hear, their distant strain,
Sweet to the soul, and tasting strong of heaven,
Soft-wafted on celestial pity's plume,
Through the vast spaces of the universe,
To cheer me in this melancholy gloom?
Oh, when will death (now stingless), like a friend,
Admit me of their choir? Oh, when will death
This mouldering, old, partition-wall throw down?
Give beings, one in nature, one abode?
O Death divine! that givest us to the skies!   660
Great future! glorious patron of the past,
And present! when shall I thy shrine adore?
From nature's continent, immensely wide,
Immensely bless'd, this little isle of life,
This dark, incarcerating colony,   665
Divides us. Happy day! that breaks our chain;
That manumits; that calls from exile home;
That leads to nature's great metropolis,
And re-admits us, through the guardian hand
Of elder brothers, to our Father's throne;
Who hears our Advocate, and, through his wounds
Beholding man, allows that tender name.   672
'Tis this makes Christian triumph a command:
'Tis this makes joy a duty to the wise;
'Tis impious in a good man to be sad.

See thou, Lorenzo! where hangs all our hope?
Touch'd by the Cross, we live; or, more than die;
That touch which touch'd not angels; more divine
Than that which touch'd confusion into form,
And darkness into glory; partial touch!   680
Ineffably pre-eminent regard!
Sacred to man, and sovereign through the whole
Long golden chain of miracles, which hangs
From heaven through all duration, and supports
In one illustrious and amazing plan,
Thy welfare, nature! and thy God's renown.
That touch, with charm celestial, heals the soul
Diseased, drives pain from guilt, lights life in death,
Turns earth to heaven, to heavenly thrones transforms
The ghastly ruins of the mouldering tomb.   690
    Dost ask me when? When He who died returns;
Returns, how changed! Where then the man of woe?
In glory's terrors all the Godhead burns;
And all his courts, exhausted by the tide
Of deities triumphant in his train,
Leave a stupendous solitude in heaven;
Replenish'd soon, replenish'd with increase
Of pomp, and multitude; a radiant band   698
Of angels new; of angels from the tomb.
    Is this by fancy thrown remote? and rise
Dark doubts between the promise and event?
I send thee not to volumes for thy cure;
Read nature; nature is a friend to truth;
Nature is Christian; preaches to mankind;
And bids dead matter aid us in our creed.
Hast thou ne'er seen the comet's flaming flight?
Th' illustrious stranger passing, terror sheds
On gazing nations; from his fiery train
Of length enormous, takes his ample round   709
Through depths of ether; coasts unnumber'd worlds,
Of more than solar glory; doubles wide
Heaven's mighty cape; and then revisits earth,
From the long travel of a thousand years.
Thus, at the destined period, shall return
He, once on earth, who bids the comet blaze:
And, with him, all our triumph o'er the tomb.
    Nature is dumb on this important point;
Or hope precarious in low whisper breathes;
Faith speaks aloud, distinct; even adders hear;
But turn, and dart into the dark again.   720
Faith builds a bridge across the gulf of death,

To break the shock blind nature cannot shun,
And lands thought smoothly on the farther shore.
Death's terror is the mountain faith removes;
That mountain barrier between man and peace.
'Tis faith disarms destruction; and absolves
From every clamorous charge, the guiltless tomb.
     Why disbelieve? Lorenzo!—"Reason bids,
All-sacred reason."—Hold her sacred still;
Nor shalt thou want a rival in thy flame: 730
All-sacred reason! source, and soul, of all
Demanding praise, on earth, or earth above!   732
My heart is thine: deep in its inmost folds,
Live thou with life; live dearer of the two.
Wear I the blessed cross, by fortune stamp'd
On passive nature, before thought was born?
My birth's blind bigot! fired with local zeal!
No; reason re-baptized me when adult;
Weigh'd true, and false, in her impartial scale;
My heart became the convert of my head;   740
And made that choice, which once was but my fate.
"On argument alone my faith is built:"
Reason pursued is faith; and, unpursued
Where proof invites, 'tis reason, then, no more:
And such our proof, that, or our faith is right,
Or reason lies, and Heaven design'd it wrong:
Absolve we this? What, then, is blasphemy?
     Fond as we are, and justly fond, of faith,
Reason, we grant, demands our first regard;
The mother honour'd, as the daughter dear.   750
Reason the root, fair faith is but the flower;
The fading flower shall die; but reason lives
Immortal, as her Father in the skies.
When faith is virtue, reason makes it so.
Wrong not the Christian; think not reason yours:
'Tis reason our great Master holds so dear;
'Tis reason's injured rights his wrath resents;
'Tis reason's voice obey'd his glories crown;
To give lost reason life, he pour'd his own:
Believe, and show the reason of a man;   760
Believe, and taste the pleasure of a God;
Believe, and look with triumph on the tomb:
Through reason's wounds alone thy faith can die;
Which dying, tenfold terror gives to death,
And dips in venom his twice-mortal sting.
     Learn hence what honours, what loud pæans, due   766
To those, who push our antidote aside;

74

Those boasted friends to reason, and to man,
Whose fatal love stabs every joy, and leaves
Death's terror heighten'd, gnawing on his heart.
Those pompous sons of reason idolized
And vilified at once; of reason dead,
Then deified, as monarchs were of old; 773
What conduct plants proud laurels on their brow?
While love of truth through all their camp resounds,
They draw pride's curtain o'er the noontide ray,
Spike up their inch of reason, on the point
Of philosophic wit, call'd argument;
And then, exulting in their taper, cry,
"Behold the sun!" and, Indian-like, adore. 780
    Talk they of morals? O thou bleeding Love!
Thou maker of new morals to mankind!
The grand morality is love of thee.
As wise as Socrates, if such they were
(Nor will they bate of that sublime renown),
As wise as Socrates, might justly stand
The definition of a modern fool.
    A Christian is the highest style of man:
And is there, who the blessed cross wipes off,
As a foul blot from his dishonour'd brow? 790
If angels tremble, 'tis at such a sight:
The wretch they quit, desponding of their charge,
More struck with grief or wonder, who can tell?
    Ye sold to sense! ye citizens of earth!
(For such alone the Christian banner fly)
Know ye how wise your choice, how great your gain?
Behold the picture of earth's happiest man:
"He calls his wish, it comes; he sends it back,
And says, he call'd another; that arrives,
Meets the same welcome; yet he still calls on; 800
Till one calls him, who varies not his call,
But holds him fast, in chains of darkness bound,
Till nature dies, and judgment sets him free;
A freedom far less welcome than his chain."
    But grant man happy; grant him happy long;
Add to life's highest prize her latest hour;
That hour, so late, is nimble in approach,
That, like a post, comes on in full career:
How swift the shuttle flies that weaves thy shroud!
Where is the fable of thy former years? 810
Thrown down the gulf of time; as far from thee
As they had ne'er been thine; the day in hand,
Like a bird struggling to get loose, is going;

Scarce now possess'd, so suddenly 'tis gone;
And each swift moment fled, is death advanced
By strides as swift. Eternity is all;
And whose eternity? Who triumphs there?
Bathing for ever in the font of bliss!
For ever basking in the Deity!
Lorenzo! who?—Thy conscience shall reply.   820

     O give it leave to speak! 'twill speak ere long,
Thy leave unask'd; Lorenzo! hear it now,
While useful its advice, its accents mild.
By the great edict, the divine decree,
Truth is deposited with man's last hour;
An honest hour, and faithful to her trust;
Truth, eldest daughter of the Deity;
Truth, of his council, when he made the worlds;
Nor less, when he shall judge the worlds he made;
Though silent long, and sleeping ne'er so sound,   830
Smother'd with errors, and oppress'd with toys,
That heaven-commission'd hour no sooner calls,
But from her cavern in the soul's abyss,
Like him they fable under Ætna whelm'd,   834
The goddess bursts in thunder, and in flame;
Loudly convinces, and severely pains.
Dark demons I discharge, and hydra-stings;
The keen vibration of bright truth—is hell:
Just definition! though by schools untaught.
Ye deaf to truth! peruse this parson'd page,   840
And trust, for once, a prophet, and a priest;
"Men may live fools, but fools they cannot die."

NIGHT FIFTH.

THE RELAPSE.

TO THE RIGHT HONOURABLE

THE EARL OF LICHFIELD.

LORENZO! to recriminate is just.
Fondness for fame is avarice of air.
I grant the man is vain who writes for praise.
Praise no man e'er deserved, who sought no more.
    As just thy second charge. I grant the Muse
Has often blush'd at her degenerate sons,
Retain'd by sense to plead her filthy cause;
To raise the low, to magnify the mean,
And subtilize the gross into refined:
As if to magic numbers' powerful charm   10
'Twas given, to make a civet of their song
Obscene, and sweeten ordure to perfume.
Wit, a true Pagan, deifies the brute,
And lifts our swine-enjoyments from the mire.
    The fact notorious, nor obscure the cause.
We wear the chains of pleasure and of pride.
These share the man; and these distract him too;
Draw different ways, and clash in their commands.
Pride, like an eagle, builds among the stars;
But pleasure, lark-like, nests upon the ground.   20
Joys shared by brute creation, pride resents;   21
Pleasure embraces: man would both enjoy,
And both at once: a point so hard, how gain!
But, what can't wit, when stung by strong desire?
    Wit dares attempt this arduous enterprise.
Since joys of sense can't rise to reason's taste;
In subtle sophistry's laborious forge,
Wit hammers out a reason new, that stoops
To sordid scenes, and meets them with applause.
Wit calls the graces the chaste zone to loose;   30
Nor less than a plump god to fill the bowl:
A thousand phantoms, and a thousand spells,
A thousand opiates scatters, to delude,
To fascinate, inebriate, lay asleep,
And the fool'd mind delightfully confound.

Thus that which shock'd the judgment, shocks no more;
That which gave Pride offence, no more offends.
Pleasure and Pride, by nature mortal foes,
At war eternal, which in man shall reign,
By Wit's address, patch up a fatal peace,   40
And hand in hand lead on the rank debauch,
From rank refined to delicate and gay.
Art, cursed Art! wipes off th' indebted blush
From Nature's cheek, and bronzes every shame.
Man smiles in ruin, glories in his guilt,
And infamy stands candidate for praise.
    All writ by man in favour of the soul,
These sensual ethics far, in bulk, transcend.
The flowers of eloquence, profusely pour'd
O'er spotted vice, fill half the letter'd world.   50
Can powers of genius exorcise their page,
And consecrate enormities with song?
    But let not these inexpiable strains
Condemn the Muse that knows her dignity;
Nor meanly stops at time, but holds the world   55
As 'tis, in nature's ample field, a point,
A point in her esteem; from whence to start,
And run the round of universal space,
To visit being universal there,
And being's source, that utmost flight of mind!
Yet, spite of this so vast circumference,
Well knows, but what is moral, nought is great.   62
Sing syrens only? Do not angels sing?
There is in Poesy a decent pride,
Which well becomes her when she speaks to Prose,
Her younger sister; haply, not more wise.
    Think'st thou, Lorenzo! to find pastimes here?
No guilty passion blown into a flame,
No foible flatter'd, dignity disgraced,
No fairy field of fiction, all on flower,   70
No rainbow colours here, or silken tale:
But solemn counsels, images of awe,
Truths, which eternity lets fall on man
With double weight, through these revolving spheres,
This death-deep silence, and incumbent shade:
Thoughts, such as shall revisit your last hour;
Visit uncall'd, and live when life expires;
And thy dark pencil, Midnight! darker still
In melancholy dipp'd, embrowns the whole.
    Yet this, even this, my laughter-loving friends!   80
Lorenzo! and thy brothers of the smile!

If, what imports you most, can most engage,
Shall steal your ear, and chain you to my song.
Or if you fail me, know, the wise shall taste
The truths I sing; the truths I sing shall feel;
And, feeling, give assent; and their assent
Is ample recompence; is more than praise.
But chiefly thine, O Lichfield! nor mistake;
Think not unintroduced I force my way;   89
Narcissa, not unknown, not unallied,
By virtue, or by blood, illustrious youth!
To thee, from blooming amaranthine bowers,
Where all the language harmony, descends
Uncall'd, and asks admittance for the Muse:
A Muse that will not pain thee with thy praise;
Thy praise she drops, by nobler still inspired.

    O Thou! Blest Spirit! whether the supreme,
Great antemundane Father! in whose breast
Embryo creation, unborn being, dwelt,
And all its various revolutions roll'd   100
Present, though future; prior to themselves;
Whose breath can blow it into nought again;
Or, from his throne some delegated power,
Who, studious of our peace, dost turn the thought
From vain and vile, to solid and sublime!
Unseen thou lead'st me to delicious draughts
Of inspiration, from a purer stream,
And fuller of the god, than that which burst
From famed Castalia: nor is yet allay'd
My sacred thirst; though long my soul has ranged   110
Through pleasing paths of moral, and divine,
By Thee sustain'd, and lighted by the stars.

    By them best lighted are the paths of thought:
Nights are their days, their most illumined hours.
By day, the soul, o'erborne by life's career,
Stunn'd by the din, and giddy with the glare,
Reels far from reason, jostled by the throng.
By day the soul is passive, all her thoughts
Imposed, precarious, broken ere mature.
By night, from objects free, from passion cool,   120
Thoughts uncontroll'd, and unimpress'd, the births
Of pure election, arbitrary range,
Not to the limits of one world confined;   123
But from ethereal travels light on earth,
As voyagers drop anchor, for repose.

    Let Indians, and the gay, like Indians, fond
Of feather'd fopperies, the sun adore:

Darkness has more divinity for me;
It strikes thought inward; it drives back the soul
To settle on herself, our point supreme!　　　　　　130
There lies our theatre; there sits our judge.
Darkness the curtain drops o'er life's dull scene;
'Tis the kind hand of Providence stretch'd out
'Twixt man and vanity; 'tis reason's reign,
And virtue's too; these tutelary shades
Are man's asylum from the tainted throng.
Night is the good man's friend, and guardian too;
It no less rescues virtue, than inspires.

　　　Virtue, for ever frail, as fair, below,
Her tender nature suffers in the crowd,　　　　　　140
Nor touches on the world, without a stain:
The world's infectious; few bring back at eve.
Immaculate, the manners of the morn.
Something we thought, is blotted; we resolved,
Is shaken; we renounced, returns again.
Each salutation may slide in a sin
Unthought before, or fix a former flaw.
Nor is it strange: light, motion, concourse, noise,
All, scatter us abroad; thought outward-bound,
Neglectful of our home affairs, flies off　　　　　　150
In fume and dissipation, quits her charge,
And leaves the breast unguarded to the foe.

　　　Present example gets within our guard,
And acts with double force, by few repell'd.
Ambition fires ambition; love of gain
Strikes, like a pestilence, from breast to breast;
Riot, pride, perfidy, blue vapours breathe;　　　　　157
And inhumanity is caught from man,
From smiling man. A slight, a single glance,
And shot at random, often has brought home
A sudden fever, to the throbbing heart,
Of envy, rancour, or impure desire.
We see, we hear, with peril; safety dwells　　　　　163
Remote from multitude; the world's a school
Of wrong, and what proficients swarm around!
We must, or imitate, or disapprove;
Must list as their accomplices, or foes;
That stains our innocence; this wounds our peace.
From nature's birth, hence, wisdom has been smit
With sweet recess, and languish'd for the shade.　　170

　　　This sacred shade, and solitude, what is it?
'Tis the felt presence of the Deity.
Few are the faults we flatter when alone.

Vice sinks in her allurements, is ungilt,
And looks, like other objects, black by night.
By night an atheist half believes a God.
    Night is fair virtue's immemorial friend;
The conscious moon, through every distant age,
Has held a lamp to wisdom, and let fall,
On contemplation's eye, her purging ray.   180
The famed Athenian,[1] he who woo'd from heaven
Philosophy the fair, to dwell with men,
And form their manners, not inflame their pride,
While o'er his head, as fearful to molest
His labouring mind, the stars in silence slide,
And seem all gazing on their future guest,
See him soliciting his ardent suit
In private audience: all the live-long night,
Rigid in thought, and motionless, he stands;
Nor quits his theme, or posture, till the sun   190
(Rude drunkard rising rosy from the main!)
Disturbs his nobler intellectual beam,
And gives him to the tumult of the world.
Hail, precious moments! stolen from the black waste
Of murder'd time! Auspicious midnight! hail!
The world excluded, every passion hush'd,
And open'd a calm intercourse with Heaven,
Here the soul sits in council; ponders past,
Predestines future, action; sees, not feels,
Tumultuous life, and reasons with the storm;   200
All her lies answers, and thinks down her charms.
    What awful joy! what mental liberty!
I am not pent in darkness; rather say
(If not too bold) in darkness I'm embower'd.
Delightful gloom! the clustering thoughts around
Spontaneous rise, and blossom in the shade;
But droop by day, and sicken in the sun.
Thought borrows light elsewhere; from that first fire,
Fountain of animation! whence descends
Urania, my celestial guest! who deigns   210
Nightly to visit me, so mean; and now,
Conscious how needful discipline to man,
From pleasing dalliance with the charms of Night
My wandering thought recalls, to what excites
Far other beat of heart! Narcissa's tomb!
Or is it feeble nature calls me back,
And breaks my spirit into grief again?

[1] 'Athenian:' Socrates.

Is it a Stygian vapour in my blood?
A cold, slow puddle, creeping through my veins?
Or is it thus with all men?—Thus with all. 220
What are we? how unequal! Now we soar,
And now we sink; to be the same, transcends
Our present prowess. Dearly pays the soul
For lodging ill; too dearly rents her clay. 224
Reason, a baffled counsellor! but adds
The blush of weakness to the bane of woe.
The noblest spirit fighting her hard fate,
In this damp, dusky region, charged with storms,
But feebly flutters, yet untaught to fly;
Or, flying, short her flight, and sure her fall.
Our utmost strength, when down, to rise again;
And not to yield, though beaten, all our praise. 232
　　'Tis vain to seek in men for more than man.
Though proud in promise, big in previous thought,
Experience damps our triumph. I, who late,
Emerging from the shadows of the grave,
Where grief detain'd me prisoner, mounting high,
Threw wide the gates of everlasting day,
And call'd mankind to glory, shook off pain,
Mortality shook off, in ether pure, 240
And struck the stars; now feel my spirits fail;
They drop me from the zenith; down I rush,
Like him whom fable fledged[1] with waxen wings,
In sorrow drown'd—but not in sorrow lost.
How wretched is the man who never mourn'd!
I dive for precious pearl in sorrow's stream:
Not so the thoughtless man that only grieves;
Takes all the torment, and rejects the gain;
(Inestimable gain!) and gives Heaven leave
To make him but more wretched, not more wise. 250
　　If wisdom is our lesson (and what else
Ennobles man? what else have angels learn'd?),
Grief! more proficients in thy school are made,
Than genius, or proud learning, e'er could boast.
Voracious learning, often over-fed,
Digests not into sense her motley meal.
This book-case, which dark booty almost burst, 257
This forager on others' wisdom, leaves
Her native farm, her reason, quite untill'd.
With mix'd manure she surfeits the rank soil,
Dung'd, but not dress'd; and rich to beggary.

---

[1] 'Fable fledged:' Icarus.

A pomp untameable of weeds prevails.
Her servant's wealth, encumber'd wisdom mourns.   263
    And what says Genius? "Let the dull be wise."
Genius, too hard for right, can prove it wrong;
And loves to boast, where blush men less inspired.
It pleads exemption from the laws of sense;
Considers reason as a leveller;
And scorns to share a blessing with the crowd.
That wise it could be, thinks an ample claim   270
To glory, and to pleasure gives the rest.
Crassus but sleeps, Ardelio is undone.
Wisdom less shudders at a fool, than wit.
    But Wisdom smiles, when humbled mortals weep.
When sorrow wounds the breast, as ploughs the glebe,
And hearts obdurate feel her softening shower;
Her seed celestial, then, glad wisdom sows;
Her golden harvest triumphs in the soil.
If so, Narcissa, welcome my Relapse;
I'll raise a tax on my calamity,   280
And reap rich compensation from my pain.
I'll range the plenteous intellectual field;
And gather every thought of sovereign power
To chase the moral maladies of man;
Thoughts, which may bear transplanting to the skies,
Though natives of this coarse penurious soil;
Nor wholly wither there, where seraphs sing,
Refined, exalted, not annull'd, in heaven.
Reason, the sun that gives them birth, the same
In either clime, though more illustrious there.   290
These choicely cull'd, and elegantly ranged,   291
Shall form a garland for Narcissa's tomb;
And, peradventure, of no fading flowers.
    Say on what themes shall puzzled choice descend?
"Th' importance of contemplating the tomb;
Why men decline it; suicide's foul birth;
The various kind of grief; the faults of age;
And Death's dread character—invite my song."
    And, first th' importance of our end survey'd.
Friends counsel quick dismission of our grief: 300
Mistaken kindness! our hearts heal too soon.
Are they more kind than He, who struck the blow?
Who bid it do his errand in our hearts,
And banish peace, till nobler guests arrive,
And bring it back, a true and endless peace?
Calamities are friends: as glaring day
Of these unnumber'd lustres robs our sight;

Prosperity puts out unnumber'd thoughts
Of import high, and light divine, to man.
　　　The man how blest, who, sick of gaudy scenes,　　　310
(Scenes apt to thrust between us and ourselves!)
Is led by choice to take his favourite walk,
Beneath death's gloomy, silent, cypress shades,
Unpierced by vanity's fantastic ray;
To read his monuments, to weigh his dust,
Visit his vaults, and dwell among the tombs!
Lorenzo read with me Narcissa's stone;
(Narcissa was thy favourite) let us read
Her moral stone; few doctors preach so well;
Few orators so tenderly can touch　　　320
The feeling heart. What pathos in the date!
Apt words can strike: and yet in them we see
Faint images of what we here enjoy.
What cause have we to build on length of life?
Temptations seize, when fear is laid asleep;　　　325
And ill foreboded is our strongest guard.
　　　See from her tomb, as from an humble shrine,
Truth, radiant goddess! sallies on my soul,
And puts delusion's dusky train to flight;
Dispels the mists our sultry passions raise,
From objects low, terrestrial, and obscene;
And shows the real estimate of things;　　　332
Which no man, unafflicted, ever saw;
Pulls off the veil from virtue's rising charms;
Detects temptation in a thousand lies.
Truth bids me look on men, as autumn leaves,
And all they bleed for, as the summer's dust,
Driven by the whirlwind: lighted by her beams,
I widen my horizon, gain new powers,
See things invisible, feel things remote,　　　340
Am present with futurities; think nought
To man so foreign, as the joys possess'd;
Nought so much his, as those beyond the grave.
　　　No folly keeps its colour in her sight;
Pale worldly wisdom loses all her charms;
In pompous promise, from her schemes profound,
If future fate she plans, 'tis all in leaves,
Like Sibyl, unsubstantial, fleeting bliss!
At the first blast it vanishes in air.
Not so, celestial: would'st thou know, Lorenzo!　　　350
How differ worldly wisdom, and divine?
Just as the waning and the waxing moon.
More empty worldly wisdom every day;

And every day more fair her rival shines.
When later, there's less time to play the fool.
Soon our whole term for wisdom is expired
(Thou know'st she calls no council in the grave):
And everlasting fool is writ in fire,   358
Or real wisdom wafts us to the skies.
    As worldly schemes resemble Sibyl's leaves,
The good man's days to Sibyl's books compare,
(In ancient story read, thou know'st the tale),
In price still rising, as in number less,
Inestimable quite his final hour.   364
For that who thrones can offer, offer thrones;
Insolvent worlds the purchase cannot pay.
"O let me die his death!" all nature cries.
"Then live his life"—all nature falters there;
Our great physician daily to consult,
To commune with the grave, our only cure.   370
    What grave prescribes the best?—A friend's; and yet,
From a friend's grave, how soon we disengage!
Even to the dearest, as his marble, cold.
Why are friends ravish'd from us? 'Tis to bind,
By soft affection's ties, on human hearts,
The thought of death, which reason, too supine,
Or misemploy'd, so rarely fastens there.
Nor reason, nor affection, no, nor both
Combined, can break the witchcrafts of the world.
Behold, th' inexorable hour at hand!   380
Behold, th' inexorable hour forgot!
And to forget it, the chief aim of life,
Though well to ponder it, is life's chief end.
    Is Death, that ever threatening, ne'er remote,
That all-important, and that only sure
(Come when he will), an unexpected guest?
Nay, though invited by the loudest calls
Of blind imprudence, unexpected still;
Though numerous messengers are sent before,
To warn his great arrival. What the cause,   390
The wondrous cause, of this mysterious ill?   391
All heaven looks down astonish'd at the sight.
Is it, that life has sown her joys so thick,
We can't thrust in a single care between?
Is it, that life has such a swarm of cares,
The thought of death can't enter for the throng?
    Is it, that time steals on with downy feet,
Nor wakes indulgence from her golden dream?
To-day is so like yesterday, it cheats;

We take the lying sister for the same. 400
Life glides away, Lorenzo, like a brook;
For ever changing, unperceived the change.
In the same brook none ever bathed him twice:
To the same life none ever twice awoke.
We call the brook the same; the same we think
Our life, though still more rapid in its flow;
Nor mark the much, irrevocably lapsed,
And mingled with the sea. Or shall we say
(Retaining still the brook to bear us on)
That life is like a vessel on the stream? 410
In life embark'd, we smoothly down the tide
Of time descend, but not on time intent;
Amused, unconscious of the gliding wave;
Till on a sudden we perceive a shock;
We start, awake, look out; what see we there?
Our brittle bark is burst on Charon's shore.
    Is this the cause death flies all human thought?
Or is it judgment, by the will struck blind,
That domineering mistress of the soul!
Like him so strong, by Dalilah the fair? 420
Or is it fear turns startled reason back,
From looking down a precipice so steep?
'Tis dreadful; and the dread is wisely placed,
By nature, conscious of the make of man.
A dreadful friend it is, a terror kind, 425
A flaming sword to guard the tree of life.
By that unawed, in life's most smiling hour,
The good man would repine; would suffer joys,
And burn impatient for his promised skies.
The bad, on each punctilious pique of pride,
Or gloom of humour, would give rage the rein;
Bound o'er the barrier, rush into the dark, 432
And mar the schemes of Providence below.
    What groan was that, Lorenzo?—Furies! rise,
And drown in your less execrable yell
Britannia's shame. There took her gloomy flight,
On wing impetuous, a black sullen soul,
Blasted from hell, with horrid lust of death;
Thy friend, the brave, the gallant Altamont,
So call'd, so thought—and then he fled the field. 440
Less base the fear of death, than fear of life.
O Britain, infamous for suicide!
An island in thy manners! far disjoin'd
From the whole world of rationals beside!
In ambient waves plunge thy polluted head,

Wash the dire stain, nor shock the Continent.
    But thou be shock'd, while I detect the cause
Of self-assault, expose the monster's birth,
And bid abhorrence hiss it round the world.
Blame not thy clime, nor chide the distant sun;   450
The sun is innocent, thy clime absolved:
Immoral climes kind nature never made.
The cause I sing, in Eden might prevail,
And proves, it is thy folly, not thy fate.
    The soul of man (let man in homage bow,
Who names his soul), a native of the skies!
High-born, and free, her freedom should maintain,
Unsold, unmortgaged for earth's little bribes.
Th' illustrious stranger, in this foreign land,   459
Like strangers, jealous of her dignity,
Studious of home, and ardent to return,
Of earth suspicious, earth's enchanted cup
With cool reserve light touching, should indulge
On immortality her godlike taste;
There take large draughts, make her chief banquet there.
    But some reject this sustenance divine;
To beggarly vile appetites descend;
Ask alms of earth, for guests that came from heaven!
Sink into slaves; and sell, for present hire,
Their rich reversion, and (what shares its fate)   470
Their native freedom, to the prince who sways
This nether world. And when his payments fail,
When his foul basket gorges them no more,
Or their pall'd palates loathe the basket full;
Are instantly, with wild demoniac rage,
For breaking all the chains of Providence,
And bursting their confinement; though fast barr'd
By laws divine and human; guarded strong
With horrors doubled to defend the pass,
The blackest, nature, or dire guilt, can raise;   480
And moated round with fathomless destruction,
Sure to receive, and whelm them in their fall.
    Such, Britons! is the cause, to you unknown,
Or worse, o'erlook'd; o'erlook'd by magistrates,
Thus criminals themselves. I grant the deed
Is madness, but the madness of the heart.
And what is that? Our utmost bound of guilt.
A sensual, unreflecting life, is big
With monstrous births, and suicide, to crown
The black infernal brood. The bold to break   490
Heaven's law supreme, and desperately rush,

Through sacred Nature's murder, on their own,
Because they never think of death, they die.   493
'Tis equally man's duty, glory, gain,
At once to shun, and meditate, his end.
When by the bed of languishment we sit
(The seat of wisdom! if our choice, not fate),
Or, o'er our dying friends, in anguish hang,
Wipe the cold dew, or stay the sinking head,
Number their moments, and, in every clock,   500
Start at the voice of an eternity;
See the dim lamp of life just feebly lift
An agonizing beam, at us to gaze,
Then sink again, and quiver into death,
That most pathetic herald of our own;
How read we such sad scenes? As sent to man
In perfect vengeance? No; in pity sent,
To melt him down, like wax, and then impress,
Indelible, Death's image on his heart;
Bleeding for others, trembling for himself.   510
We bleed, we tremble, we forget, we smile.
The mind turns fool, before the cheek is dry.
Our quick-returning folly cancels all;
As the tide rushing razes what is writ
In yielding sands, and smooths the letter'd shore.
     Lorenzo! hast thou ever weigh'd a sigh?
Or studied the philosophy of tears?
(A science, yet unlectured in our schools!)
Hast thou descended deep into the breast,
And seen their source? If not, descend with me,   520
And trace these briny rivulets to their springs.
     Our funeral tears from different causes rise,
As if from separate cisterns in the soul,
Of various kinds, they flow. From tender hearts,
By soft contagion call'd, some burst at once,
And stream obsequious to the leading eye.
Some ask more time, by curious art distill'd.   527
Some hearts, in secret hard, unapt to melt,
Struck by the magic of the public eye,
Like Moses' smitten rock, gush out amain.
Some weep to share the fame of the deceased,
So high in merit, and to them so dear.
They dwell on praises, which they think they share;   533
And thus, without a blush, commend themselves.
Some mourn, in proof that something they could love:
They weep not to relieve their grief, but show.
Some weep in perfect justice to the dead,

As conscious all their love is in arrear.
Some mischievously weep, not unapprised
Tears, sometimes, aid the conquest of an eye.   540
With what address the soft Ephesians draw
Their sable network o'er entangled hearts!
As seen through crystal, how their roses glow,
While liquid pearl runs trickling down their cheek!
Of hers not prouder Egypt's wanton queen,
Carousing gems, herself dissolved in love.
Some weep at death, abstracted from the dead,
And celebrate, like Charles,[1] their own decease.
By kind construction some are deem'd to weep,
Because a decent veil conceals their joy.   550
    Some weep in earnest, and yet weep in vain;
As deep in indiscretion, as in woe.
Passion, blind Passion! impotently pours
Tears, that deserve more tears; while Reason sleeps;
Or gazes like an idiot, unconcern'd;
Nor comprehends the meaning of the storm;
Knows not it speaks to her, and her alone.
Irrationals all sorrow are beneath,
That noble gift! that privilege of man!
From sorrow's pang, the birth of endless joy.   560
But these are barren of that birth divine:
They weep impetuous, as the summer storm,
And full as short! The cruel grief soon tamed,
They make a pastime of the stingless tale;
Far as the deep resounding knell, they spread
The dreadful news, and hardly feel it more.
No grain of wisdom pays them for their woe.
    Half-round the globe, the tears pump'd up by Death
Are spent in watering vanities of life;
In making folly flourish still more fair,   570
When the sick soul, her wonted stay withdrawn,
Reclines on earth, and sorrows in the dust;
Instead of learning, there, her true support,
Though there thrown down her true support to learn.
Without Heaven's aid, impatient to be bless'd,
She crawls to the next shrub, or bramble vile,
Though from the stately cedar's arms she fell;
With stale, forsworn embraces, clings anew,
The stranger weds, and blossoms, as before,
In all the fruitless fopperies of life: 580
Presents her weed, well-fancied, at the ball,

---

[1] 'Charles:' Charles V.

And raffles for the Death's-head on the ring.
    So wept Aurelia, till the destined youth
Stepp'd in, with his receipt for making smiles,
And blanching sables into bridal bloom.
So wept Lorenzo fair Clarissa's fate;
Who gave that angel boy, on whom he doats;
And died to give him, orphan'd in his birth!
Not such, Narcissa, my distress for thee.
I'll make an altar of thy sacred tomb,   590
To sacrifice to wisdom.—What wast thou?
"Young, gay, and fortunate!" Each yields a theme.
I'll dwell on each, to shun thought more severe;
(Heaven knows I labour with severer still!)   594
I'll dwell on each, and quite exhaust thy death.
A soul without reflection, like a pile
Without inhabitant, to ruin runs.
    And, first, thy youth. What says it to grey hairs?
Narcissa, I'm become thy pupil now—
Early, bright, transient, chaste, as morning dew,
She sparkled, was exhaled, and went to heaven.
Time on this head has snow'd; yet still 'tis borne   602
Aloft; nor thinks but on another's grave.
Cover'd with shame I speak it, age severe
Old worn-out vice sets down for virtue fair;
With graceless gravity, chastising youth,
That youth chastised surpassing in a fault,
Father of all, forgetfulness of death:
As if, like objects pressing on the sight,
Death had advanced too near us to be seen: 610
Or, that life's loan Time ripen'd into right;
And men might plead prescription from the grave;
Deathless, from repetition of reprieve.
Deathless? far from it! such are dead already;
Their hearts are buried, and the world their grave.
    Tell me, some god! my guardian angel! tell,
What thus infatuates? what enchantment plants
The phantom of an age 'twixt us, and Death
Already at the door? He knocks, we hear,
And yet we will not hear. What mail defends   620
Our untouch'd hearts? what miracle turns off
The pointed thought, which from a thousand quivers
Is daily darted, and is daily shunn'd?
We stand, as in a battle, throngs on throngs
Around us falling; wounded oft ourselves;
Though bleeding with our wounds, immortal still!
We see Time's furrows on another's brow,

And Death intrench'd, preparing his assault;   628
How few themselves, in that just mirror, see,
Or, seeing, draw their inference as strong!
There, death is certain; doubtful here: he must,
And soon; we may, within an age, expire.
Though grey our heads, our thoughts and aims are green;
Like damaged clocks, whose hand and bell dissent;
Folly sings six, while Nature points at twelve.
    Absurd longevity! More, more! it cries:
More life, more wealth, more trash of every kind.
And wherefore mad for more, when relish fails?
Object, and appetite, must club for joy;
Shall Folly labour hard to mend the bow,   640
Baubles, I mean, that strike us from without,
While Nature is relaxing every string?
Ask thought for joy; grow rich, and hoard within.
Think you the soul, when this life's rattles cease,
Has nothing of more manly to succeed?
Contract the taste immortal; learn even now
To relish what alone subsists hereafter.
Divine, or none, henceforth your joys for ever.
Of age the glory is, to wish to die.
That wish is praise, and promise; it applauds   650
Past life, and promises our future bliss.
What weakness see not children in their sires?
Grand-climacterical absurdities!
Grey-hair'd authority, to faults of youth,
How shocking! it makes folly thrice a fool;
And our first childhood might our last despise.
Peace and esteem is all that age can hope.
Nothing but wisdom gives the first; the last,
Nothing, but the repute of being wise.
Folly bars both; our age is quite undone.   660
    What folly can be ranker? Like our shadows,
Our wishes lengthen, as our sun declines.   662
No wish should loiter, then, this side the grave.
Our hearts should leave the world, before the knell
Calls for our carcases to mend the soil.
Enough to live in tempest, die in port;
Age should fly concourse, cover in retreat
Defects of judgment; and the will subdue;
Walk thoughtful on the silent, solemn shore
Of that vast ocean it must sail so soon;   670
And put good works on board; and wait the wind
That shortly blows us into worlds unknown:
If unconsider'd too, a dreadful scene!

All should be prophets to themselves; foresee
Their future fate; their future fate foretaste;
This art would waste the bitterness of death.
The thought of death alone, the fear destroys.
A disaffection to that precious thought
Is more than midnight darkness on the soul,
Which sleeps beneath it, on a precipice,   680
Puff'd off by the first blast, and lost for ever.

    Dost ask, Lorenzo, why so warmly press'd,
By repetition hammer'd on thine ear,
The thought of death? That thought is the machine,
The grand machine, that heaves us from the dust,
And rears us into men. That thought, plied home,
Will soon reduce the ghastly precipice
O'er-hanging hell, will soften the descent,
And gently slope our passage to the grave;
How warmly to be wish'd! What heart of flesh   690
Would trifle with tremendous? dare extremes?
Yawn o'er the fate of infinite? What hand,
Beyond the blackest brand of censure bold,
(To speak a language too well known to thee),
Would at a moment give its all to chance,   695
And stamp the die for an eternity?

    Aid me, Narcissa! aid me to keep pace
With Destiny; and ere her scissors cut
My thread of life, to break this tougher thread
Of moral death, that ties me to the world.
Sting thou my slumbering reason to send forth
A thought of observation on the foe;   702
To sally; and survey the rapid march
Of his ten thousand messengers to man;
Who, Jehu-like, behind him turns them all.
All accident apart, by Nature sign'd,
My warrant is gone out, though dormant yet;
Perhaps behind one moment lurks my fate.

    Must I then forward only look for Death?
Backward I turn mine eye, and find him there.   710
Man is a self-survivor every year.
Man, like a stream, is in perpetual flow.
Death's a destroyer of quotidian prey.
My youth, my noontide, his; my yesterday;
The bold invader shares the present hour.
Each moment on the former shuts the grave.
While man is growing, life is in decrease;
And cradles rock us nearer to the tomb.
Our birth is nothing but our death begun;

As tapers waste, that instant they take fire. 720
     Shall we then fear, lest that should come to pass,
Which comes to pass each moment of our lives?
If fear we must, let that Death turn us pale,
Which murders strength and ardour; what remains
Should rather call on Death, than dread his call.
Ye partners of my fault, and my decline!
Thoughtless of death, but when your neighbour's knell
(Rude visitant!) knocks hard at your dull sense,
And with its thunder scarce obtains your ear! 729
Be death your theme, in every place and hour;
Nor longer want, ye monumental sires!
A brother tomb to tell you ye shall die.
That death you dread (so great is Nature's skill)
Know, you shall court before you shall enjoy.
     But you are learn'd; in volumes deep, you sit;
In wisdom, shallow: pompous ignorance!
Would you be still more learned than the learn'd?
Learn well to know how much need not be known,
And what that knowledge, which impairs your sense.
Our needful knowledge, like our needful food, 740
Unhedged, lies open in life's common field;
And bids all welcome to the vital feast.
You scorn what lies before you in the page
Of Nature, and Experience, moral truth;
Of indispensable, eternal fruit;
Fruit, on which mortals feeding, turn to gods:
And dive in science for distinguish'd names,
Dishonest fomentation of your pride!
Sinking in virtue, as you rise in fame.
Your learning, like the lunar beam, affords 750
Light, but not heat; it leaves you indevout,
Frozen at heart, while speculation shines.
Awake, ye curious indagators! fond
Of knowing all, but what avails you known.
If you would learn Death's character, attend.
All casts of conduct, all degrees of health,
All dies of fortune, and all dates of age,
Together shook in his impartial urn,
Come forth at random: or, if choice is made,
The choice is quite sarcastic, and insults 760
All bold conjecture, and fond hopes of man.
What countless multitudes not only leave,
But deeply disappoint us, by their deaths! 763
Though great our sorrow, greater our surprise.
     Like other tyrants, Death delights to smite,

What, smitten, most proclaims the pride of power,
And arbitrary nod. His joy supreme,
To bid the wretch survive the fortunate;
The feeble wrap th' athletic in his shroud;
And weeping fathers build their children's tomb: 770
Me thine, Narcissa!—What though short thy date?
Virtue, not rolling suns, the mind matures.
That life is long, which answers life's great end.
The time that bears no fruit, deserves no name;
The man of wisdom is the man of years.
In hoary youth Methusalems may die;
O how misdated on their flattering tombs!
    Narcissa's youth has lectured me thus far.
And can her gaiety give counsel too?
That, like the Jews' famed oracle of gems, [1]   780
Sparkles instruction; such as throws new light,
And opens more the character of Death;
Ill known to thee, Lorenzo! This thy vaunt:
"Give Death his due, the wretched, and the old;
Even let him sweep his rubbish to the grave;
Let him not violate kind Nature's laws,
But own man born to live as well as die."
Wretched and old thou givest him; young and gay
He takes; and plunder is a tyrant's joy.
What if I prove, "The farthest from the fear,   790
Are often nearest to the stroke of Fate?"
All, more than common, menaces an end.
A blaze betokens brevity of life:
As if bright embers should emit a flame,
Glad spirits sparkled from Narcissa's eye,
And made youth younger, and taught life to live,   796
As Nature's opposites wage endless war,
For this offence, as treason to the deep
Inviolable stupor of his reign,
Where Lust, and turbulent Ambition, sleep,
Death took swift vengeance. As he life detests,
More life is still more odious; and, reduced
By conquest, aggrandizes more his power.   803
But wherefore aggrandized? By Heaven's decree,
To plant the soul on her eternal guard,
In awful expectation of our end.
Thus runs Death's dread commission: "Strike, but so
As most alarms the living by the dead."
Hence stratagem delights him, and surprise,

---

[1] 'Oracle of gems:' the Urim and Thummim.

And cruel sport with man's securities.   810
Not simple conquest, triumph is his aim;
And, where least fear'd, there conquest triumphs most.
This proves my bold assertion not too bold.
      What are his arts to lay our fears asleep?
Tiberian arts his purposes wrap up
In deep dissimulation's darkest night.
Like princes unconfess'd in foreign courts,
Who travel under cover, Death assumes
The name and look of life, and dwells among us.
He takes all shapes that serve his black designs: 820
Though master of a wider empire far
Than that o'er which the Roman eagle flew.
Like Nero, he's a fiddler, charioteer,
Or drives his phaeton, in female guise;
Quite unsuspected, till, the wheel beneath,
His disarray'd oblation he devours.
      He most affects the forms least like himself,
His slender self. Hence burly corpulence
Is his familiar wear, and sleek disguise.
Behind the rosy bloom he loves to lurk,   830
Or ambush in a smile; or wanton dive
In dimples deep; love's eddies, which draw in
Unwary hearts, and sink them in despair.
Such, on Narcissa's couch he loiter'd long
Unknown; and, when detected, still was seen
To smile; such peace has innocence in death!
Most happy they! whom least his arts deceive.
One eye on Death, and one full fix'd on heaven,
Becomes a mortal, and immortal man.
Long on his wiles a piqued and jealous spy,   840
I've seen, or dreamt I saw, the tyrant dress;
Lay by his horrors, and put on his smiles.
Say, Muse, for thou remember'st, call it back,
And show Lorenzo the surprising scene;
If 'twas a dream, his genius can explain.
      'Twas in a circle of the gay I stood.
Death would have enter'd; Nature push'd him back;
Supported by a doctor of renown,
His point he gain'd. Then artfully dismiss'd
The sage; for Death design'd to be conceal'd.   850
He gave an old vivacious usurer
His meagre aspect, and his naked bones;
In gratitude for plumping up his prey,
A pamper'd spendthrift; whose fantastic air,
Well-fashion'd figure, and cockaded brow,

He took in change, and underneath the pride
Of costly linen, tuck'd his filthy shroud.
His crooked bow he straighten'd to a cane;
And hid his deadly shafts in Myra's eye.
    The dreadful masquerader, thus equipp'd, 860
Out sallies on adventures. Ask you where?
Where is he not? For his peculiar haunts,
Let this suffice; sure as night follows day,
Death treads in pleasure's footsteps round the world, 864
When pleasure treads the paths, which reason shuns.
When, against reason, riot shuts the door,
And gaiety supplies the place of sense,
Then, foremost at the banquet, and the ball,
Death leads the dance, or stamps the deadly die;
Nor ever fails the midnight bowl to crown. 870
Gaily carousing to his gay compeers,
Inly he laughs, to see them laugh at him,
As absent far: and when the revel burns,
When fear is banish'd, and triumphant thought,
Calling for all the joys beneath the moon,
Against him turns the key; and bids him sup
With their progenitors—He drops his mask;
Frowns out at full; they start, despair, expire.
    Scarce with more sudden terror and surprise,
From his black mask of nitre, touch'd by fire, 880
He bursts, expands, roars, blazes, and devours.
And is not this triumphant treachery,
And more than simple conquest, in the fiend?
    And now, Lorenzo, dost thou wrap thy soul
In soft security, because unknown
Which moment is commission'd to destroy?
In death's uncertainty thy danger lies.
Is death uncertain? Therefore thou be fix'd;
Fix'd as a sentinel, all eye, all ear,
All expectation of the coming foe. 890
Rouse, stand in arms, nor lean against thy spear;
Lest slumber steal one moment o'er thy soul,
And Fate surprise thee nodding. Watch, be strong:
Thus give each day the merit, and renown,
Of dying well; though doom'd but once to die.
Nor let life's period hidden (as from most)
Hide too from thee the precious use of life.
    Early, not sudden, was Narcissa's fate. 898
Soon, not surprising, Death his visit paid.
Her thought went forth to meet him on his way,
Nor gaiety forgot it was to die:

Though Fortune too (our third and final theme),
As an accomplice, play'd her gaudy plumes,
And every glittering gewgaw, on her sight,   904
To dazzle, and debauch it from its mark.
Death's dreadful advent is the mark of man;
And every thought that misses it, is blind.
Fortune, with youth and gaiety, conspired
To weave a triple wreath of happiness
(If happiness on earth) to crown her brow.   910
And could Death charge through such a shining shield?
        That shining shield invites the tyrant's spear.
As if to damp our elevated aims,
And strongly preach humility to man.
O how portentous is prosperity!
How, comet-like, it threatens, while it shines!
Few years but yield us proof of Death's ambition,
To cull his victims from the fairest fold,
And sheath his shafts in all the pride of life.
When flooded with abundance, purpled o'er   920
With recent honours, bloom'd with every bliss,
Set up in ostentation, made the gaze,
The gaudy centre, of the public eye,
When Fortune thus has toss'd her child in air,
Snatch'd from the covert of an humble state,
How often have I seen him dropp'd at once,
Our morning's envy! and our evening's sigh!
As if her bounties were the signal given,
The flowery wreath to mark the sacrifice,
And call Death's arrows on the destined prey.   930
        High Fortune seems in cruel league with Fate.
Ask you for what? To give his war on man   932
The deeper dread, and more illustrious spoil;
Thus to keep daring mortals more in awe.
And burns Lorenzo still for the sublime
Of life? to hang his airy nest on high,
On the slight timber of the topmost bough,
Rock'd at each breeze, and menacing a fall?
Granting grim Death at equal distance there;
Yet peace begins just where ambition ends.   940
What makes man wretched? Happiness denied?
Lorenzo! no: 'tis happiness disdain'd.
She comes too meanly dress'd to win our smile;
And calls herself Content, a homely name!
Our flame is transport, and Content our scorn.
Ambition turns, and shuts the door against her,
And weds a toil, a tempest, in her stead;

A tempest to warm transport near of kin.
Unknowing what our mortal state admits,
Life's modest joys we ruin, while we raise;   950
And all our ecstasies are wounds to peace;
Peace, the full portion of mankind below.
     And since thy peace is dear, ambitious youth!
Of fortune fond! as thoughtless of thy fate!
As late I drew Death's picture, to stir up
Thy wholesome fears; now, drawn in contrast, see
Gay Fortune's, thy vain hopes to reprimand.
See, high in air, the sportive goddess hangs,
Unlocks her casket, spreads her glittering ware,
And calls the giddy winds to puff abroad   960
Her random bounties o'er the gaping throng.
All rush rapacious; friends o'er trodden friends;
Sons o'er their fathers, subjects o'er their kings,
Priests o'er their gods, and lovers o'er the fair
(Still more adored), to snatch the golden shower.
     Gold glitters most, where virtue shines no more;
As stars from absent suns have leave to shine.   967
O what a precious pack of votaries
Unkennell'd from the prisons, and the stews,
Pour in, all opening in their idol's praise;
All, ardent, eye each wafture of her hand,
And, wide-expanding their voracious jaws,
Morsel on morsel swallow down unchew'd,   973
Untasted, through mad appetite for more;
Gorged to the throat, yet lean and ravenous still.
Sagacious all, to trace the smallest game,
And bold to seize the greatest. If (bless'd chance!)
Court-zephyrs sweetly breathe, they launch, they fly,
O'er just, o'er sacred, all-forbidden ground,
Drunk with the burning scent of place or power,   980
Staunch to the foot of lucre, till they die.
     Or, if for men you take them, as I mark
Their manners, thou their various fates survey.
With aim mismeasured, and impetuous speed,
Some darting, strike their ardent wish far off,
Through fury to possess it: some succeed,
But stumble, and let fall the taken prize.
From some, by sudden blasts, 'tis whirl'd away,
And lodged in bosoms that ne'er dreamt of gain.
To some it sticks so close, that, when torn off,   990
Torn is the man, and mortal is the wound.
Some, o'er-enamour'd of their bags, run mad,
Groan under gold, yet weep for want of bread.

Together some (unhappy rivals!) seize,
And rend abundance into poverty;
Loud croaks the raven of the law, and smiles:
Smiles too the goddess; but smiles most at those
(Just victims of exorbitant desire!)
Who perish at their own request, and, whelm'd
Beneath her load of lavish grants, expire.   1000
Fortune is famous for her numbers slain,
The number small, which happiness can bear.   1002
Though various for a while their fates; at last
One curse involves them all: at Death's approach,
All read their riches backward into loss,
And mourn, in just proportion to their store.
      And Death's approach (if orthodox my song)
Is hasten'd by the lure of Fortune's smiles.
And art thou still a glutton of bright gold?
And art thou still rapacious of thy ruin?   1010
Death loves a shining mark, a signal blow;
A blow, which, while it executes, alarms;
And startles thousands with a single fall.
As when some stately growth of oak, or pine,
Which nods aloft, and proudly spreads her shade,
The sun's defiance, and the flock's defence;
By the strong strokes of labouring hinds subdued,
Loud groans her last, and, rushing from her height,
In cumbrous ruin, thunders to the ground:
The conscious forest trembles at the shock,   1020
And hill, and stream, and distant dale, resound.
      These high-aim'd darts of Death, and these alone,
Should I collect, my quiver would be full.
A quiver, which, suspended in mid-air,
Or near heaven's archer, in the zodiac, hung,
(So could it be) should draw the public eye,
The gaze and contemplation of mankind!
A constellation awful, yet benign,
To guide the gay through life's tempestuous wave;
Nor suffer them to strike the common rock,   1030
"From greater danger to grow more secure,
And, wrapt in happiness, forget their fate."
      Lysander, happy past the common lot,
Was warn'd of danger, but too gay to fear.
He woo'd the fair Aspasia: she was kind:
In youth, form, fortune, fame, they both were bless'd:
All who knew, envied; yet in envy loved: 1037
Can fancy form more finish'd happiness?
Fix'd was the nuptial hour. Her stately dome

Rose on the sounding beach. The glittering spires
Float in the wave, and break against the shore:
So break those glittering shadows, human joys.
The faithless morning smiled: he takes his leave, 1043
To re-embrace, in ecstasies, at eve.
The rising storm forbids. The news arrives:
Untold, she saw it in her servant's eye.
She felt it seen (her heart was apt to feel);
And, drown'd, without the furious ocean's aid,
In suffocating sorrows, shares his tomb.
Now, round the sumptuous bridal monument, 1050
The guilty billows innocently roar;
And the rough sailor passing, drops a tear.
A tear?—can tears suffice?—But not for me.
How vain our efforts! and our arts, how vain!
The distant train of thought I took, to shun,
Has thrown me on my fate—these died together;
Happy in ruin! undivorced by death!
Or ne'er to meet, or ne'er to part,[1] is peace—
Narcissa! pity bleeds at thought of thee.
Yet thou wast only near me; not myself. 1060
Survive myself?—That cures all other woe.
Narcissa lives; Philander is forgot.
O the soft commerce! O the tender ties,
Close twisted with the fibres of the heart!
Which, broken, break them; and drain off the soul
Of human joy; and make it pain to live—
And is it then to live? When such friends part,
'Tis the survivor dies—My heart! no more. 1068

---

[1] 'Ne'er to meet, or ne'er to part:' hence Burns's famous line in his verses to Clarinda:—

> 'Never met, or never parted,
> We had ne'er been broken-hearted.'

NIGHT SIXTH.

THE

INFIDEL RECLAIMED,

IN TWO PARTS;
CONTAINING

THE NATURE, PROOF, AND IMPORTANCE OF IMMORTALITY.

PART I.
WHERE, AMONG OTHER THINGS, GLORY AND RICHES ARE PARTICULARLY CONSIDERED.

TO THE

RIGHT HON. HENRY PELHAM,
FIRST LORD COMMISSIONER OF THE TREASURY, AND CHANCELLOR OF THE EXCHEQUER.

PREFACE.

FEW ages have been deeper in dispute about religion than this. The dispute about religion, and the practice of it, seldom go together. The shorter, therefore, the dispute, the better. I think it may be reduced to this single question, *Is man immortal, or is he not?* If he is not, all our disputes are mere amusements, or trials of skill. In this case, truth, reason, religion, which give our discourses such pomp and solemnity, are (as will be shown) mere empty sound, without any meaning in them. But if man is immortal, it will behove him to be very serious about eternal consequences; or, in other words, to be truly religious. And this great fundamental truth, unestablished, or unawakened in the minds of men, is, I conceive, the real source and support of all our infidelity; how remote soever the particular objections advanced may seem to be from it.

Sensible appearances affect most men much more than abstract reasonings; and we daily see bodies drop around us, but the soul is invisible. The power which inclination has over the judgment, is greater than can be well conceived by those that have not had an experience of it; and of what numbers is it the sad interest that souls should not survive! The heathen world confessed, that they rather hoped, than firmly believed, immortality; and how many heathens have we still amongst us! The sacred page assures us, that life and immortality are brought to light by the Gospel: but by how

101

many is the Gospel rejected or overlooked? From these considerations, and from my being accidentally privy to the sentiments of some particular persons, I have been long persuaded that most, if not all, our infidels (whatever name they take, and whatever scheme, for argument's sake, and to keep themselves in countenance, they patronise), are supported in their deplorable error, by some doubt of their immortality, at the bottom. And I am satisfied, that men once thoroughly convinced of their immortality, are not far from being Christians. For it is hard to conceive, that a man fully conscious eternal pain or happiness will certainly be his lot, should not earnestly and impartially inquire after the surest means of escaping the one, and securing the other. And of such an earnest and impartial inquiry I well know the consequence.

Here, therefore, in proof of this most fundamental truth, some plain arguments are offered; arguments derived from principles which infidels admit in common with believers; arguments which appear to me altogether irresistible; and such as, I am satisfied, will have great weight with all who give themselves the small trouble of looking seriously into their own bosoms, and of observing, with any tolerable degree of attention, what daily passes round about them in the world. If some arguments shall here occur, which others have declined, they are submitted, with all deference, to better judgments in this, of all points the most important. For, as to the being of a God, that is no longer disputed; but it is undisputed for this reason only, viz., because, where the least pretence to reason is admitted, it must for ever be indisputable. And of consequence no man can be betrayed into a dispute of that nature by vanity; which has a principal share in animating our modern combatants against other articles of our belief.

NIGHT SIXTH.

THE INFIDEL RECLAIMED.

PART I.

SHE[1] (for I know not yet her name in heaven),
Not early, like Narcissa, left the scene;
Nor sudden, like Philander. What avail?
This seeming mitigation but inflames;
This fancied medicine heightens the disease.
The longer known, the closer still she grew;
And gradual parting is a gradual death.
'Tis the grim tyrant's engine, which extorts,
By tardy pressure's still-increasing weight,
From hardest hearts, confession of distress.   10

    Oh, the long, dark approach through years of pain,
Death's gallery! (might I dare to call it so)
With dismal doubt, and sable terror, hung;
Sick hope's pale lamp its only glimmering ray:
There, fate my melancholy walk ordain'd,
Forbid self-love itself to flatter, there.
How oft I gazed, prophetically sad!
How oft I saw her dead, while yet in smiles!   18
In smiles she sunk her grief to lessen mine.
She spoke me comfort, and increased my pain.
Like powerful armies trenching at a town,
By slow, and silent, but resistless sap,
In his pale progress gently gaining ground,
Death urged his deadly siege; in spite of art,
Of all the balmy blessings nature lends
To succour frail humanity. Ye stars!
(Not now first made familiar to my sight)
And thou, O moon! bear witness, many a night
He tore the pillow from beneath my head,
Tied down my sore attention to the shock,   30
By ceaseless depredations on a life
Dearer than that he left me. Dreadful post
Of observation! darker every hour!
Less dread the day that drove me to the brink,
And pointed at eternity below;
When my soul shudder'd at futurity;
When, on a moment's point, th' important die
Of life and death spun doubtful, ere it fell,

----

[1] 'She:' his wife, it is supposed.

And turn'd up life; my title to more woe.

But why more woe? More comfort let it be. 40
Nothing is dead, but that which wish'd to die;
Nothing is dead, but wretchedness and pain;
Nothing is dead, but what encumber'd, gall'd,
Block'd up the pass, and barr'd from real life.
Where dwells that wish most ardent of the wise?
Too dark the sun to see it; highest stars
Too low to reach it; Death, great Death alone,
O'er stars and sun, triumphant, lands us there.

Nor dreadful our transition; though the mind,
An artist at creating self-alarms, 50
Rich in expedients for inquietude,
Is prone to paint it dreadful. Who can take 52
Death's portrait true? The tyrant never sat.
Our sketch all random strokes, conjecture all;
Close shuts the grave, nor tells one single tale.
Death, and his image rising in the brain,
Bear faint resemblance; never are alike;
Fear shakes the pencil; Fancy loves excess;
Dark Ignorance is lavish of her shades:
And these the formidable picture draw. 60

But grant the worst; 'tis past; new prospects rise;
And drop a veil eternal o'er her tomb.
Far other views our contemplation claim,
Views that o'erpay the rigours of our life;
Views that suspend our agonies in death.
Wrapt in the thought of immortality,
Wrapt in the single, the triumphant thought!
Long life might lapse, age unperceived come on;
And find the soul unsated with her theme.
Its nature, proof, importance, fire my song. 70
O that my song could emulate my soul!
Like her, immortal. No!—the soul disdains
A mark so mean; far nobler hope inflames;
If endless ages can outweigh an hour,
Let not the laurel, but the palm, inspire.

Thy nature, Immortality! who knows?
And yet who knows it not? It is but life
In stronger thread of brighter colour spun,
And spun for ever; dipp'd by cruel Fate
In Stygian dye, how black, how brittle here! 80
How short our correspondence with the sun!
And while it lasts, inglorious! Our best deeds,
How wanting in their weight! our highest joys
Small cordials to support us in our pain,

And give us strength to suffer. But how great
To mingle interests, converse, amities, 86
With all the sons of Reason, scatter'd wide
Through habitable space, wherever born,
Howe'er endow'd! to live free citizens
Of universal nature! to lay hold
By more than feeble faith on the Supreme!
To call heaven's rich unfathomable mines
(Mines, which support archangels in their state) 93
Our own! To rise in science, as in bliss,
Initiate in the secrets of the skies!
To read creation; read its mighty plan
In the bare bosom of the Deity!
The plan, and execution, to collate!
To see, before each glance of piercing thought,
All cloud, all shadow, blown remote; and leave 100
No mystery—but that of Love Divine,
Which lifts us on the seraph's flaming wing,
From earth's Aceldama, this field of blood,
Of inward anguish, and of outward ill,
From darkness, and from dust, to such a scene!
Love's element! true joy's illustrious home!
From earth's sad contrast (now deplored) more fair!
What exquisite vicissitude of fate!
Bless'd absolution of our blackest hour!
　　Lorenzo, these are thoughts that make man Man, 110
The wise illumine, aggrandize the great.
How great (while yet we tread the kindred clod,
And every moment fear to sink beneath
The clod we tread; soon trodden by our sons);
How great, in the wild whirl of Time's pursuits,
To stop, and pause, involved in high presage,
Through the long vista of a thousand years,
To stand contemplating our distant selves,
As in a magnifying mirror seen,
Enlarged, ennobled, elevate, divine! 120
To prophesy our own futurities!
To gaze in thought on what all thought transcends!
To talk, with fellow-candidates, of joys
As far beyond conception as desert,
Ourselves th' astonish'd talkers, and the tale!
　　Lorenzo, swells thy bosom at the thought?
The swell becomes thee: 'tis an honest pride.
Revere thyself;—and yet thyself despise.
His nature no man can o'er-rate; and none
Can under-rate his merit. Take good heed, 130

Nor there be modest, where thou should'st be proud;
That almost universal error shun.
How just our pride, when we behold those heights!
Not those Ambition paints in air, but those
Reason points out, and ardent Virtue gains,
And angels emulate; our pride how just!
When mount we? when these shackles cast? when quit
This cell of the creation? this small nest,
Stuck in a corner of the universe,
Wrapt up in fleecy cloud, and fine-spun air?   140
Fine-spun to sense; but gross and feculent
To souls celestial; souls ordain'd to breathe
Ambrosial gales, and drink a purer sky;
Greatly triumphant on Time's farther shore,
Where Virtue reigns, enrich'd with full arrears;
While Pomp imperial begs an alms of peace.
    In empire high, or in proud science deep,
Ye born of earth! on what can you confer,
With half the dignity, with half the gain,
The gust, the glow of rational delight,   150
As on this theme, which angels praise and share?
Man's fates and favours are a theme in heaven.
    What wretched repetition cloys us here!
What periodic potions for the sick!   154
Distemper'd bodies! and distemper'd minds!
In an eternity, what scenes shall strike!
Adventures thicken! novelties surprise!
What webs of wonder shall unravel, there!
What full day pour on all the paths of heaven,
And light th' Almighty's footsteps in the deep!
How shall the blessed day of our discharge
Unwind, at once, the labyrinths of fate,   162
And straighten its inextricable maze!
    If inextinguishable thirst in man
To know; how rich, how full, our banquet there!
There, not the moral world alone unfolds;
The world material, lately seen in shades,
And, in those shades, by fragments only seen,
And seen those fragments by the labouring eye,
Unbroken, then, illustrious, and entire,   170
Its ample sphere, its universal frame,
In full dimensions, swells to the survey;
And enters, at one glance, the ravish'd sight.
From some superior point (where, who can tell?
Suffice it, 'tis a point where gods reside)
How shall the stranger man's illumined eye,

In the vast ocean of unbounded space,
Behold an infinite of floating worlds
Divide the crystal waves of ether pure,
In endless voyage, without port? The least   180
Of these disseminated orbs, how great!
Great as they are, what numbers these surpass,
Huge, as Leviathan, to that small race,
Those twinkling multitudes of little life,
He swallows unperceived! Stupendous these!
Yet what are these stupendous to the whole?
As particles, as atoms ill perceived;
As circulating globules in our veins;   188
So vast the plan. Fecundity divine!
Exuberant Source! perhaps, I wrong thee still.
    If admiration is a source of joy,
What transport hence! Yet this the least in heaven.
What this to that illustrious robe He wears,
Who toss'd this mass of wonders from his hand,
A specimen, an earnest of his power?
'Tis to that glory, whence all glory flows,
As the mead's meanest floweret to the sun,
Which gave it birth. But what, this sun of heaven?
This bliss supreme of the supremely blest?
Death, only death, the question can resolve.   200
By death, cheap bought th' ideas of our joy;
The bare ideas! solid happiness
So distant from its shadow chased below.
    And chase we still the phantom through the fire,
O'er bog, and brake, and precipice, till death?
And toil we still for sublunary pay?
Defy the dangers of the field and flood,
Or, spider-like, spin out our precious all,
Our more than vitals spin (if no regard
To great futurity) in curious webs   210
Of subtle thought, and exquisite design;
(Fine network of the brain!) to catch a fly!
The momentary buzz of vain renown!
A name! a mortal immortality!
    Or (meaner still!) instead of grasping air,
For sordid lucre plunge we in the mire,
Drudge, sweat, through every shame, for every gain,
For vile contaminating trash; throw up
Our hope in heaven, our dignity with man?
And deify the dirt, matured to gold?   220
Ambition, Avarice; the two demons these,
Which goad through every slough our human herd,   222

Hard-travell'd from the cradle to the grave.
How low the wretches stoop! how steep they climb!
These demons burn mankind; but most possess
Lorenzo's bosom, and turn out the skies.
    Is it in time to hide eternity?
And why not in an atom on the shore
To cover ocean? or a mote, the sun?
Glory and wealth! have they this blinding power?   230
What if to them I prove Lorenzo blind?
Would it surprise thee? Be thou then surprised;
Thou neither know'st: their nature learn from me.
    Mark well, as foreign as these subjects seem,
What close connexion ties them to my theme.
First, what is true ambition? The pursuit
Of glory, nothing less than man can share.
Were they as vain, as gaudy-minded man,
As flatulent with fumes of self-applause,
Their arts and conquests animals might boast,   240
And claim their laurel crowns, as well as we;
But not celestial. Here we stand alone;
As in our form, distinct, pre-eminent;
If prone in thought, our stature is our shame;
And man should blush, his forehead meets the skies.
The visible and present are for brutes,
A slender portion, and a narrow bound!
These Reason, with an energy divine,
O'erleaps; and claims the future and unseen;
The vast unseen! the future fathomless!   250
When the great soul buoys up to this high point,
Leaving gross nature's sediments below,
Then, and then only, Adam's offspring quits
The sage and hero of the fields and woods,
Asserts his rank, and rises into man.   255
This is ambition: this is human fire.
    Can Parts or Place (two bold pretenders!) make
Lorenzo great, and pluck him from the throng?
    Genius and Art, ambition's boasted wings,
Our boast but ill deserve. A feeble aid!
Dedalian enginery! If these alone
Assist our flight, Fame's flight is Glory's fall.
Heart merit wanting, mount we ne'er so high,   263
Our height is but the gibbet of our name.
A celebrated wretch, when I behold,
When I behold a genius bright, and base,
Of towering talents, and terrestrial aims;
Methinks I see, as thrown from her high sphere,

The glorious fragments of a soul immortal,
With rubbish mix'd, and glittering in the dust.   270
Struck at the splendid, melancholy sight,
At once compassion soft, and envy, rise—
But wherefore envy? Talents angel-bright,
If wanting worth, are shining instruments
In false ambition's hand, to finish faults
Illustrious, and give infamy renown.
    Great ill is an achievement of great powers.
Plain sense but rarely leads us far astray.
Reason the means, affections choose our end;
Means have no merit, if our end amiss.   280
If wrong our hearts, our heads are right in vain:
What is a Pelham's head, to Pelham's heart?
Hearts are proprietors of all applause.
Right ends, and means, make wisdom: worldly-wise
Is but half-witted, at its highest praise.
    Let Genius then despair to make thee great;
Nor flatter Station: what is station high?
'Tis a proud mendicant; it boasts, and begs;
It begs an alms of homage from the throng,   289
And oft the throng denies its charity.
Monarchs and ministers, are awful names;
Whoever wear them, challenge our devoir.
Religion, public order, both exact
External homage, and a supple knee,
To beings pompously set up, to serve
The meanest slave: all more is merit's due,
Her sacred and inviolable right;
Nor ever paid the monarch, but the man.
Our hearts ne'er bow but to superior worth;
Nor ever fail of their allegiance there.   300
Fools, indeed, drop the man in their account,
And vote the mantle into majesty.
Let the small savage boast his silver fur;
His royal robe unborrow'd, and unbought,
His own, descending fairly from his sires.
Shall man be proud to wear his livery,
And souls in ermine scorn a soul without?
Can place or lessen us, or aggrandize?
Pigmies are pigmies still, though perch'd on Alps;
And pyramids are pyramids in vales.   310
Each man makes his own stature, builds himself:
Virtue alone outbuilds the pyramids:
Her monuments shall last, when Egypt's fall.
    Of these sure truths dost thou demand the cause?

The cause is lodged in immortality.
Hear, and assent. Thy bosom burns for power;
What station charms thee? I'll install thee there;
'Tis thine. And art thou greater than before?
Then thou before wast something less than man.
Has thy new post betray'd thee into pride? 320
That treacherous pride betrays thy dignity;
That pride defames humanity, and calls
The being mean, which staffs or strings can raise. 323
That pride, like hooded hawks, in darkness soars,
From blindness bold, and towering to the skies.
'Tis born of ignorance, which knows not man:
An angel's second; nor his second, long.
A Nero quitting his imperial throne,
And courting glory from the tinkling string,
But faintly shadows an immortal soul, 330
With empire's self, to pride, or rapture, fired.
If nobler motives minister no cure,
Even vanity forbids thee to be vain.
    High worth is elevated place: 'tis more;
It makes the post stand candidate for thee;
Makes more than monarchs, makes an honest man;
Though no exchequer it commands, 'tis wealth;
And though it wears no riband, 'tis renown;
Renown, that would not quit thee, though disgraced,
Nor leave thee pendent on a master's smile. 340
Other ambition Nature interdicts;
Nature proclaims it most absurd in man,
By pointing at his origin, and end;
Milk, and a swathe, at first, his whole demand;
His whole domain, at last, a turf, or stone;
To whom, between, a world may seem too small.
    Souls truly great dart forward on the wing
Of just ambition, to the grand result,
The curtain's fall; there, see the buskin'd chief
Unshod behind this momentary scene; 350
Reduced to his own stature, low or high,
As vice, or virtue, sinks him, or sublimes;
And laugh at this fantastic mummery,
This antic prelude of grotesque events,
Where dwarfs are often stilted, and betray
A littleness of soul by worlds o'errun,
And nations laid in blood. Dread sacrifice 357
To Christian pride! which had with horror shock'd
The darkest Pagans, offer'd to their gods.

O thou most Christian[1] enemy to peace!
Again in arms? Again provoking fate?
That prince, and that alone, is truly great,
Who draws the sword reluctant, gladly sheathes;   363
On empire builds what empire far outweighs,
And makes his throne a scaffold to the skies.
    Why this so rare? Because forgot of all
The day of death; that venerable day,
Which sits as judge; that day, which shall pronounce
On all our days, absolve them, or condemn.
Lorenzo, never shut thy thought against it;   370
Be levees ne'er so full, afford it room,
And give it audience in the cabinet.
That friend consulted, flatteries apart,
Will tell thee fair, if thou art great, or mean.
    To doat on aught may leave us, or be left,
Is that ambition? Then let flames descend,
Point to the centre their inverted spires,
And learn humiliation from a soul,
Which boasts her lineage from celestial fire.
Yet these are they, the world pronounces wise;   380
The world, which cancels nature's right and wrong,
And casts new wisdom: even the grave man lends
His solemn face, to countenance the coin.
Wisdom for parts is madness for the whole.
This stamps the paradox, and gives us leave
To call the wisest weak, the richest poor,
The most ambitious, unambitious, mean;
In triumph, mean; and abject, on a throne.
Nothing can make it less than mad in man,
To put forth all his ardour, all his art,   390
And give his soul her full unbounded flight,
But reaching Him, who gave her wings to fly.
When blind Ambition quite mistakes her road,
And downwards pores, for that which shines above,
Substantial happiness, and true renown;
Then, like an idiot, gazing on the brook,
We leap at stars, and fasten in the mud;
At glory grasp, and sink in infamy.
    Ambition! powerful source of good and ill!
Thy strength in man, like length of wing in birds,   400
When disengaged from earth, with greater ease,
And swifter flight, transports us to the skies;
By toys entangled, or in guilt bemired,

---

[1] 'Most Christian:' Louis XIV., King of France.

It turns a curse; it is our chain, and scourge,
In this dark dungeon, where confined we lie,
Close grated by the sordid bars of Sense;
All prospect of eternity shut out;
And, but for execution, ne'er set free.
    With error in ambition justly charged,
Find we Lorenzo wiser in his wealth?   410
What if thy rental I reform? and draw
An inventory new, to set thee right?
Where thy true treasure? Gold says, "Not in me:"
And, "Not in me," the diamond. Gold is poor;
India's insolvent: seek it in thyself,
Seek in thy naked self, and find it there;
In being, so descended, form'd, endow'd;
Sky-born, sky-guided, sky-returning race!
Erect, immortal, rational, divine!
In senses, which inherit earth, and heavens;   420
Enjoy the various riches Nature yields;
Far nobler! give the riches they enjoy;
Give taste to fruits; and harmony to groves;
Their radiant beams to gold, and gold's bright fire;   424
Take in, at once, the landscape of the world,
At a small inlet, which a grain might close,
And half create the wondrous world they see.
Our senses, as our reason, are divine.
But for the magic organ's powerful charm,
Earth were a rude, uncolour'd chaos still.
Objects are but th' occasion; ours th' exploit;
Ours is the cloth, [1] the pencil, and the paint,   432
Which nature's admirable picture draws;
And beautifies creation's ample dome.
Like Milton's Eve, when gazing on the lake,
Man makes the matchless image man admires.
Say then, shall man, his thoughts all sent abroad,
Superior wonders in himself forgot,
His admiration waste on objects round,
When Heaven makes him the soul of all he sees?   440
Absurd! not rare! so great, so mean, is man.
    What wealth in senses such as these! What wealth
In Fancy, fired to form a fairer scene
Than Sense surveys! In memory's firm record,
Which, should it perish, could this world recall
From the dark shadows of o'erwhelming years!

[1] 'Ours is the cloth,' &c.: how like the lines of Coleridge!—
                'O Lady, we receive but what we give,' &c.

In colours fresh, originally bright,
Preserve its portrait, and report its fate!
What wealth in Intellect, that sovereign power!
Which Sense and Fancy summons to the bar;   450
Interrogates, approves, or reprehends;
And from the mass those underlings import,
From their materials sifted, and refined,
And in Truth's balance accurately weigh'd,
Forms art, and science, government, and law;
The solid basis, and the beauteous frame,   456
The vitals, and the grace of civil life!
And manners (sad exception!) set aside,
Strikes out, with master hand, a copy fair
Of His idea, whose indulgent thought
Long, long, ere chaos teem'd, plann'd human bliss.
     What wealth in souls that soar, dive, range around,
Disdaining limit, or from place, or time;   463
And hear at once, in thought extensive, hear
Th' Almighty fiat, and the trumpet's sound!
Bold, on creation's outside walk, and view
What was, and is, and more than e'er shall be;
Commanding, with omnipotence of thought,
Creations new in fancy's field to rise!
Souls, that can grasp whate'er th' Almighty made,   470
And wander wild through things impossible!
What wealth, in faculties of endless growth,
In quenchless passions violent to crave,
In liberty to choose, in power to reach,
And in duration (how thy riches rise!)
Duration to perpetuate—boundless bliss!
     Ask you, what power resides in feeble man
That bliss to gain? Is Virtue's, then, unknown?
Virtue, our present peace, our future prize.
Man's unprecarious, natural estate,   480
Improveable at will, in virtue lies;
Its tenure sure; its income is divine.
     High-built abundance, heap on heap! for what?
To breed new wants, and beggar us the more;
Then make a richer scramble for the throng?
Soon as this feeble pulse, which leaps so long
Almost by miracle, is tired with play,
Like rubbish from disploding engines thrown,
Our magazines of hoarded trifles fly;
Fly diverse; fly to foreigners, to foes;   490
New masters court, and call the former fools
(How justly!), for dependence on their stay.

Wide scatter, first, our playthings; then, our dust.
    Dost court abundance for the sake of peace?
Learn, and lament thy self-defeated scheme:
Riches enable to be richer still;
And, richer still, what mortal can resist?
Thus wealth (a cruel taskmaster!) enjoins
New toils, succeeding toils, an endless train!
And murders peace, which taught it first to shine.   500
The poor are half as wretched as the rich;
Whose proud and painful privilege it is
At once, to bear a double load of woe;
To feel the stings of envy, and of want,
Outrageous want! both Indies cannot cure.
    A competence is vital to content.
Much wealth is corpulence, if not disease;
Sick, or encumber'd, is our happiness,
A competence is all we can enjoy.
Oh, be content, where Heaven can give no more!   510
More, like a flash of water from a lock,
Quickens our spirits' movement for an hour;
But soon its force is spent, nor rise our joys
Above our native temper's common stream.
Hence disappointment lurks in every prize,
As bees in flowers; and stings us with success.
    The rich man, who denies it, proudly feigns;
Nor knows the wise are privy to the lie.
Much learning shows how little mortals know;
Much wealth, how little worldlings can enjoy: 520
At best, it babies us with endless toys,
And keeps us children till we drop to dust.
As monkeys at a mirror stand amazed,
They fail to find what they so plainly see;   524
Thus men, in shining riches, see the face
Of happiness, nor know it is a shade;
But gaze, and touch, and peep, and peep again,
And wish, and wonder it is absent still.
    How few can rescue opulence from want!
Who lives to Nature, rarely can be poor;
Who lives to Fancy, never can be rich.
Poor is the man in debt; the man of gold,   532
In debt to Fortune, trembles at her power.
The man of reason smiles at her, and Death.
Oh! what a patrimony this! a being
Of such inherent strength and majesty,
Not worlds possess'd can raise it; worlds destroy'd
Can't injure; which holds on its glorious course,

When thine, O Nature! ends; too blest to mourn
Creation's obsequies. What treasure, this!   540
The monarch is a beggar to the man.
  Immortal! Ages past, yet nothing gone!
Morn without eve! a race without a goal!
Unshorten'd by progression infinite!
Futurity for ever future! Life
Beginning still where computation ends!
'Tis the description of a deity!
'Tis the description of the meanest slave:
The meanest slave dares then Lorenzo scorn?
The meanest slave thy sovereign glory shares.   550
Proud youth! fastidious of the lower world!
Man's lawful pride includes humility;
Stoops to the lowest; is too great to find
Inferiors; all immortal! brothers all!
Proprietors eternal of thy love.
  Immortal! What can strike the sense so strong,
As this the soul? It thunders to the thought;
Reason amazes; gratitude o'erwhelms;   558
No more we slumber on the brink of fate;
Roused at the sound, th' exulting soul ascends,
And breathes her native air; an air that feeds
Ambitions high, and fans ethereal fires;
Quick kindles all that is divine within us;
Nor leaves one loitering thought beneath the stars.
  Has not Lorenzo's bosom caught the flame?
Immortal! Were but one immortal, how
Would others envy! how would thrones adore!
Because 'tis common, is the blessing lost?
How this ties up the bounteous hand of Heaven!   569
Oh, vain, vain, vain, all else! Eternity!
A glorious and a needful refuge, that,
From vile imprisonment, in abject views.
'Tis immortality, 'tis that alone,
Amid life's pains, abasements, emptiness,
The soul can comfort, elevate, and fill.
That only, and that amply, this performs;
Lifts us above life's pains, her joys above;
Their terror those, and these their lustre lose;
Eternity depending covers all;
Eternity depending all achieves;   580
Sets earth at distance; casts her into shades;
Blends her distinctions; abrogates her powers;
The low, the lofty, joyous, and severe,
Fortune's dread frowns, and fascinating smiles,

Make one promiscuous and neglected heap,
The man beneath; if I may call him man,
Whom immortality's full force inspires.
Nothing terrestrial touches his high thought;
Suns shine unseen, and thunders roll unheard,
By minds quite conscious of their high descent,   590
Their present province, and their future prize;
Divinely darting upward every wish,   592
Warm on the wing, in glorious absence lost!
     Doubt you this truth? Why labours your belief?
If earth's whole orb by some due distanced eye
Were seen at once, her towering Alps would sink,
And levell'd Atlas leave an even sphere.
Thus earth, and all that earthly minds admire,
Is swallow'd in eternity's vast round.
To that stupendous view, when souls awake,   600
So large of late, so mountainous to man,
Time's toys subside; and equal all below.
     Enthusiastic, this? Then all are weak,
But rank enthusiasts. To this godlike height
Some souls have soar'd; or martyrs ne'er had bled,
And all may do, what has by man been done.
Who, beaten by these sublunary storms,
Boundless, interminable joys can weigh,
Unraptured, unexalted, uninflamed?
What slave unblest, who from to-morrow's dawn   610
Expects an empire? He forgets his chain,
And, throned in thought, his absent sceptre waves.
     And what a sceptre waits us! what a throne!
Her own immense appointments to compute,
Or comprehend her high prerogatives,
In this her dark minority, how toils,
How vainly pants, the human soul divine!
Too great the bounty seems for earthly joy;
What heart but trembles at so strange a bliss?
     In spite of all the truths the Muse has sung,   620
Ne'er to be prized enough! enough revolved!
Are there who wrap the world so close about them,
They see no farther than the clouds; and dance
On heedless vanity's fantastic toe,
Till, stumbling at a straw, in their career,
Headlong they plunge, where end both dance and song?
Are there, Lorenzo? is it possible?   627
Are there on earth (let me not call them men)
Who lodge a soul immortal in their breasts;
Unconscious as the mountain of its ore;

Or rock of its inestimable gem?
When rocks shall melt, and mountains vanish, these
Shall know their treasure; treasure, then, no more. 633
    Are there (still more amazing!) who resist
The rising thought? who smother, in its birth,
The glorious truth? who struggle to be brutes?
Who through this bosom-barrier burst their way,
And, with reversed ambition, strive to sink?
Who labour downwards through th' opposing powers
Of instinct, reason, and the world against them, 640
To dismal hopes, and shelter in the shock
Of endless night; night darker than the grave's?
Who fight the proofs of immortality?
With horrid zeal, and execrable arts,
Work all their engines, level their black fires,
To blot from man this attribute divine
(Than vital blood far dearer to the wise),
Blasphemers, and rank atheists to themselves?
    To contradict them, see all nature rise!
What object, what event, the moon beneath, 650
But argues, or endears, an after-scene?
To reason proves, or weds it to desire?
All things proclaim it needful; some advance
One precious step beyond, and prove it sure.
A thousand arguments swarm round my pen,
From heaven, and earth, and man. Indulge a few,
By Nature, as her common habit, worn;
So pressing Providence a truth to teach,
Which truth untaught, all other truths were vain.
    Thou! whose all-providential eye surveys, 660
Whose hand directs, whose Spirit fills and warms
Creation, and holds empire far beyond!
Eternity's inhabitant august!
Of two eternities amazing Lord!
One past, ere man's, or angel's, had begun
Aid! while I rescue from the foe's assault
Thy glorious immortality in man:
A theme for ever, and for all, of weight,
Of moment infinite! but relish'd most
By those who love Thee most, who most adore. 670
    Nature, thy daughter, ever-changing birth
Of Thee the Great Immutable, to man
Speaks wisdom, is his oracle supreme;
And he who most consults her, is most wise.
Lorenzo, to this heavenly Delphos haste;
And come back all-immortal, all-divine:

Look nature through, 'tis revolution all;
All change; no death. Day follows night; and night
The dying day; stars rise, and set, and rise;
Earth takes th' example. See, the summer gay,   680
With her green chaplet, and ambrosial flowers,
Droops into pallid autumn: winter grey,
Horrid with frost, and turbulent with storm,
Blows autumn, and his golden fruits, away:
Then melts into the spring: soft spring, with breath
Favonian, from warm chambers of the south,
Recalls the first. All, to re-flourish, fades;
As in a wheel, all sinks, to re-ascend.
Emblems of man, who passes, not expires.
      With this minute distinction, emblems just,   690
Nature revolves, but man advances; both
Eternal, that a circle, this a line.
That gravitates, this soars. Th' aspiring soul,
Ardent, and tremulous, like flame, ascends,   694
Zeal and humility her wings, to heaven.
The world of matter, with its various forms,
All dies into new life. Life born from death
Rolls the vast mass, and shall for ever roll.
No single atom, once in being, lost,
With change of counsel charges the Most High.
      What hence infers Lorenzo? Can it be?
Matter immortal? And shall Spirit die?   702
Above the nobler, shall less noble rise?
Shall Man alone, for whom all else revives,
No resurrection know? Shall Man alone,
Imperial Man! be sown in barren ground,
Less privileged than grain, on which he feeds?
Is Man, in whom alone is power to prize
The bliss of being, or with previous pain
Deplore its period, by the spleen of fate,   710
Severely doom'd Death's single unredeem'd?
      If Nature's revolution speaks aloud,
In her gradation, hear her louder still.
Look nature through, 'tis neat gradation all.
By what minute degrees her scale ascends!
Each middle nature join'd at each extreme,
To that above it join'd, to that beneath.
Parts, into parts reciprocally shot,
Abhor divorce: what love of union reigns!
Here, dormant matter waits a call to life;   720
Half life, half death, join there; here, life and sense;
There, sense from reason steals a glimmering ray;

118

Reason shines out in man. But how preserved
The chain unbroken upward, to the realms
Of incorporeal life? those realms of bliss,
Where Death hath no dominion? Grant a make
Half mortal, half immortal; earthy, part,
And part ethereal; grant the soul of man   728
Eternal; or in man the series ends.
Wide yawns the gap; connexion is no more;
Check'd Reason halts; her next step wants support;
Striving to climb, she tumbles from her scheme;
A scheme, analogy pronounced so true;
Analogy, man's surest guide below.   734
     Thus far, all nature calls on thy belief.
And will Lorenzo, careless of the call,
False attestation on all nature charge,
Rather than violate his league with Death?
Renounce his reason, rather than renounce
The dust beloved, and run the risk of heaven?   740
Oh, what indignity to deathless souls!
What treason to the majesty of man!
Of man immortal! Hear the lofty style:
"If so decreed, th' Almighty Will be done.
Let earth dissolve, yon ponderous orbs descend,
And grind us into dust. The soul is safe;
The man emerges; mounts above the wreck,
As towering flame[1] from Nature's funeral pyre;
O'er devastation, as a gainer, smiles;
His charter, his inviolable rights,   750
Well pleased to learn from thunder's impotence,
Death's pointless darts, and hell's defeated storms."
     But these chimeras touch not thee, Lorenzo!
The glories of the world thy sevenfold shield.
Other ambition than of crowns in air,
And superlunary felicities,
Thy bosom warm. I'll cool it, if I can;
And turn those glories that enchant, against thee.
What ties thee to this life, proclaims the next.   759
If wise, the cause that wounds thee is thy cure.
     Come, my ambitious! let us mount together
(To mount, Lorenzo never can refuse);
And from the clouds, where pride delights to dwell,
Look down on earth.—What seest thou? Wondrous things!
Terrestrial wonders, that eclipse the skies.

---

[1] 'Towering flame,' &c.: these lines are *reproduced* in the close of Campbell's 'Pleasures of Hope.'

What lengths of labour'd lands! what loaded seas!
Loaded by man, for pleasure, wealth, or war!
Seas, winds, and planets, into service brought,
His art acknowledge, and promote his ends.
Nor can th' eternal rocks his will withstand;   770
What levell'd mountains! and what lifted vales!
O'er vales and mountains sumptuous cities swell.
And gild our landscape with their glittering spires.
Some mid the wondering waves majestic rise;
And Neptune holds a mirror to their charms.
Far greater still! (what cannot mortal might?)
See, wide dominions ravish'd from the deep!
The narrow'd deep with indignation foams.
Or southward turn; to delicate and grand,
The finer arts there ripen in the sun.   780
How the tall temples, as to meet their gods,
Ascend the skies! the proud triumphal arch
Shows us half heaven beneath its ample bend.
High through mid-air, here, streams are taught to flow;
Whole rivers, there, laid by in basins, sleep.
Here, plains turn oceans; there, vast oceans join
Through kingdoms channell'd deep from shore to shore;
And changed creation takes its face from man.
Beats thy brave breast for formidable scenes,
Where fame and empire wait upon the sword?   790
See fields in blood; hear naval thunders rise;
Britannia's voice! that awes the world to peace.
How yon enormous mole projecting breaks   793
The mid-sea, furious waves! Their roar amidst,
Out-speaks the Deity, and says, "O main!
Thus far, nor farther; new restraints obey."
Earth's disembowell'd! measured are the skies!
Stars are detected in their deep recess!
Creation widens! vanquish'd Nature yields!
Her secrets are extorted! Art prevails!   800
What monument of genius, spirit, power!
    And now, Lorenzo! raptured at this scene,
Whose glories render heaven superfluous! say,
Whose footsteps these?—Immortals have been here.
Could less than souls immortal this have done?
Earth's cover'd o'er with proofs of souls immortal;
And proofs of immortality forgot.
    To flatter thy grand foible, I confess,
These are Ambition's works: and these are great:
But this, the least immortal souls can do;   810
Transcend them all—but what can these transcend?

120

Dost ask me what?—One sigh for the distress'd.
What then for infidels? A deeper sigh.
'Tis moral grandeur makes the mighty man:
How little they, who think aught great below!
All our ambitions death defeats, but one;
And that it crowns.—Here cease we: but, ere long,
More powerful proof shall take the field against thee,
Stronger than death, and smiling at the tomb.   819

NIGHT SEVENTH.

THE

INFIDEL RECLAIMED,

PART II.

CONTAINING

THE NATURE, PROOF, AND IMPORTANCE OF IMMORTALITY.

PREFACE.

As we are at war with the power, it were well if we were at war with the manners, of France. A land of levity is a land of guilt. A serious mind is the native soil of every virtue; and the single character that does true honour to mankind. The soul's immortality has been the favourite theme with the serious of all ages. Nor is it strange: it is a subject by far the most interesting and important that can enter the mind of man. Of highest moment this subject always was, and always will be. Yet this its highest moment seems to admit of increase, at this day; a sort of occasional importance is superadded to the natural weight of it; if that opinion which is advanced in the Preface to the preceding Night be just. It is there supposed, that all our infidels, whatever scheme, for argument's sake, and to keep themselves in countenance, they patronise, are betrayed into their deplorable error, by some doubts of their immortality, at the bottom. And the more I consider this point, the more I am persuaded of the truth of that opinion. Though the distrust of a futurity is a strange error; yet it is an error into which bad men may naturally be distressed. For it is impossible to bid defiance to final ruin, without some refuge in imagination, some presumption of escape. And what presumption is there? There are but two in nature; but two, within the compass of human thought. And these are,—That either God will not, or cannot, punish. Considering the divine attributes, the first is too gross to be digested by our strongest wishes. And since omnipotence is as much a divine attribute as holiness, that God cannot punish, is as absurd a supposition as the former. God certainly can punish as long as wicked men exist. In non-existence, therefore, is their only refuge; and, consequently, non-existence is their strongest wish. And strong wishes have a strange influence on our opinions; they bias the judgment in a manner almost incredible. And since on this member of their alternative, there are some very small appearances in their favour, and none at all on the other, they catch at this reed, they lay hold on this chimera, to save themselves from the shock and horror of an immediate and absolute despair.

On reviewing my subject, by the light which this argument, and others of like tendency, threw upon it, I was more inclined than ever to pursue it, as it appeared to me to strike directly at the main root of all our infidelity. In the following pages it is, accordingly, pursued at large; and some arguments for immortality, new at least to me, are ventured on in them. There also the writer has made an attempt to set the gross absurdities and horrors of annihilation in a fuller and more affecting view than is (I think) to be met with elsewhere.

The gentlemen, for whose sake this attempt was chiefly made, profess great admiration for the wisdom of heathen antiquity: what pity it is they are not sincere! If they were sincere, how would it mortify them to consider, with what contempt and abhorrence their notions would have been received by those whom they so much admire! What degree of contempt and abhorrence would fall to their share, may be conjectured by the following matter of fact (in my opinion) extremely memorable. Of all their heathen worthies, Socrates (it is well known) was the most guarded, dispassionate, and composed: yet this great master of temper was angry; and angry at his last hour; and angry with his friend; and angry for what deserved acknowledgment; angry for a right and tender instance of true friendship towards him. Is not this surprising? What could be the cause? The cause was for his honour; it was a truly noble, though, perhaps, a too punctilious, regard for immortality. For his friend asking him, with such an affectionate concern as became a friend, "where he should deposit his remains," it was resented by Socrates, as implying a dishonourable supposition, that he could be so mean, as to have a regard for anything, even in himself, that was not immortal.

This fact well considered, would make our infidels withdraw their admiration from Socrates; or make them endeavour, by their imitation of this illustrious example, to share his glory: and, consequently, it would incline them to peruse the following pages with candour and impartiality; which is all I desire; and that, for their sakes: for I am persuaded, that an unprejudiced infidel must, necessarily, receive some advantageous impressions from them.

July 7, 1744.

NIGHT SIXTH.

THE INFIDEL RECLAIMED.

PART I.

CONTENTS.

HEAVEN gives the needful, but neglected, call.
What day, what hour, but knocks at human hearts,
To wake the soul to sense of future scenes?   3
Deaths stand, like Mercuries, in every way,
And kindly point us to our journey's end.
Pope, who could'st make immortals! art thou dead?
I give thee joy: nor will I take my leave;
So soon to follow. Man but dives in death;
Dives from the sun, in fairer day to rise;
The grave, his subterranean road to bliss.   10
Yes, infinite indulgence plann'd it so;
Through various parts our glorious story runs;
Time gives the preface, endless age unrolls

The volume (ne'er unroll'd!) of human fate.
    This, earth and skies already[1] have proclaim'd.
The world's a prophecy of worlds to come;
And who, what God foretells (who speaks in things,
Still louder than in words) shall dare deny?
If Nature's arguments appear too weak,
Turn a new leaf, and stronger read in Man.   20
If man sleeps on, untaught by what he sees,
Can he prove infidel to what he feels?
He, whose blind thought futurity denies,
Unconscious bears, Bellerophon![2] like thee,
His own indictment; he condemns himself;
Who reads his bosom, reads immortal life;
Or, Nature, there, imposing on her sons,
Has written fables; man was made a lie.
    Why Discontent for ever harbour'd there?
Incurable consumption of our peace!   30
Resolve me, why, the cottager, and king,
He, whom sea-sever'd realms obey, and he
Who steals his whole dominion from the waste,
Repelling winter blasts with mud and straw   34
Disquieted alike, draw sigh for sigh,
In fate so distant, in complaint so near?
    Is it, that things terrestrial can't content?
Deep in rich pasture will thy flocks complain?
Not so; but to their master is denied
To share their sweet serene. Man, ill at ease,
In this, not his own place, this foreign field,
Where Nature fodders him with other food,   42
Than was ordain'd his cravings to suffice,
Poor in abundance, famish'd at a feast,
Sighs on for something more, when most enjoy'd.
    Is Heaven, then, kinder to thy flocks than thee?
Not so; thy pasture richer, but remote;
In part, remote; for that remoter part
Man bleats from instinct, though perhaps, debauch'd
By sense, his reason sleeps, nor dreams the cause.   50
The cause how obvious, when his reason wakes!
His grief is but his grandeur in disguise;
And discontent is immortality.
    Shall sons of ether, shall the blood of heaven,

---

[1] 'Already:' Night Sixth.
[2] 'Bellerophon:' who carried letters from Proctus to Jobates, King of Lycia, which contained an order in cipher for his execution after nine days. He contrived, however, to escape.

Set up their hopes on earth, and stable here,
With brutal acquiescence in the mire?
Lorenzo, no! they shall be nobly pain'd;
The glorious foreigners, distress'd, shall sigh
On thrones; and thou congratulate the sigh:
Man's misery declares him born for bliss;   60
His anxious heart asserts the truth I sing,
And gives the sceptic in his head the lie.
    Our heads, our hearts, our passions, and our powers,
Speak the same language; call us to the skies:
Unripen'd these in this inclement clime,
Scarce rise above conjecture, and mistake;
And for this land of trifles those too strong
Tumultuous rise, and tempest human life: 68
What prize on earth can pay us for the storm?
Meet objects for our passions Heaven ordain'd,
Objects that challenge all their fire, and leave
No fault, but in defect: bless'd Heaven! avert
A bounded ardour for unbounded bliss!
O for a bliss unbounded! Far beneath
A soul immortal, is a mortal joy.
Nor are our powers to perish immature;
But, after feeble effort here, beneath
A brighter sun, and in a nobler soil,
Transplanted from this sublunary bed,
Shall flourish fair, and put forth all their bloom.   80
    Reason progressive, Instinct is complete;
Swift Instinct leaps; slow Reason feebly climbs.
Brutes soon their zenith reach; their little all
Flows in at once; in ages they no more
Could know, or do, or covet, or enjoy.
Were man to live coeval with the sun,
The patriarch-pupil would be learning still;
Yet, dying, leave his lesson half unlearn'd.
Men perish in advance, as if the sun
Should set ere noon, in eastern oceans drown'd;   90
If fit, with dim, illustrious to compare,
The sun's meridian with the soul of man.
To man, why, stepdame Nature! so severe?
Why thrown aside thy masterpiece half wrought,
While meaner efforts thy last hand enjoy?
Or, if abortively, poor man must die,
Nor reach, what reach he might, why die in dread?
Why cursed with foresight? wise to misery?
Why of his proud prerogative the prey?
Why less pre-eminent in rank than pain?   100

His immortality alone can tell;
Full ample fund to balance all amiss,   102
And turn the scale in favour of the just!
　　His immortality alone can solve
The darkest of enigmas, human hope;
Of all the darkest, if at death we die.
Hope, eager Hope, th' assassin of our joy,
All present blessings treading under foot,
Is scarce a milder tyrant than Despair.
With no past toils content, still planting new,   110
Hope turns us o'er to death alone for ease.
Possession, why more tasteless than pursuit?
Why is a wish far dearer than a crown?
That wish accomplish'd, why the grave of bliss?
Because, in the great future buried deep,
Beyond our plans of empire and renown,
Lies all that man with ardour should pursue;
And He who made him, bent him to the right.
Man's heart th' Almighty to the future sets,
By secret and inviolable springs;   120
And makes his hope his sublunary joy.
　　Man's heart eats all things, and is hungry still;
"More, more!" the glutton cries: for something new
So rages appetite, if man can't mount,
He will descend. He starves on the possess'd.
Hence, the world's master, from ambition's spire,
In Caprea plunged; and dived beneath the brute.
In that rank sty why wallow'd empire's son
Supreme? Because he could no higher fly;
His riot was ambition in despair.   130
　　Old Rome consulted birds; Lorenzo! thou
With more success, the flight of Hope survey;
Of restless Hope, for ever on the wing.
High perch'd o'er every thought that falcon sits,
To fly at all that rises in her sight;
And never stooping, but to mount again   136
Next moment, she betrays her aim's mistake,
And owns her quarry lodged beyond the grave.
　　There should it fail us (it must fail us there,
If being fails), more mournful riddles rise,
And Virtue vies with Hope in mystery.
Why Virtue? where its praise, its being, fled?
Virtue is true self-interest pursued: 143
What true self-interest of quite-mortal man?
To close with all that makes him happy here.
If vice (as sometimes) is our friend on earth,

Then vice is virtue; 'tis our sovereign good.
In self-applause is virtue's golden prize;
No self-applause attends it on thy scheme:
Whence self-applause? From conscience of the right.
And what is right, but means of happiness? 151
No means of happiness when virtue yields;
That basis failing, falls the building too,
And lays in ruin every virtuous joy.
The rigid guardian of a blameless heart,
So long revered, so long reputed wise,
Is weak; with rank knight-errantries o'errun.
Why beats thy bosom with illustrious dreams
Of self-exposure, laudable, and great?
Of gallant enterprise, and glorious death? 160
Die for thy country!—Thou romantic fool!
Seize, seize the plank thyself, and let her sink:
Thy country! what to thee?—the Godhead, what?
(I speak with awe!) though He should bid thee bleed?
If, with thy blood, thy final hope is spilt,
Nor can Omnipotence reward the blow,
Be deaf; preserve thy being; disobey.
        Nor is it disobedience: know, Lorenzo!
Whate'er th' Almighty's subsequent command,
His first command is this:—"Man, love thyself." 170
In this alone, free agents are not free.
Existence is the basis, bliss the prize;
If virtue costs existence, 'tis a crime;
Bold violation of our law supreme,
Black suicide; though nations, which consult
Their gain, at thy expence, resound applause.
        Since Virtue's recompence is doubtful, here,
If man dies wholly, well may we demand,
Why is man suffer'd to be good in vain?
Why to be good in vain, is man enjoin'd? 180
Why to be good in vain, is man betray'd?
Betray'd by traitors lodged in his own breast,
By sweet complacencies from virtue felt?
Why whispers Nature lies on Virtue's part?
Or if blind Instinct (which assumes the name
Of sacred conscience) plays the fool in man,
Why Reason made accomplice in the cheat?
Why are the wisest loudest in her praise?
Can man by Reason's beam be led astray?
Or, at his peril, imitate his God? 190
Since virtue sometimes ruins us on earth,
Or both are true, or man survives the grave.

Or man survives the grave, or own, Lorenzo,
Thy boast supreme, a wild absurdity.
Dauntless thy spirit; cowards are thy scorn.
Grant man immortal, and thy scorn is just.
The man immortal, rationally brave,
Dares rush on death—because he cannot die.
But if man loses all, when life is lost,
He lives a coward, or a fool expires.   200
A daring infidel (and such there are,
From pride, example, lucre, rage, revenge,
Or pure heroical defect of thought),   203
Of all earth's madmen, most deserves a chain.
  When to the grave we follow the renown'd
For valour, virtue, science, all we love,
And all we praise; for worth, whose noontide beam,
Enabling us to think in higher style,
Mends our ideas of ethereal powers;
Dream we, that lustre of the moral world   210
Goes out in stench, and rottenness the close?
Why was he wise to know, and warm to praise,
And strenuous to transcribe, in human life,
The Mind Almighty? Could it be, that Fate,
Just when the lineaments began to shine,
And dawn the Deity, should snatch the draught,
With night eternal blot it out, and give
The skies alarm, lest angels too might die?
  If human souls, why not angelic too
Extinguish'd? and a solitary God,   220
O'er ghastly ruin, frowning from his throne?
Shall we this moment gaze on God in man?
The next, lose man for ever in the dust?
From dust we disengage, or man mistakes;
And there, where least his judgment fears a flaw.
Wisdom and worth, how boldly he commends!
Wisdom and worth, are sacred names; revered,
Where not embraced; applauded; deified;
Why not compassion'd too? If spirits die,
Both are calamities, inflicted both,   230
To make us but more wretched: Wisdom's eye
Acute, for what? to spy more miseries;
And worth, so recompensed, new-points their stings.
Or man surmounts the grave, or gain is loss,
And worth exalted humbles us the more.
Thou wilt not patronise a scheme that makes   236
Weakness and vice the refuge of mankind.
  "Has virtue, then, no joys?"—Yes, joys dear-bought.

Talk ne'er so long, in this imperfect state,
Virtue and vice are at eternal war,
Virtue's a combat; and who fights for nought?
Or for precarious, or for small reward?
Who virtue's self-reward so loud resound, 243
Would take degrees angelic here below,
And virtue, while they compliment, betray,
By feeble motives, and unfaithful guards.
The crown, th' unfading crown, her soul inspires:
'Tis that, and that alone, can countervail
The body's treacheries, and the world's assaults:
On earth's poor pay our famish'd virtue dies. 250
Truth incontestible! in spite of all
A Bayle has preach'd, or a Voltaire believed.
    In man the more we dive, the more we see
Heaven's signet stamping an immortal make.
Dive to the bottom of his soul, the base
Sustaining all; what find we? knowledge, love.
As light and heat, essential to the sun,
These to the soul. And why, if souls expire?
How little lovely here? how little known?
Small knowledge we dig up with endless toil; 260
And love unfeign'd may purchase perfect hate.
Why starved, on earth, our angel appetites;
While brutal are indulged their fulsome fill?
Were then capacities divine conferr'd,
As a mock-diadem, in savage sport,
Rank insult of our pompous poverty,
Which reaps but pain, from seeming claims so fair?
In future age lies no redress? and shuts
Eternity the door on our complaint?
If so, for what strange ends were mortals made! 270
The worst to wallow, and the best to weep;
The man who merits most, must most complain:
Can we conceive a disregard in heaven,
What the worst perpetrate, or best endure?
    This cannot be. To love, and know, in man
Is boundless appetite, and boundless power;
And these demonstrate boundless objects too.
Objects, powers, appetites, Heaven suits in all;
Nor, nature through, e'er violates this sweet,
Eternal concord, on her tuneful string. 280
Is Man the sole exception from her laws?
Eternity struck off from human hope
(I speak with truth, but veneration too),
Man is a monster, the reproach of Heaven,

A stain, a dark impenetrable cloud
On Nature's beauteous aspect; and deforms
(Amazing blot!), deforms her with her lord.
If such is man's allotment, what is heaven?
Or own the soul immortal, or blaspheme.
    Or own the soul immortal, or invert   290
All order. Go, mock-majesty! go, man!
And bow to thy superiors of the stall;
Through every scene of sense superior far:
They graze the turf untill'd; they drink the stream
Unbrew'd, and ever full, and unembitter'd
With doubts, fears, fruitless hopes, regrets, despairs;
Mankind's peculiar! reason's precious dower!
No foreign clime they ransack for their robes;
Nor brothers cite to the litigious bar;
Their good is good entire, unmix'd, unmarr'd;   300
They find a paradise in every field,
On boughs forbidden where no curses hang:
Their ill no more than strikes the sense; unstretch'd
By previous dread, or murmur in the rear: 304
When the worst comes, it comes unfear'd; one stroke
Begins, and ends, their woe: they die but once;
Bless'd, incommunicable privilege! for which
Proud man, who rules the globe, and reads the stars,
Philosopher, or hero, sighs in vain.
    Account for this prerogative in brutes.
No day, no glimpse of day, to solve the knot,
But what beams on it from eternity.   312
O sole and sweet solution! that unties
The difficult, and softens the severe;
The cloud on nature's beauteous face dispels;
Restores bright order; casts the brute beneath;
And re-enthrones us in supremacy
Of joy, even here: admit immortal life,
And virtue is knight-errantry no more;
Each virtue brings in hand a golden dower,   320
Far richer in reversion: Hope exults;
And though much bitter in our cup is thrown,
Predominates, and gives the taste of heaven.
O wherefore is the Deity so kind?
Astonishing beyond astonishment!
Heaven our reward—for heaven enjoy'd below.
    Still unsubdued thy stubborn heart?—for there
The traitor lurks who doubts the truth I sing.
Reason is guiltless; will alone rebels.
What, in that stubborn heart, if I should find   330

New, unexpected witnesses against thee?
Ambition, pleasure, and the love of gain!
Canst thou suspect that these, which make the soul
The slave of earth, should own her heir of heaven?
Canst thou suspect what makes us disbelieve
Our immortality, should prove it sure?

    First, then, Ambition summon to the bar.
Ambition's shame, extravagance, disgust   338
And inextinguishable nature, speak.
Each much deposes; hear them in their turn.

    Thy soul, how passionately fond of fame!
How anxious, that fond passion to conceal!
We blush, detected in designs on praise,
Though for best deeds, and from the best of men:
And why? Because immortal. Art divine
Has made the body tutor to the soul;
Heaven kindly gives our blood a moral flow;
Bids it ascend the glowing cheek, and there
Upbraid that little heart's inglorious aim,
Which stoops to court a character from man;   350
While o'er us, in tremendous judgment sit
Far more than man, with endless praise, and blame.

    Ambition's boundless appetite outspeaks
The verdict of its shame. When souls take fire
At high presumptions of their own desert,
One age is poor applause; the mighty shout,
The thunder by the living few begun,
Late time must echo; worlds unborn resound.
We wish our names eternally to live:
Wild dream! which ne'er had haunted human thought,
Had not our natures been eternal too.   361
Instinct points out an interest in hereafter;
But our blind reason sees not where it lies;
Or, seeing, gives the substance for the shade.

    Fame is the shade of immortality,
And in itself a shadow. Soon as caught,
Contemn'd; it shrinks to nothing in the grasp.
Consult th' ambitious, 'tis ambition's cure.
"And is this all?" cried Cæsar at his height,
Disgusted. This third proof Ambition brings   370
Of immortality. The first in fame.
Observe him near, your envy will abate: 372
Shamed at the disproportion vast, between
The passion and the purchase, he will sigh
At such success, and blush at his renown.
And why? Because far richer prize invites

His heart; far more illustrious glory calls:
It calls in whispers, yet the deafest hear.
　　And can Ambition a fourth proof supply?
It can, and stronger than the former three;　　　　　　　380
Yet quite o'erlook'd by some reputed wise.
Though disappointments in ambition pain,
And though success disgusts; yet still, Lorenzo!
In vain we strive to pluck it from our hearts;
By Nature planted for the noblest ends.
Absurd the famed advice to Pyrrhus[1] given,
More praised, than ponder'd; specious, but unsound;
Sooner that hero's sword the world had quell'd,
Than Reason, his ambition. Man must soar.
An obstinate activity within,　　　　　　　　　　　390
An insuppressive spring, will toss him up
In spite of Fortune's load. Not kings alone,
Each villager has his ambition too;
No Sultan prouder than his fetter'd slave:
Slaves build their little Babylons of straw,
Echo the proud Assyrian, in their hearts,
And cry,—"Behold the wonders of my might!"
And why? Because immortal as their lord;
And souls immortal must for ever heave
At something great; the glitter, or the gold;　　　　400
The praise of mortals, or the praise of Heaven.
　　Nor absolutely vain is human praise,
When human is supported by divine.
I'll introduce Lorenzo to himself;　　　　　　　　404
Pleasure and Pride (bad masters!) share our hearts.
As love of pleasure is ordain'd to guard
And feed our bodies, and extend our race;
The love of praise is planted to protect,
And propagate the glories of the mind.
What is it, but the love of praise, inspires,
Matures, refines, embellishes, exalts,
Earth's happiness? From that, the delicate,　　　　412
The grand, the marvellous, of civil life,
Want and convenience, underworkers, lay
The basis, on which love of glory builds.
Nor is thy life, O Virtue! less in debt
To praise, thy secret stimulating friend.
Were men not proud, what merit should we miss!
Pride made the virtues of the Pagan world.

[1] 'To Pyrrhus:' by a philosopher who told him he would have been as happy had he stayed at home, instead of pursuing a career of conquest.

133

Praise is the salt that seasons right to man,   420
And whets his appetite for moral good.
Thirst of applause is Virtue's second guard;
Reason, her first; but reason wants an aid;
Our private reason is a flatterer;
Thirst of applause calls public judgment in,
To poise our own, to keep an even scale,
And give endanger'd Virtue fairer play.
        Here a fifth proof arises, stronger still:
Why this so nice construction of our hearts?
These delicate moralities of sense;   430
This constitutional reserve of aid
To succour virtue, when our reason fails;
If virtue, kept alive by care and toil,
And oft, the mark of injuries on earth,
When labour'd to maturity (its bill
Of disciplines, and pains, unpaid), must die?
Why freighted rich, to dash against a rock?
Were man to perish when most fit to live,   438
O how misspent were all these stratagems,
By skill divine inwoven in our frame!
Where are Heaven's holiness and mercy fled?
Laughs Heaven, at once, at Virtue, and at Man?
If not, why that discouraged, this destroy'd?
        Thus far Ambition. What says Avarice?
This her chief maxim, which has long been thine:
"The wise and wealthy are the same,"—I grant it.
To store up treasure with incessant toil,
This is man's province, this his highest praise.
To this great end keen Instinct stings him on.
To guide that instinct, Reason! is thy charge;   450
'Tis thine to tell us where true treasure lies:
But, Reason failing to discharge her trust,
Or to the deaf discharging it in vain,
A blunder follows; and blind Industry,
Gall'd by the spur, but stranger to the course
(The course where stakes of more than gold are won),
O'erloading, with the cares of distant age,
The jaded spirits of the present hour,
Provides for an eternity below.
        "Thou shalt not covet," is a wise command;   460
But bounded to the wealth the sun surveys:
Look farther, the command stands quite reversed,
And avarice is a virtue most divine.
Is faith a refuge for our happiness?
Most sure: and is it not for reason too?

Nothing this world unriddles, but the next.
Whence inextinguishable thirst of gain?
From inextinguishable life in man.
Man, if not meant, by worth, to reach the skies,
Had wanted wing to fly so far in guilt. 470
Sour grapes, I grant, ambition, avarice,
Yet still their root is immortality: 472
These its wild growths so bitter, and so base,
(Pain and reproach!) Religion can reclaim,
Refine, exalt, throw down their poisonous lee,
And make them sparkle in the bowl of bliss.
    See, the third witness laughs at bliss remote,
And falsely promises an Eden here:
Truth she shall speak for once, though prone to lie,
A common cheat, and Pleasure is her name. 480
To Pleasure never was Lorenzo deaf;
Then hear her now, now first thy real friend.
    Since Nature made us not more fond than proud
Of happiness (whence hypocrites in joy!
Makers of mirth! artificers of smiles!),
Why should the joy most poignant sense affords,
Burn us with blushes, and rebuke our pride?—
Those heaven-born blushes tell us man descends,
Even in the zenith of his earthly bliss:
Should Reason take her infidel repose, 490
This honest instinct speaks our lineage high;
This instinct calls on darkness to conceal
Our rapturous relation to the stalls.
Our glory covers us with noble shame,
And he that's unconfounded, is unmann'd.
The man that blushes, is not quite a brute.
Thus far with thee, Lorenzo, will I close:
Pleasure is good, and man for pleasure made;
But pleasure full of glory, as of joy;
Pleasure, which neither blushes, nor expires. 500
    The witnesses are heard; the cause is o'er;
Let Conscience file the sentence in her court,
Dearer than deeds that half a realm convey;
Thus seal'd by Truth, th' authentic record runs:
    "Know all; know, infidels,—unapt to know!
'Tis immortality your nature solves; 506
'Tis immortality deciphers man,
And opens all the mysteries of his make.
Without it, half his instincts are a riddle;
Without it, all his virtues are a dream.
His very crimes attest his dignity;

His sateless thirst of pleasure, gold, and fame,
Declares him born for blessings infinite: 513
What less than infinite makes unabsurd
Passions, which all on earth but more inflames?
Fierce passions, so mismeasured to this scene,
Stretch'd out, like eagles' wings, beyond our nest,
Far, far beyond the worth of all below,
For earth too large, presage a nobler flight,
And evidence our title to the skies."   520
    Ye gentle theologues, of calmer kind!
Whose constitution dictates to your pen,
Who, cold yourselves, think ardour comes from hell!
Think not our passions from Corruption sprung,
Though to Corruption now they lend their wings;
That is their mistress, not their mother. All
(And justly) Reason deem divine: I see,
I feel a grandeur in the passions too,
Which speaks their high descent, and glorious end;
Which speaks them rays of an eternal fire.   530
In Paradise itself they burn'd as strong,
Ere Adam fell; though wiser in their aim.
Like the proud Eastern,[1] struck by Providence,
What though our passions are run mad, and stoop
With low, terrestrial appetite, to graze
On trash, on toys, dethroned from high desire?
Yet still, through their disgrace, no feeble ray
Of greatness shines, and tells us whence they fell:
But these (like that fallen monarch when reclaim'd),   539
When Reason moderates the rein aright,
Shall reascend, remount their former sphere,
Where once they soar'd illustrious; ere seduced
By wanton Eve's debauch, to stroll on earth,
And set the sublunary world on fire.
    But grant their phrensy lasts; their phrensy fails
To disappoint one providential end,
For which Heaven blew up ardour in our hearts:
Were Reason silent, boundless Passion speaks
A future scene of boundless objects too,
And brings glad tidings of eternal day.   550
Eternal day! 'tis that enlightens all;
And all, by that enlighten'd, proves it sure.
Consider man as an immortal being,
Intelligible all; and all is great;
A crystalline transparency prevails,

---

[1] 'Proud Eastern:' Nebuchadnezzar.

And strikes full lustre through the human sphere:
Consider man as mortal, all is dark,
And wretched; Reason weeps at the survey.
     The learn'd Lorenzo cries, "And let her weep,
Weak, modern Reason: ancient times were wise.   560
Authority, that venerable guide,
Stands on my part; the famed Athenian porch
(And who for wisdom so renown'd as they?)
Denied this immortality to man."
I grant it; but affirm, they proved it too.
A riddle this!—have patience; I'll explain.
     What noble vanities, what moral flights,
Glittering through their romantic wisdom's page,
Make us at once despise them, and admire?
Fable is flat to these high-season'd sires;   570
They leave th' extravagance of song below.
"Flesh shall not feel; or, feeling, shall enjoy
The dagger, or the rack; to them, alike   573
A bed of roses, or the burning bull."
In men exploding all beyond the grave,
Strange doctrine, this! As doctrine, it was strange;
But not, as prophecy; for such it proved,
And, to their own amazement, was fulfill'd:
They feign'd a firmness Christians need not feign.
The Christian truly triumph'd in the flame: 580
The Stoic saw, in double wonder lost,
Wonder at them, and wonder at himself,
To find the bold adventures of his thought
Not bold, and that he strove to lie in vain.
     Whence, then, those thoughts? those towering thoughts, that flew
Such monstrous heights?—From instinct, and from pride.
The glorious instinct of a deathless soul,
Confusedly conscious of her dignity,
Suggested truths they could not understand.
In Lust's dominion, and in Passion's storm,   590
Truth's system broken, scatter'd fragments lay,
As light in chaos, glimmering through the gloom:
Smit with the pomp of lofty sentiments,
Pleased Pride proclaim'd, what Reason disbelieved.
Pride, like the Delphic priestess, with a swell,
Raved nonsense, destined to be future sense,
When life immortal, in full day, shall shine;
And death's dark shadows fly the Gospel sun.
They spoke, what nothing but immortal souls
Could speak; and thus the truth they question'd, proved.
     Can then absurdities, as well as crimes,   601

Speak man immortal? All things speak him so.
Much has been urged; and dost thou call for more?
Call; and with endless questions be distress'd,
All unresolvable, if earth is all.
　　"Why life, a moment; infinite, desire?　　　　　606
Our wish, eternity? Our home, the grave?
Heaven's promise dormant lies in human hope;
Who wishes life immortal, proves it too.
Why happiness pursued, though never found?
Man's thirst of happiness declares it is,
(For nature never gravitates to nought);
That thirst unquench'd declares it is not here.　　613
My Lucia, thy Clarissa call to thought;
Why cordial friendship riveted so deep,
As hearts to pierce at first, at parting, rend,
If friend, and friendship, vanish in an hour?
Is not this torment in the mask of joy?
Why by reflection marr'd the joys of sense?
Why past, and future, preying on our hearts,　　620
And putting all our present joys to death?
Why labours Reason? Instinct were as well;
Instinct far better; what can choose, can err:
O how infallible the thoughtless brute!
'Twere well his Holiness were half as sure.
Reason with inclination, why at war?
Why sense of guilt? why Conscience up in arms?"
　　Conscience of guilt, is prophecy of pain,
And bosom-council to decline the blow.
Reason with inclination ne'er had jarr'd,　　　　630
If nothing future paid forbearance here:
Thus on—these, and a thousand pleas uncall'd,
All promise, some insure, a second scene;
Which, were it doubtful, would be dearer far
Than all things else most certain; were it false,
What truth on earth so precious as the lie?
This world it gives us, let what will ensue;
This world it gives, in that high cordial, hope:
The future of the present is the soul.
How this life groans, when sever'd from the next!　　640
Poor mutilated wretch, that disbelieves!
By dark distrust his being cut in two,
In both parts perishes; life void of joy,
Sad prelude of eternity in pain!
　　Couldst thou persuade me, the next life could fail
Our ardent wishes; how should I pour out
My bleeding heart in anguish, new, as deep!

Oh! with what thoughts, thy hope, and my despair,
Abhorr'd annihilation! blasts the soul,
And wide extends the bounds of human woe!   650
Could I believe Lorenzo's system true,
In this black channel would my ravings run:
"Grief from the future borrow'd peace, erewhile.
The future vanish'd! and the present pain'd!
Strange import of unprecedented ill!
Fall, how profound! Like Lucifer's, the fall!
Unequal fate! his fall, without his guilt!
From where fond Hope built her pavilion high,
The gods among, hurl'd headlong, hurl'd at once
To night! to nothing! darker still than night.   660
If 'twas a dream, why wake me, my worst foe,
Lorenzo! boastful of the name of friend?
O for delusion! O for error still!
Could vengeance strike much stronger than to plant
A thinking being in a world like this,
Not over-rich before, now beggar'd quite;
More cursed than at the fall?—The sun goes out!
The thorns shoot up! What thorns in every thought!
Why sense of better? It embitters worse.
Why sense? why life? If but to sigh, then sink   670
To what I was! twice nothing! and much woe!
Woe, from Heaven's bounties! woe from what was wont
To flatter most, high intellectual powers.
Thought, virtue, knowledge!—blessings, by thy scheme,
All poison'd into pains. First, knowledge, once   675
My soul's ambition, now her greatest dread.
To know myself, true wisdom?—No, to shun
That shocking science, parent of despair!
Avert thy mirror: if I see, I die.
     "Know my Creator! climb his bless'd abode
By painful speculation, pierce the veil,
Dive in his nature, read his attributes,
And gaze in admiration—on a foe,   683
Obtruding life, withholding happiness!
From the full rivers that surround his throne,
Not letting fall one drop of joy on man;
Man gasping for one drop, that he might cease
To curse his birth, nor envy reptiles more!
Ye sable clouds! ye darkest shades of night!
Hide him, for ever hide him, from my thought,   690
Once all my comfort; source, and soul of joy!

139

Now leagued with furies, and with thee,[1] against me.
    "Know his achievements? study his renown?
Contemplate this amazing universe,
Dropp'd from his hand, with miracles replete!
For what? 'Mid miracles of nobler name,
To find one miracle of misery?
To find the being, which alone can know
And praise his works, a blemish on his praise?
Through nature's ample range, in thought, to stroll,   700
And start at man, the single mourner there,
Breathing high hope, chain'd down to pangs, and death?
Knowing is suffering: and shall Virtue share
The sigh of knowledge?—Virtue shares the sigh.
By straining up the steep of excellent,
By battles fought, and, from temptation won,
What gains she, but the pang of seeing worth,   707
Angelic worth, soon shuffled in the dark
With every vice, and swept to brutal dust?
Merit is madness; virtue is a crime;
A crime to reason, if it costs us pain
Unpaid: what pain, amidst a thousand more,
To think the most abandon'd, after days   713
Of triumph o'er their betters, find in death
As soft a pillow, nor make fouler clay!
    "Duty! Religion!—these, our duty done,
Imply reward. Religion is mistake.
Duty!—there's none, but to repel the cheat.
Ye cheats, away! ye daughters of my pride!
Who feign yourselves the favourites of the skies: 720
Ye towering hopes! abortive energies!
That toss, and struggle, in my lying breast,
To scale the skies, and build presumptions there,
As I were heir of an eternity.
Vain, vain ambitions! trouble me no more.
Why travel far in quest of sure defeat?
As bounded as my being, be my wish.
All is inverted; wisdom is a fool.
Sense! take the rein; blind Passion! drive us on;
And, Ignorance! befriend us on our way;   730
Ye new, but truest patrons of our peace!
Yes; give the pulse full empire; live the brute,
Since, as the brute, we die. The sum of man,
Of godlike man! to revel, and to rot.
    "But not on equal terms with other brutes:

---

[1] 'Thee:' Lorenzo.

140

Their revels a more poignant relish yield,
And safer too; they never poisons choose.
Instinct, than reason, makes more wholesome meals,
And sends all-marring murmur far away.
For sensual life they best philosophize;   740
Theirs, that serene, the sages sought in vain: 741
'Tis man alone expostulates with Heaven;
His all the power, and all the cause, to mourn.
Shall human eyes alone dissolve in tears?
And bleed, in anguish, none but human hearts?
The wide-stretch'd realm of intellectual woe,
Surpassing sensual far, is all our own.
In life so fatally distinguish'd, why
Cast in one lot, confounded, lump'd, in death?
    "Ere yet in being, was mankind in guilt?   750
Why thunder'd this peculiar clause against us,
All-mortal, and all-wretched!—Have the skies
Reasons of state, their subjects may not scan,
Nor humbly reason, when they sorely sigh?
All-mortal, and all-wretched!—'Tis too much:
Unparallell'd in nature: 'tis too much
On being unrequested at thy hands,
Omnipotent! for I see nought but power.
    "And why see that? Why thought? To toil, and eat,
Then make our bed in darkness, needs no thought.   760
What superfluities are reasoning souls!
Oh give eternity! or thought destroy.
But without thought our curse were half unfelt;
Its blunted edge would spare the throbbing heart;
And, therefore, 'tis bestow'd, I thank thee, Reason!
For aiding life's too small calamities,
And giving being to the dread of Death.
Such are thy bounties!—was it then too much
For me, to trespass on the brutal rights?
Too much for Heaven to make one emmet more?   770
Too much for chaos to permit my mass
A longer stay with essences unwrought,
Unfashion'd, untormented into man?
Wretched preferment to this round of pains!
Wretched capacity of phrensy, thought!   775
Wretched capacity of dying, life!
Life, thought, worth, wisdom, all (O foul revolt!)
Once friends to peace, gone over to the foe.
    "Death, then, has changed his nature too: O Death!
Come to my bosom, thou best gift of Heaven!
Best friend of man! since man is man no more.

Why in this thorny wilderness so long,
Since there's no promised land's ambrosial bower,   783
To pay me with its honey for my stings?
If needful to the selfish schemes of Heaven
To sting us sore, why mock'd our misery?
Why this so sumptuous insult o'er our heads?
Why this illustrious canopy display'd?
Why so magnificently lodged Despair?
At stated periods, sure returning, roll   790
These glorious orbs, that mortals may compute
Their length of labours, and of pains; nor lose
Their misery's full measure?—Smiles with flowers,
And fruits, promiscuous, ever-teeming earth,
That man may languish in luxurious scenes,
And in an Eden mourn his wither'd joys?
Claim earth and skies man's admiration, due
For such delights! Blest animals! too wise
To wonder, and too happy to complain!
    "Our doom decreed demands a mournful scene: 800
Why not a dungeon dark, for the condemn'd?
Why not the dragon's subterranean den,
For man to howl in? Why not his abode
Of the same dismal colour with his fate?
A Thebes, a Babylon, at vast expence
Of time, toil, treasure, art, for owls and adders,
As congruous as, for man, this lofty dome,
Which prompts proud thought, and kindles high desire;
If, from her humble chamber in the dust,   809
While proud thought swells, and high desire inflames,
The poor worm calls us for her inmates there;
And, round us, Death's inexorable hand
Draws the dark curtain close; undrawn no more.
    "Undrawn no more!—Behind the cloud of death,
Once I beheld a sun; a sun which gilt
That sable cloud, and turn'd it all to gold:
How the grave's alter'd! fathomless, as hell!
A real hell to those who dreamt of heaven.
Annihilation! how it yawns before me!
Next moment I may drop from thought, from sense,   820
The privilege of angels, and of worms,
An outcast from existence! and this spirit,
This all-pervading, this all-conscious soul,
This particle of energy divine,
Which travels nature, flies from star to star,
And visits gods, and emulates their powers,
For ever is extinguish'd. Horror! death!

Death of that death I fearless once survey'd!—
When horror universal shall descend,
And heaven's dark concave urn all human race,   830
On that enormous, unrefunding tomb,
How just this verse! this monumental sigh!"

    Beneath the lumber of demolish'd worlds,
Deep in the rubbish of the general wreck,
Swept ignominious to the common mass
Of matter, never dignified with life,
Here lie proud rationals; the sons of heaven!
The lords of earth! the property of worms!
Beings of yesterday, and no to-morrow!
Who lived in terror, and in pangs expired!   840
All gone to rot in chaos; or to make
Their happy transit into blocks or brutes,   842
Nor longer sully their Creator's name.

    Lorenzo! hear, pause, ponder, and pronounce.
Just is this history? If such is man,
Mankind's historian, though divine, might weep.
And dares Lorenzo smile!—I know thee proud;
For once let Pride befriend thee; Pride looks pale
At such a scene, and sighs for something more.
Amid thy boasts, presumptions, and displays,   850
And art thou then a shadow? less than shade?
A nothing? less than nothing? To have been,
And not to be, is lower than unborn.
Art thou ambitious? Why then make the worm
Thine equal? Runs thy taste of pleasure high?
Why patronise sure death of every joy?
Charm riches? Why choose beggary in the grave,
Of every hope a bankrupt! and for ever?
Ambition, pleasure, avarice, persuade thee
To make that world of glory, rapture, wealth,   860
They lately proved,[1] the soul's supreme desire.
    What art thou made of? Rather, how unmade?
Great Nature's master-appetite destroy'd!
Is endless life, and happiness, despised?
Or both wish'd, here, where neither can be found?
Such man's perverse, eternal war with Heaven!
Darest thou persist? And is there nought on earth
But a long train of transitory forms,
Rising, and breaking, millions in an hour?
Bubbles of a fantastic deity, blown up   870

---

[1] 'Lately proved:' in the Sixth Night.

In sport, and then in cruelty destroy'd?
Oh! for what crime, unmerciful Lorenzo!
Destroys thy scheme the whole of human race?
Kind is fell Lucifer, compared to thee: 874
Oh! spare this waste of being half divine;
And vindicate th' economy of Heaven.
    Heaven is all love; all joy in giving joy:
It never had created, but to bless:
And shall it, then, strike off the list of life,
A being bless'd, or worthy so to be?
Heaven starts at an annihilating God.
    Is that, all Nature starts at, thy desire?   882
Art such a clod to wish thyself all clay?
What is that dreadful wish?—The dying groan
Of Nature, murder'd by the blackest guilt.
What deadly poison has thy nature drank?
To Nature undebauch'd no shock so great;
Nature's first wish is endless happiness;
Annihilation is an after-thought,
A monstrous wish, unborn till virtue dies.   900
And, oh! what depth of horror lies enclosed!
For non-existence no man ever wish'd,
But, first, he wish'd the Deity destroy'd.
    If so; what words are dark enough to draw
Thy picture true? The darkest are too fair.
Beneath what baleful planet, in what hour
Of desperation, by what fury's aid,
In what infernal posture of the soul,
All hell invited, and all hell in joy
At such a birth, a birth so near of kin,   900
Did thy foul fancy whelp so black a scheme
Of hopes abortive, faculties half-blown,
And deities begun, reduced to dust?
    There's nought (thou say'st) but one eternal flux
Of feeble essences, tumultuous driven
Through Time's rough billows into Night's abyss.
Say, in this rapid tide of human ruin,
Is there no rock, on which man's tossing thought   908
Can rest from terror, dare his fate survey,
And boldly think it something to be born?
Amid such hourly wrecks of being fair,
Is there no central, all-sustaining base,
All-realising, all-connecting power,
Which, as it call'd forth all things, can recall,
And force Destruction to refund her spoil?
Command the grave restore her taken prey?

Bid death's dark vale its human harvest yield,
And earth, and ocean, pay their debt of man,
True to the grand deposit trusted there?
Is there no potentate, whose outstretch'd arm, 920
When ripening time calls forth th' appointed hour,
Pluck'd from foul Devastation's famish'd maw,
Binds present, past, and future, to his throne?
His throne, how glorious, thus divinely graced,
By germinating beings clustering round!
A garland worthy the divinity!
A throne, by Heaven's omnipotence in smiles,
Built (like a Pharos towering in the waves)
Amidst immense effusions of his love!
An ocean of communicated bliss! 930
    An all-prolific, all-preserving God!
This were a God indeed.—And such is man,
As here presumed: he rises from his fall.
Think'st thou Omnipotence a naked root,
Each blossom fair of Deity destroy'd?
Nothing is dead; nay, nothing sleeps; each soul,
That ever animated human clay,
Now wakes; is on the wing: and where, oh! where,
Will the swarm settle?—When the trumpet's call,
As sounding brass, collects us, round Heaven's throne
Conglobed, we bask in everlasting day, 941
(Paternal splendour!) and adhere for ever. 942
Had not the soul this outlet to the skies,
In this vast vessel of the universe,
How should we gasp, as in an empty void!
How in the pangs of famish'd hope expire?
    How bright my prospect shines! how gloomy, thine!
A trembling world! and a devouring God!
Earth, but the shambles of Omnipotence!
Heaven's face all stain'd with causeless massacres 950
Of countless millions, born to feel the pang
Of being lost. Lorenzo! can it be?
This bids us shudder at the thoughts of life.
Who would be born to such a phantom world,
Where nought substantial but our misery?
Where joy (if joy) but heightens our distress,
So soon to perish, and revive no more?
The greater such a joy, the more it pains.
A world, so far from great, (and yet how great
It shines to thee!) there's nothing real in it; 960
Being, a shadow; consciousness, a dream!
A dream, how dreadful! universal blank

Before it, and behind! Poor man, a spark
From non-existence struck by wrath divine,
Glittering a moment, nor that moment sure,
'Midst upper, nether, and surrounding night,
His sad, sure, sudden, and eternal tomb!
    Lorenzo! dost thou feel these arguments?
Or is there nought but vengeance can be felt?
How hast thou dared the Deity dethrone?   970
How dared indict Him of a world like this?
If such the world, creation was a crime;
For what is crime, but cause of misery?
Retract, blasphemer! and unriddle this,
Of endless arguments above, below,
Without us, and within, the short result—   976
"If man's immortal, there's a God in heaven."
    But wherefore such redundancy? such waste
Of argument? One sets my soul at rest!
One obvious, and at hand, and, oh!—at heart.
So just the skies, Philander's life so pain'd,
His heart so pure; that, or succeeding scenes
Have palms to give, or ne'er had he been born.   983
    "What an old tale is this!" Lorenzo cries.—
I grant this argument is old; but truth
No years impair; and had not this been true,
Thou never hadst despised it for its age.
Truth is immortal as thy soul; and fable
As fleeting as thy joys: be wise, nor make
Heaven's highest blessing, vengeance; oh, be wise! 990
Nor make a curse of immortality.
    Say, know'st thou what it is, or what thou art?
Know'st thou th' importance of a soul immortal?
Behold this midnight glory: worlds on worlds!
Amazing pomp! redouble this amaze;
Ten thousand add; add twice ten thousand more;
Then weigh the whole; one soul outweighs them all;
And calls th' astonishing magnificence
Of unintelligent creation, poor.
    For this, believe not me; no man believe: 1000
Trust not in words, but deeds; and deeds no less
Than those of the Supreme; nor His, a few;
Consult them all; consulted, all proclaim
Thy soul's importance: tremble at thyself;
For whom Omnipotence has waked so long:
Has waked, and work'd, for ages; from the birth
Of Nature to this unbelieving hour.
    In this small province of His vast domain

(All nature bow, while I pronounce His Name!)
What has God done, and not for this sole end, 1010
To rescue souls from death? The soul's high price
Is writ in all the conduct of the skies.
The soul's high price is the creation's key,
Unlocks its mysteries, and naked lays
The genuine cause of every deed divine:
That is the chain of ages, which maintains
Their obvious correspondence, and unites
Most distant periods in one bless'd design:
That is the mighty hinge, on which have turn'd
All revolutions, whether we regard 1020
The natural, civil, or religious, world;
The former two but servants to the third:
To that their duty done, they both expire,
Their mass new-cast, forgot their deeds renown'd;
And angels ask, "Where once they shone so fair?"
　　　To lift us from this abject, to sublime;
This flux, to permanent; this dark, to day;
This foul, to pure; this turbid, to serene;
This mean, to mighty!—for this glorious end
Th' Almighty, rising, his long Sabbath broke! 1030
The world was made; was ruin'd; was restored;
Laws from the skies were publish'd; were repeal'd;
On earth, kings, kingdoms, rose; kings, kingdoms, fell;
Famed sages lighted up the Pagan world;
Prophets from Sion darted a keen glance
Through distant age; saints travell'd; martyrs bled;
By wonders sacred nature stood controll'd;
The living were translated; dead were raised;
Angels, and more than angels, came from heaven;
And, oh! for this, descended lower still; 1040
Guilt was hell's gloom; astonish'd at his guest,
For one short moment Lucifer adored:
Lorenzo! and wilt thou do less?—For this,
That hallow'd page, fools scoff at, was inspired, 1044
Of all these truths thrice venerable code!
Deists! perform your quarantine; and then
Fall prostrate, ere you touch it, lest you die.
　　　Nor less intensely bent infernal powers
To mar, than those of light, this end to gain.
Oh, what a scene is here!—Lorenzo, wake!
Rise to the thought; exert, expand thy soul
To take the vast idea: it denies 1052
All else the name of great. Two warring worlds!
Not Europe against Afric; warring worlds!

Of more than mortal! mounted on the wing!
On ardent wings of energy, and zeal,
High hovering o'er this little brand of strife!
This sublunary ball—but strife, for what?
In their own cause conflicting? No; in thine,
In Man's. His single interest blows the flame;   1060
His the sole stake; his fate the trumpet sounds,
Which kindles war immortal. How it burns!
Tumultuous swarms of deities in arms!
Force, force opposing, till the waves run high,
And tempest nature's universal sphere.
Such opposites eternal, steadfast, stern,
Such foes implacable, are Good, and Ill;
Yet man, vain man, would mediate peace between them.
     Think not this fiction, "There was war in heaven."
From heaven's high crystal mountain, where it hung,
Th' Almighty's outstretch'd arm took down his bow,   1071
And shot his indignation at the deep:
Re-thunder'd hell, and darted all her fires.—
And seems the stake of little moment still?
And slumbers man, who singly caused the storm?
He sleeps.—And art thou shock'd at mysteries?
The greatest, thou. How dreadful to reflect,
What ardour, care, and counsel, mortals cause   1078
In breasts divine! how little in their own!
     Where'er I turn, how new proofs pour upon me!
How happily this wondrous view supports
My former argument! How strongly strikes
Immortal life's full demonstration, here!
Why this exertion? Why this strange regard
From heaven's Omnipotent indulged to man?—
Because, in man, the glorious dreadful power,
Extremely to be pain'd, or bless'd, for ever.
Duration gives importance; swells the price
An angel, if a creature of a day,
What would he be? a trifle of no weight;   1090
Or stand, or fall; no matter which; he's gone.
Because immortal, therefore is indulged
This strange regard of deities to dust.
Hence, Heaven looks down on earth with all her eyes;
Hence, the soul's mighty moment in her sight:
Hence, every soul has partisans above,
And every thought a critic in the skies:
Hence, clay, vile clay! has angels for its guard,
And every guard a passion for his charge:
Hence, from all age, the cabinet divine 1100

Has held high counsel o'er the fate of man.
  Nor have the clouds those gracious counsels hid,
Angels undrew the curtain of the throne,
And Providence came forth to meet mankind:
In various modes of emphasis and awe,
He spoke his will, and trembling Nature heard;
He spoke it loud, in thunder and in storm.
Witness, thou Sinai! whose cloud-cover'd height,
And shaken basis, own'd the present God:
Witness, ye billows! whose returning tide,   1110
Breaking the chain that fasten'd it in air,
Swept Egypt, and her menaces, to hell: 1112
Witness, ye flames! th' Assyrian tyrant blew
To sevenfold rage, as impotent, as strong:
And thou, earth! witness, whose expanding jaws
Closed o'er Presumption's sacrilegious sons:[1]
Has not each element, in turn, subscribed
The soul's high price, and sworn it to the wise?
Has not flame, ocean, ether, earthquake, strove
To strike this truth, through adamantine man?   1120
If not all-adamant, Lorenzo! hear;
All is delusion; Nature is wrapt up,
In tenfold night, from Reason's keenest eye;
There's no consistence, meaning, plan, or end,
In all beneath the sun, in all above
(As far as man can penetrate), or heaven
Is an immense, inestimable prize;
Or all is nothing, or that prize is all.—
And shall each toy be still a match for Heaven,
And full equivalent for groans below?   1130
Who would not give a trifle to prevent
What he would give a thousand worlds to cure?
  Lorenzo! thou hast seen (if thine to see)
All nature, and her God (by nature's course,
And nature's course controll'd), declare for me:
The skies above proclaim, "Immortal man!"
And, "Man immortal!" all below resounds.
The world's a system of theology,
Read by the greatest strangers to the schools:
If honest, learn'd; and sages o'er a plough.   1140
Is not, Lorenzo, then, imposed on thee
This hard alternative; or, to renounce
Thy reason, or thy sense; or, to believe?
What then is unbelief? 'Tis an exploit;

---

[1] 'Presumption's sacrilegious sons:' Korah, &c.

A strenuous enterprise: to gain it, man   1145
Must burst through every bar of common sense,
Of common shame, magnanimously wrong:
And what rewards the sturdy combatant?
His prize, repentance; infamy, his crown.
  But wherefore infamy?—For want of faith,
Down the steep precipice of wrong he slides;
There's nothing to support him in the right.   1152
Faith in the future wanting, is, at least
In embryo, every weakness, every guilt;
And strong temptation ripens it to birth.
If this life's gain invites him to the deed,
Why not his country sold, his father slain?
'Tis virtue to pursue our good supreme;
And his supreme, his only good, is here.
Ambition, avarice, by the wise disdain'd,   1160
Is perfect wisdom, while mankind are fools,
And think a turf, or tombstone, covers all:
These find employment, and provide for Sense
A richer pasture, and a larger range;
And Sense by right divine ascends the throne,
When Virtue's prize and prospect are no more;
Virtue no more we think the will of Heaven.
Would Heaven quite beggar Virtue, if beloved?
  "Has Virtue charms?"—I grant her heavenly fair;
But if unportion'd, all will Interest wed;   1170
Though that our admiration, this our choice.
The virtues grow on immortality;
That root destroy'd, they wither and expire.
A Deity believed, will nought avail;
Rewards and punishments make God adored;
And hopes and fears give Conscience all her power.
  As in the dying parent dies the child,
Virtue, with immortality, expires.
Who tells me he denies his soul immortal,   1179
Whate'er his boast, has told me, he's a knave.
His duty 'tis, to love himself alone;
Nor care though mankind perish, if he smiles.
Who thinks ere long the man shall wholly die,
Is dead already; nought but brute survives.
  And are there such?—Such candidates there are
For more than death; for utter loss of being,
Being, the basis of the Deity!
Ask you the cause?—The cause they will not tell:
Nor need they: oh the sorceries of Sense!
They work this transformation on the soul;   1190

Dismount her, like the serpent at the fall,
Dismount her from her native wing (which soar'd
Erewhile ethereal heights), and throw her down,
To lick the dust, and crawl in such a thought.
    Is it in words to paint you? O ye fallen!
Fallen from the wings of Reason, and of Hope!
Erect in stature, prone in appetite!
Patrons of pleasure, posting into pain!
Lovers of argument, averse to sense!
Boasters of liberty, fast bound in chains!   1200
Lords of the wide creation, and the shame!
More senseless than th' irrationals you scorn!
More base than those you rule! than those you pity,
Far more undone! O ye most infamous
Of beings, from superior dignity!
Deepest in woe, from means of boundless bliss!
Ye cursed by blessings infinite! because
Most highly favour'd, most profoundly lost!
Ye motley mass of contradiction strong!
And are you, too, convinced, your souls fly off   1210
In exhalation soft, and die in air,
From the full flood of evidence against you?
In the coarse drudgeries, and sinks of Sense,   1213
Your souls have quite worn out the make of Heaven,
By vice new-cast, and creatures of your own:
But though you can deform, you can't destroy;
To curse, not uncreate, is all your power.
    Lorenzo! this black brotherhood renounce;
Renounce St Evremont, and read St Paul.
Ere rapt by miracle, by Reason wing'd,   1220
His mounting mind made long abode in heaven.
This is freethinking, unconfined to parts,
To send the soul, on curious travel bent,
Through all the provinces of human thought;
To dart her flight, through the whole sphere of man;
Of this vast universe to make the tour;
In each recess of space, and time, at home;
Familiar with their wonders; diving deep;
And, like a prince of boundless interests there,
Still most ambitious of the most remote;   1230
To look on truth unbroken, and entire;
Truth in the system, the full orb; where truths
By truths enlighten'd, and sustain'd, afford
An arch-like, strong foundation, to support
Th' incumbent weight of absolute, complete
Conviction; here, the more we press, we stand

More firm; who most examine, most believe.
Parts, like half sentences, confound; the whole
Conveys the sense, and God is understood;
Who not in fragments writes to human race: 1240
Read his whole volume, sceptic! then reply.
     This, this, is thinking free, a thought that grasps
Beyond a grain, and looks beyond an hour.
Turn up thine eye, survey this midnight scene;
What are earth's kingdoms, to yon boundless orbs,
Of human souls, one day, the destined range?
And what yon boundless orbs, to godlike man?   1247
Those numerous worlds that throng the firmament,
And ask more space in heaven, can roll at large
In man's capacious thought, and still leave room
For ampler orbs, for new creations, there.
Can such a soul contract itself, to gripe
A point of no dimension, of no weight?   1253
It can; it does: the world is such a point;
And, of that point, how small a part enslaves!
     How small a part—of nothing, shall I say?
Why not?—Friends, our chief treasure! how they drop!
Lucia,[1] Narcissa fair, Philander, gone!
The grave, like fabled Cerberus, has oped
A triple mouth; and, in an awful voice,   1260
Loud calls my soul, and utters all I sing.
How the world falls to pieces round about us,
And leaves us in a ruin of our joy!
What says this transportation of my friends?
It bids me love the place where now they dwell,
And scorn this wretched spot, they leave so poor.
Eternity's vast ocean lies before thee;
There, there, Lorenzo! thy Clarissa sails.
Give thy mind sea-room; keep it wide of earth,
That rock of souls immortal; cut thy cord;   1270
Weigh anchor; spread thy sails; call every wind;
Eye thy great Pole-star; make the land of life.
     Two kinds of life has double-natured man,
And two of death; the last far more severe.
Life animal is nurtured by the sun;
Thrives on his bounties, triumphs in his beams.
Life rational subsists on higher food,
Triumphant in His beams, who made the day.
When we leave that sun, and are left by this
(The fate of all who die in stubborn guilt),   1280

---

[1] 'Lucia:' probably his wife.

'Tis utter darkness; strictly double death.
We sink by no judicial stroke of Heaven,
But nature's course; as sure as plummets fall.
Since God, or man, must alter, ere they meet
(Since light and darkness blend not in one sphere),
'Tis manifest, Lorenzo! who must change.
    If, then, that double death should prove thy lot,
Blame not the bowels of the Deity;
Man shall be blest, as far as man permits.
Not man alone, all rationals, Heaven arms   1290
With an illustrious, but tremendous, power
To counteract its own most gracious ends;
And this, of strict necessity, not choice;
That power denied, men, angels, were no more
But passive engines, void of praise, or blame.
A nature rational implies the power
Of being blest, or wretched, as we please;
Else idle Reason would have nought to do;
And he that would be barr'd capacity
Of pain, courts incapacity of bliss.   1300
Heaven wills our happiness, allows our doom;
Invites us ardently, but not compels.
Heaven but persuades, almighty man decrees;
Man is the maker of immortal fates.
Man falls by man, if finally he falls;
And fall he must, who learns from Death alone,
The dreadful secret,—that he lives for ever.
    Why this to thee?—thee yet, perhaps, in doubt
Of second life? But wherefore doubtful still?
Eternal life is nature's ardent wish: 1310
What ardently we wish, we soon believe:
Thy tardy faith declares that wish destroy'd:
What has destroy'd it?—Shall I tell thee what?
When fear'd the future, 'tis no longer wish'd;   1314
And, when unwish'd, we strive to disbelieve.
"Thus infidelity our guilt betrays."
Nor that the sole detection! blush, Lorenzo!
Blush for hypocrisy, if not for guilt.
The future fear'd?—an infidel, and fear?
Fear what? a dream? a fable?—How thy dread,
Unwilling evidence, and therefore strong,
Affords my cause an undesign'd support!   1322
How disbelief affirms, what it denies!
"It, unawares, asserts immortal life."—
Surprising! infidelity turns out
A creed, and a confession of our sins:

Apostates, thus, are orthodox divines.
    Lorenzo! with Lorenzo clash no more;
Nor longer a transparent visor wear.
Think'st thou, Religion only has her mask?   1330
Our infidels are Satan's hypocrites,
Pretend the worst, and, at the bottom, fail.
When visited by thought (thought will intrude),
Like him they serve, they tremble, and believe.
Is there hypocrisy so foul as this?
So fatal to the welfare of the world?
What detestation, what contempt, their due!
And, if unpaid, be thank'd for their escape
That Christian candour they strive hard to scorn.
If not for that asylum, they might find   1340
A hell on earth; nor 'scape a worse below.
    With insolence, and impotence of thought,
Instead of racking fancy, to refute,
Reform thy manners, and the truth enjoy.—
But shall I dare confess the dire result?
Can thy proud reason brook so black a brand?
From purer manners, to sublimer faith,
Is nature's unavoidable ascent;   1348
An honest deist, where the Gospel shines,
Matured to nobler, in the Christian ends.
When that bless'd change arrives, even cast aside
This song superfluous; life immortal strikes
Conviction, in a flood of light divine.
A Christian dwells, like Uriel,[1] in the sun;
Meridian evidence puts doubt to flight;
And ardent Hope anticipates the skies.
Of that bright sun, Lorenzo! scale the sphere;
'Tis easy! it invites thee; it descends
From heaven to woo, and waft thee whence it came:
Read and revere the sacred page; a page   1360
Where triumphs immortality; a page
Which not the whole creation could produce;
Which not the conflagration shall destroy;
'Tis printed in the mind of gods for ever,
In nature's ruins not one letter lost.
    In proud disdain of what even gods adore,
Dost smile?—Poor wretch! thy guardian angel weeps.
Angels, and men, assent to what I sing;
Wits smile, and thank me for my midnight dream.
How vicious hearts fume phrensy to the brain!   1370

[1] 'Uriel:' see Milton.

Parts push us on to pride, and pride to shame;
Pert infidelity is Wit's cockade,
To grace the brazen brow that braves the skies,
By loss of being, dreadfully secure.
Lorenzo! if thy doctrine wins the day,
And drives my dreams, defeated, from the field;
If this is all, if earth a final scene,
Take heed; stand fast; be sure to be a knave;
A knave in grain! ne'er deviate to the right:
Should'st thou be good—how infinite thy loss!   1380
Guilt only makes annihilation gain.   1381
Bless'd scheme! which life deprives of comfort, death
Of hope; and which Vice only recommends.
If so, where, infidels! your bait thrown out
To catch weak converts? where your lofty boast
Of zeal for virtue, and of love to man?
Annihilation! I confess, in these.
       What can reclaim you? Dare I hope profound
Philosophers the converts of a song?
Yet know, its title[1] flatters you, not me;   1390
Yours be the praise to make my title good;
Mine, to bless Heaven, and triumph in your praise.
But since so pestilential your disease,
Though sovereign is the medicine I prescribe,
As yet, I'll neither triumph, nor despair:
But hope, ere long, my midnight dream will wake
Your hearts, and teach your wisdom—to be wise:
For why should souls immortal, made for bliss,
E'er wish (and wish in vain!) that souls could die?
What ne'er can die, oh! grant to live; and crown   1400
The wish, and aim, and labour of the skies;
Increase, and enter on the joys of heaven:
Thus shall my title pass a sacred seal,
Receive an imprimatur from above,
While angels shout—An Infidel Reclaimed!
       To close, Lorenzo! spite of all my pains,
Still seems it strange, that thou should'st live for ever?
Is it less strange, that thou should'st live at all?
This is a miracle; and that no more.
Who gave beginning, can exclude an end.   1410
Deny thou art: then, doubt if thou shalt be.
A miracle with miracles enclosed,
Is man; and starts his faith at what is strange?
What less than wonders, from the Wonderful;   1414

---

[1] 'Title:' The Infidel Reclaimed.

What less than miracles, from God, can flow?
Admit a God—that mystery supreme!
That Cause uncaused! all other wonders cease;
Nothing is marvellous for Him to do:
Deny Him—all is mystery besides;
Millions of mysteries! each darker far,
Than that thy wisdom would, unwisely, shun.
If weak thy faith, why choose the harder side?   1422
We nothing know, but what is marvellous;
Yet what is marvellous, we can't believe.
So weak our reason, and so great our God,
What most surprises in the sacred page,
Or full as strange, or stranger, must be true.
Faith is not reason's labour, but repose.
     To faith, and virtue, why so backward, man?
From hence:—the present strongly strikes us all;   1430
The future, faintly: can we, then, be men?
If men, Lorenzo! the reverse is right.
Reason is man's peculiar: Sense, the brute's.
The present is the scanty realm of Sense;
The future, Reason's empire unconfined:
On that expending all her godlike power,
She plans, provides, expatiates, triumphs, there;
There, builds her blessings; there, expects her praise;
And nothing asks of Fortune, or of men.
And what is Reason? Be she thus defined;   1440
Reason is upright stature in the soul.
Oh! be a man;—and strive to be a god.
     "For what? (thou say'st)—to damp the joys of life?"
No; to give heart and substance to thy joys.
That tyrant, Hope; mark how she domineers;
She bids us quit realities, for dreams;
Safety and peace, for hazard and alarm;
That tyrant o'er the tyrants of the soul,   1448
She bids Ambition quit its taken prize,
Spurn the luxuriant branch on which it sits,
Though bearing crowns, to spring at distant game;
And plunge in toils and dangers—for repose.
If hope precarious, and of things, when gain'd,
Of little moment, and as little stay,
Can sweeten toils and dangers into joys;
What then, that hope, which nothing can defeat,
Our leave unask'd? rich hope of boundless bliss!
Bliss, past Man's power to paint it; Time's, to close!
     This hope is earth's most estimable prize:
This is man's portion, while no more than man: 1460

Hope, of all passions, most befriends us here;
Passions of prouder name befriend us less.
Joy has her tears; and Transport has her death;
Hope, like a cordial, innocent, though strong,
Man's heart, at once, inspirits, and serenes;
Nor makes him pay his wisdom for his joys;
'Tis all our present state can safely bear,
Health to the frame! and vigour to the mind!
A joy attemper'd! a chastised delight!
Like the fair summer evening, mild, and sweet!   1470
'Tis man's full cup; his paradise below!

    A blest hereafter, then, or hoped, or gain'd,
Is all;—our whole of happiness: full proof,
I chose no trivial or inglorious theme.
And know, ye foes to song! (well-meaning men,
Though quite forgotten half your Bible's[1] praise!)
Important truths, in spite of verse, may please:
Grave minds you praise; nor can you praise too much:
If there is weight in an eternity,
Let the grave listen;—and be graver still.   1480

---

[1] 'Bible:' the poetical parts of it.

NIGHT EIGHTH.

VIRTUE'S APOLOGY;

OR,

THE MAN OF THE WORLD ANSWERED.

IN WHICH ARE CONSIDERED,

THE LOVE OF THIS LIFE; THE AMBITION AND PLEASURE, WITH THE WIT
AND WISDOM, OF THE WORLD.

AND has all nature, then, espoused my part?
Have I bribed heaven, and earth, to plead against thee?
And is thy soul immortal?—What remains?
All, all, Lorenzo!—Make immortal blest.
Unblest immortals!—What can shock us more?
And yet Lorenzo still affects the world;
There stows his treasure; thence his title draws,
Man of the world (for such would'st thou be call'd),
And art thou proud of that inglorious style?
Proud of reproach? for a reproach it was,   10
In ancient days; and Christian,—in an age,
When men were men, and not ashamed of heaven,
Fired their ambition, as it crown'd their joy.
Sprinkled with dews from the Castalian font,
Fain would I re-baptize thee, and confer
A purer spirit, and a nobler name.
      Thy fond attachments, fatal, and inflamed,
Point out my path, and dictate to my song:
To thee, the world how fair! how strongly strikes
Ambition! and gay pleasure stronger still!   20
Thy triple bane! the triple bolt that lays   21
Thy virtue dead! Be these my triple theme;
Nor shall thy wit, or wisdom, be forgot.
      Common the theme; not so the song; if she
My song invokes, Urania deigns to smile.
The charm that chains us to the world, her foe,
If she dissolves, the man of earth, at once,
Starts from his trance, and sighs for other scenes;
Scenes, where these sparks of night, these stars shall shine
Unnumber'd suns (for all things, as they are,   30
The blest behold); and, in one glory, pour
Their blended blaze on man's astonish'd sight;
A blaze—the least illustrious object there.
      Lorenzo! since eternal is at hand,

To swallow Time's ambitions; as the vast
Leviathan, the bubbles vain, that ride
High on the foaming billow; what avail
High titles, high descent, attainments high,
If unattain'd our highest? O Lorenzo!
What lofty thoughts, these elements above,   40
What towering hopes, what sallies from the sun,
What grand surveys of destiny divine,
And pompous presage of unfathom'd fate,
Should roll in bosoms, where a spirit burns,
Bound for eternity! in bosoms read
By Him, who foibles in archangels sees!
On human hearts He bends a jealous eye,
And marks, and in heaven's register enrols,
The rise, and progress, of each option there;
Sacred to doomsday! That the page unfolds,   50
And spreads us to the gaze of gods and men.
      And what an option, O Lorenzo, thine!
This world! and this, unrivall'd by the skies!
A world, where lust of pleasure, grandeur, gold,
Three demons that divide its realms between them,   55
With strokes alternate buffet to and fro
Man's restless heart, their sport, their flying ball;
Till, with the giddy circle sick, and tired,
It pants for peace, and drops into despair.
Such is the world Lorenzo sets above
That glorious promise angels were esteem'd
Too mean to bring; a promise, their Adored   62
Descended to communicate, and press,
By counsel, miracle, life, death, on man.
Such is the world Lorenzo's wisdom woos,
And on its thorny pillow seeks repose;
A pillow, which, like opiates ill prepared,
Intoxicates, but not composes; fills
The visionary mind with gay chimeras,
All the wild trash of sleep, without the rest;   70
What unfeign'd travel, and what dreams of joy!
      How frail, men, things! how momentary, both!
Fantastic chase of shadows hunting shades!
The gay, the busy, equal though unlike;
Equal in wisdom, differently wise!
Through flowery meadows, and through dreary wastes,
One bustling, and one dancing, into death.
There's not a day, but, to the man of thought,
Betrays some secret, that throws new reproach
On life, and makes him sick of seeing more.   80

The scenes of business tell us—"What are men;"
The scenes of pleasure—"What is all beside;"
There, others we despise; and here, ourselves:
Amid disgust eternal, dwells delight?
'Tis approbation strikes the string of joy.
     What wondrous prize has kindled this career,
Stuns with the din, and chokes us with the dust,
On life's gay stage, one inch above the grave?
The proud run up and down in quest of eyes;   89
The sensual, in pursuit of something worse;
The grave, of gold; the politic, of power;
And all, of other butterflies, as vain!
As eddies draw things frivolous, and light,
How is man's heart by vanity drawn in;
On the swift circle of returning toys,
Whirl'd, straw-like, round and round, and then engulf'd,
Where gay delusion darkens to despair!
     "This is a beaten track."—Is this a track
Should not be beaten? Never beat enough,
Till enough learn'd the truths it would inspire.   100
Shall Truth be silent, because Folly frowns?
Turn the world's history; what find we there,
But Fortune's sports, or Nature's cruel claims,
Or Woman's artifice, or Man's revenge,
And endless inhumanities on man?
Fame's trumpet seldom sounds, but, like the knell,
It brings bad tidings: how it hourly blows
Man's misadventures round the listening world!
Man is the tale of narrative old time;
Sad tale; which high as Paradise begins;   110
As if, the toil of travel to delude,
From stage to stage, in his eternal round,
The Days, his daughters, as they spin our hours
On Fortune's wheel, where accident unthought
Oft, in a moment, snaps life's strongest thread,
Each, in her turn, some tragic story tells,
With, now and then, a wretched farce between;
And fills his chronicle with human woes.
     Time's daughters, true as those of men, deceive us;
Not one, but puts some cheat on all mankind: 120
While in their father's bosom, not yet ours,
They flatter our fond hopes, and promise much
Of amiable; but hold him not o'er-wise,   123
Who dares to trust them; and laugh round the year
At still-confiding, still-confounded, man,
Confiding, though confounded; hoping on,

Untaught by trial, unconvinced by proof,
And ever looking for the never seen.
Life to the last, like harden'd felons, lies;
Nor owns itself a cheat, till it expires.   130
Its little joys go out by one and one,
And leave poor man, at length, in perfect night;
Night darker, than what, now, involves the pole.
　　O Thou, who dost permit these ills to fall,
For gracious ends, and would'st that man should mourn!
O Thou, whose hands this goodly fabric framed,
Who know'st it best, and would'st that man should know!
What is this sublunary world? A vapour;
A vapour all it holds; itself, a vapour;
From the damp bed of chaos, by Thy beam   140
Exhaled, ordain'd to swim its destined hour
In ambient air, then melt, and disappear.
Earth's days are number'd, nor remote her doom;
As mortal, though less transient, than her sons;
Yet they doat on her, as the world and they
Were both eternal, solid; Thou, a dream.
　　They doat!—on what? Immortal views apart,
A region of outsides! a land of shadows!
A fruitful field of flowery promises!
A wilderness of joys! perplex'd with doubts,   150
And sharp with thorns! a troubled ocean, spread
With bold adventurers, their all on board!
No second hope, if here their fortune frowns;
Frown soon it must. Of various rates they sail,
Of ensigns various; all alike in this,
All restless, anxious; toss'd with hopes, and fears,
In calmest skies; obnoxious all to storm;   157
And stormy the most general blast of life:
All bound for happiness; yet few provide
The chart of knowledge, pointing where it lies;
Or Virtue's helm, to shape the course design'd:
All, more or less, capricious fate lament,
Now lifted by the tide, and now resorb'd,   163
And farther from their wishes than before:
All, more or less, against each other dash.
To mutual hurt, by gusts of passion driven,
And suffering more from folly, than from fate.
　　Ocean! thou dreadful and tumultuous home
Of dangers, at eternal war with man!
Death's capital, where most he domineers,   170
With all his chosen terrors frowning round,

(Though lately feasted high at Albion's cost,)[1]
Wide-opening, and loud roaring still for more!
Too faithful mirror! how dost thou reflect
The melancholy face of human life!
The strong resemblance tempts me farther still:
And, haply, Britain may be deeper struck
By moral truth, in such a mirror seen,
Which Nature holds for ever at her eye.

    Self-flatter'd, unexperienced, high in hope,   180
When young, with sanguine cheer, and streamers gay,
We cut our cable, launch into the world,
And fondly dream each wind and star our friend;
All, in some darling enterprise embark'd:
But where is he can fathom its extent?
Amid a multitude of artless hands,
Ruin's sure perquisite! her lawful prize!
Some steer aright; but the black blast blows hard,
And puffs them wide of hope: with hearts of proof,
Full against wind and tide, some win their way;   190
And when strong effort has deserved the port,
And tugg'd it into view, 'tis won! 'tis lost!
Though strong their oar, still stronger is their fate:
They strike; and, while they triumph, they expire.
In stress of weather, most; some sink outright;
O'er them, and o'er their names, the billows close;
To-morrow knows not they were ever born.
Others a short memorial leave behind,
Like a flag floating,[2] when the bark's engulf'd;
It floats a moment, and is seen no more: 200
One Cæsar lives; a thousand are forgot.
How few, beneath auspicious planets born
(Darlings of Providence! fond Fate's elect!),
With swelling sails make good the promised port,
With all their wishes freighted! Yet even these,
Freighted with all their wishes, soon complain;
Free from misfortune, not from nature free,
They still are men; and when is man secure?
As fatal time, as storm! the rush of years
Beats down their strength; their numberless escapes   210
In ruin end: and, now, their proud success
But plants new terrors on the victor's brow:
What pain to quit the world, just made their own,

---

[1] 'Albion's cost:' Admiral Balchen, &c.
[2] 'Like a flag floating,' &c.: hence Wilson's line in his 'Address to a Wild-Deer:'—
    'Like a flag burning bright when the vessel is gone.'

Their nest so deeply down'd, and built so high!
Too low they build, who build beneath the stars.
　　Woe then apart (if woe apart can be
From mortal man), and fortune at our nod,
The gay, rich, great, triumphant, and august!
What are they?—The most happy (strange to say!)
Convince me most of human misery;　　　　　　　　　220
What are they? Smiling wretches of to-morrow!　　　221
More wretched, then, than e'er their slave can be:
Their treacherous blessings, at the day of need,
Like other faithless friends, unmask, and sting:
Then, what provoking indigence in wealth!
What aggravated impotence in power!
High titles, then, what insult of their pain!
If that sole anchor, equal to the waves,
Immortal Hope! defies not the rude storm,
Takes comfort from the foaming billow's rage,　　　　230
And makes a welcome harbour of the tomb.
　　Is this a sketch of what thy soul admires?
"But here (thou say'st) the miseries of life
Are huddled in a group. A more distinct
Survey, perhaps, might bring thee better news."
Look on life's stages: they speak plainer still;
The plainer they, the deeper wilt thou sigh.
Look on thy lovely boy; in him behold
The best that can befall the best on earth;
The boy has virtue by his mother's side:　　　　　　240
Yes, on Florello look: a father's heart
Is tender, though the man's is made of stone;
The truth, through such a medium seen, may make
Impression deep, and fondness prove thy friend.
　　Florello lately cast on this rude coast
A helpless infant; now a heedless child;
To poor Clarissa's throes, thy care succeeds;
Care full of love, and yet severe as hate!
O'er thy soul's joy how oft thy fondness frowns!
Needful austerities his will restrain;　　　　　　　250
As thorns fence in the tender plant from harm.
As yet, his reason cannot go alone;
But asks a sterner nurse to lead it on.
His little heart is often terrified;
The blush of morning, in his cheek, turns pale;　　　255
Its pearly dewdrop trembles in his eye;
His harmless eye! and drowns an angel there.
Ah! what avails his innocence? The task
Enjoin'd must discipline his early powers;

He learns to sigh, ere he is known to sin;
Guiltless, and sad! a wretch before the fall!
How cruel this! more cruel to forbear.   262
Our nature such, with necessary pains,
We purchase prospects of precarious peace:
Though not a father, this might steal a sigh.

    Suppose him disciplined aright (if not,
'Twill sink our poor account to poorer still);
Ripe from the tutor, proud of liberty,
He leaps enclosure, bounds into the world!
The world is taken, after ten years' toil,   270
Like ancient Troy; and all its joys his own.
Alas! the world's a tutor more severe;
Its lessons hard, and ill deserve his pains;
Unteaching all his virtuous nature taught,
Or books (fair Virtue's advocates!) inspired.

    For who receives him into public life?
Men of the world, the terræ-filial breed,
Welcome the modest stranger to their sphere
(Which glitter'd long, at distance, in his sight),
And, in their hospitable arms, enclose: 280
Men, who think nought so strong of the romance,
So rank knight-errant, as a real friend:
Men, that act up to Reason's golden rule,
All weakness of affection quite subdued:
Men, that would blush at being thought sincere,
And feign, for glory, the few faults they want;
That love a lie, where truth would pay as well;
As if to them, Vice shone her own reward.

    Lorenzo! canst thou bear a shocking sight?   289
Such, for Florello's sake, 'twill now appear:
See, the steel'd files of season'd veterans,
Train'd to the world, in burnish'd falsehood bright;
Deep in the fatal stratagems of peace;
All soft sensation, in the throng, rubb'd off;
All their keen purpose, in politeness, sheath'd;
His friends eternal—during interest;
His foes implacable—when worth their while;
At war with every welfare, but their own;
As wise as Lucifer; and half as good;
And by whom none, but Lucifer, can gain—   300
Naked, through these (so common fate ordains),
Naked of heart, his cruel course he runs,
Stung out of all, most amiable in life,
Prompt truth, and open thought, and smiles unfeign'd;
Affection, as his species, wide diffused;

Noble presumptions to mankind's renown;
Ingenuous trust, and confidence of love.
    These claims to joy (if mortals joy might claim)
Will cost him many a sigh; till time, and pains,
From the slow mistress of this school, Experience,   310
And her assistant, pausing, pale, Distrust,
Purchase a dear-bought clue to lead his youth
Through serpentine obliquities of life,
And the dark labyrinth of human hearts.
And happy! if the clue shall come so cheap:
For, while we learn to fence with public guilt,
Full oft we feel its foul contagion too,
If less than heavenly virtue is our guard.
Thus, a strange kind of cursed necessity
Brings down the sterling temper of his soul,   320
By base alloy, to bear the current stamp,
Below call'd wisdom; sinks him into safety;
And brands him into credit with the world;   323
Where specious titles dignify disgrace,
And nature's injuries are arts of life;
Where brighter reason prompts to bolder crimes;
And heavenly talents make infernal hearts;
That unsurmountable extreme of guilt!
    Poor Machiavel! who labour'd hard his plan,
Forgot, that genius need not go to school;
Forgot, that man, without a tutor wise,
His plan had practised, long before 'twas writ.   332
The world's all title-page; there's no contents;
The world's all face; the man who shows his heart,
Is hooted for his nudities, and scorn'd.
A man I knew, who lived upon a smile;
And well it fed him; he look'd plump and fair;
While rankest venom foam'd through every vein.
Lorenzo! what I tell thee, take not ill!
Living, he fawn'd on every fool alive;   340
And, dying, cursed the friend on whom he lived.
To such proficients thou art half a saint.
In foreign realms (for thou hast travell'd far)
How curious to contemplate two state-rooks,
Studious their nests to feather in a trice,
With all the necromantics of their art,
Playing the game of faces on each other,
Making court sweetmeats of their latent gall,
In foolish hope, to steal each other's trust;
Both cheating, both exulting, both deceived;   350
And, sometimes, both (let earth rejoice) undone!

Their parts we doubt not; but be that their shame;
Shall men of talents, fit to rule mankind,
Stoop to mean wiles, that would disgrace a fool;
And lose the thanks of those few friends they serve?
For who can thank the man, he cannot see?
        Why so much cover? It defeats itself.   357
Ye, that know all things! know ye not, men's hearts
Are therefore known, because they are conceal'd?
For why conceal'd?—The cause they need not tell.
I give him joy, that's awkward at a lie;
Whose feeble nature Truth keeps still in awe;
His incapacity is his renown.   363
'Tis great, 'tis manly, to disdain disguise;
It shows our spirit, or it proves our strength.
Thou say'st, 'tis needful: is it therefore right?
Howe'er, I grant it some small sign of grace,
To strain at an excuse: And would'st thou then
Escape that cruel need? Thou may'st, with ease;
Think no post needful that demands a knave.   370
When late our civil helm was shifting hands,
So Pulteney thought: think better, if you can.
        But this, how rare! the public path of life
Is dirty;—yet, allow that dirt its due,
It makes the noble mind more noble still:
The world's no neuter; it will wound, or save;
Or virtue quench, or indignation fire.
You say, the world, well known, will make a man:
The world, well known, will give our hearts to Heaven,
Or make us demons, long before we die.   380
        To show how fair the world, thy mistress, shines,
Take either part, sure ills attend the choice;
Sure, though not equal, detriment ensues.
Not Virtue's self is deified on earth;
Virtue has her relapses, conflicts, foes;
Foes, that ne'er fail to make her feel their hate.
Virtue has her peculiar set of pains.
True friends to virtue, last, and least, complain;
But if they sigh, can others hope to smile?
If Wisdom has her miseries to mourn,   390
How can poor Folly lead a happy life?   391
And if both suffer, what has earth to boast,
Where he most happy, who the least laments?
Where much, much patience, the most envied state,
And some forgiveness, needs, the best of friends?
For friend, or happy life, who looks not higher,
Of neither shall he find the shadow here.

The world's sworn advocate, without a fee,
Lorenzo smartly, with a smile, replies:
"Thus far thy song is right; and all must own,   400
Virtue has her peculiar set of pains.—
And joys peculiar who to Vice denies?
If vice it is, with nature to comply:
If Pride, and Sense, are so predominant,
To check, not overcome, them, makes a saint.
Can Nature in a plainer voice proclaim
Pleasure, and glory, the chief good of man?"
    Can Pride, and Sensuality, rejoice?
From purity of thought, all pleasure springs;
And, from an humble spirit, all our peace.   410
Ambition, pleasure! let us talk of these:
Of these, the Porch, and Academy, talk'd;
Of these, each following age had much to say:
Yet, unexhausted, still, the needful theme.
Who talks of these, to mankind all at once
He talks; for where the saint from either free?
Are these thy refuge?—No: these rush upon thee;
Thy vitals seize, and,—vulture-like, devour;
I'll try, if I can pluck thee from thy rock,
Prometheus! from this barren ball of earth;   420
If Reason can unchain thee, thou art free.
    And, first, thy Caucasus, Ambition, calls;
Mountain of torments! eminence of woes!
Of courted woes! and courted through mistake!
'Tis not ambition charms thee; 'tis a cheat   425
Will make thee start, as H—— at his moor.
Dost grasp at greatness? First, know what it is:
Think'st thou thy greatness in distinction lies?
Not in the feather, wave it e'er so high,
By Fortune stuck, to mark us from the throng,
Is glory lodged: 'tis lodged in the reverse;
In that which joins, in that which equals, all,   432
The monarch and his slave;—"A deathless soul,
Unbounded prospect, and immortal kin,
A Father God, and brothers in the skies;"
Elder, indeed, in time; but less remote
In excellence, perhaps, than thought by man;
Why greater what can fall, than what can rise?
    If still delirious, now, Lorenzo! go;
And with thy full-blown brothers of the world,   440
Throw scorn around thee; cast it on thy slaves;
Thy slaves, and equals: how scorn cast on them
Rebounds on thee! If man is mean, as man,

Art thou a god? If Fortune makes him so,
Beware the consequence: a maxim that,
Which draws a monstrous picture of mankind,
Where, in the drapery, the man is lost;
Externals fluttering, and the soul forgot.
Thy greatest glory, when disposed to boast,
Boast that aloud, in which thy servants share.   450
     We wisely strip the steed we mean to buy:
Judge we, in their caparisons, of men?
It nought avails thee, where, but what, thou art;
All the distinctions of this little life
Are quite cutaneous, foreign to the man,
When, through death's straits, earth's subtle serpents creep,
Which wriggle into wealth, or climb renown.
As crooked Satan the forbidden tree,   458
They leave their party-colour'd robe behind,
All that now glitters, while they rear aloft
Their brazen crests, and hiss at us below.
Of fortune's fucus strip them, yet alive;
Strip them of body, too; nay, closer still,
Away with all, but moral, in their minds;
And let what then remains, impose their name,
Pronounce them weak, or worthy; great, or mean.
How mean that snuff of glory Fortune lights,
And Death puts out! Dost thou demand a test,
A test, at once, infallible, and short,
Of real greatness? That man greatly lives,   470
Whate'er his fate, or fame, who greatly dies;
High-flush'd with hope, where heroes shall despair.
If this a true criterion, many courts,
Illustrious, might afford but few grandees.
     Th' Almighty, from his throne, on earth surveys
Nought greater, than an honest, humble heart;
An humble heart, His residence! pronounced
His second seat; and rival to the skies.
The private path, the secret acts of men,
If noble, far the noblest of our lives!   480
How far above Lorenzo's glory sits
Th' illustrious master of a name unknown;
Whose worth unrivall'd, and unwitness'd, loves
Life's sacred shades, where gods converse with men;
And Peace, beyond the world's conceptions, smiles!
As thou (now dark), before we part, shalt see.
     But thy great soul this skulking glory scorns.
Lorenzo's sick, but when Lorenzo's seen;
And, when he shrugs at public business, lies.

Denied the public eye, the public voice,   490
As if he lived on others' breath, he dies.
Fain would he make the world his pedestal;   492
Mankind the gazers, the sole figure, he.
Knows he, that mankind praise against their will,
And mix as much detraction as they can?
Knows he, that faithless Fame her whisper has,
As well as trumpet? that his vanity
Is so much tickled from not hearing all?
Knows this all-knower, that from itch of praise,
Or, from an itch more sordid, when he shines,   500
Taking his country by five hundred ears,
Senates at once admire him, and despise,
With modest laughter lining loud applause,
Which makes the smile more mortal to his fame?
His fame, which (like the mighty Cæsar), crown'd
With laurels, in full senate, greatly falls,
By seeming friends, that honour, and destroy.
We rise in glory, as we sink in pride:
Where boasting ends, there dignity begins:
And yet, mistaken beyond all mistake,   510
The blind Lorenzo's proud—of being proud;
And dreams himself ascending in his fall.
    An eminence, though fancied, turns the brain:
All vice wants hellebore; but of all vice,
Pride loudest calls, and for the largest bowl;
Because, unlike all other vice, it flies,
In fact, the point, in fancy most pursued.
Who court applause, oblige the world in this;
They gratify man's passion to refuse.
Superior honour, when assumed, is lost;   520
Even good men turn banditti, and rejoice,
Like Kouli-Kan, in plunder of the proud.
    Though somewhat disconcerted, steady still
To the world's cause, with half a face of joy,
Lorenzo cries—"Be, then, Ambition cast;
Ambition's dearer far stands unimpeach'd,   526
Gay Pleasure! proud Ambition is her slave;
For her, he soars at great, and hazards ill;
For her, he fights, and bleeds, or overcomes;
And paves his way, with crowns, to reach her smile:
Who can resist her charms?—or, should? Lorenzo!
What mortal shall resist, where angels yield?
Pleasure's the mistress of ethereal powers;   533
For her contend the rival gods above;
Pleasure's the mistress of the world below;

And well it was for man, that Pleasure charms:
How would all stagnate, but for Pleasure's ray!
How would the frozen stream of action cease!
What is the pulse of this so busy world?
The love of pleasure: that, through every vein,   540
Throws motion, warmth; and shuts out death from life.
     Though various are the tempers of mankind,
Pleasure's gay family hold all in chains:
Some most affect the black; and some, the fair;
Some honest pleasure court; and some, obscene.
Pleasures obscene are various, as the throng
Of passions, that can err in human hearts;
Mistake their objects, or transgress their bounds.
Think you there's but one whoredom? Whoredom, all,
But when our reason licenses delight.   550
Dost doubt, Lorenzo? thou shalt doubt no more.
Thy father chides thy gallantries; yet hugs
An ugly, common harlot, in the dark;
A rank adulterer with others' gold!
And that hag, Vengeance, in a corner, charms.
Hatred her brothel has, as well as Love,
Where horrid epicures debauch in blood.
Whate'er the motive, pleasure is the mark:
For her, the black assassin draws his sword;
For her, dark statesmen trim their midnight lamp,   560
To which no single sacrifice may fall;
For her, the saint abstains; the miser starves;
The Stoic proud, for Pleasure, pleasure scorn'd;
For her, Affliction's daughters grief indulge,
And find, or hope, a luxury in tears;
For her, guilt, shame, toil, danger, we defy;
And, with an aim voluptuous, rush on death.
Thus universal her despotic power!
     And as her empire wide, her praise is just.
Patron of pleasure! doater on delight!   570
I am thy rival; pleasure I profess;
Pleasure the purpose of my gloomy song.
Pleasure is nought but virtue's gayer name;
I wrong her still, I rate her worth too low;
Virtue the root, and pleasure is the flower;
And honest Epicurus' foes were fools.
     But this sounds harsh, and gives the wise offence;
If o'erstrain'd wisdom still retains the name.
How knits Austerity her cloudy brow,
And blames, as bold, and hazardous, the praise   580
Of Pleasure, to mankind, unpraised, too dear!

Ye modern Stoics! hear my soft reply;
Their senses men will trust: we can't impose;
Or, if we could, is imposition right?
Own honey sweet; but, owning, add this sting;
"When mix'd with poison, it is deadly too."
Truth never was indebted to a lie.
Is nought but virtue to be praised, as good?
Why then is health preferr'd before disease?
What nature loves is good, without our leave. 590
And where no future drawback cries, "Beware!"
Pleasure, though not from virtue, should prevail.
'Tis balm to life, and gratitude to Heaven;
How cold our thanks for bounties unenjoy'd! 594
The love of pleasure is man's eldest-born,
Born in his cradle, living to his tomb;
Wisdom, her younger sister, though more grave,
Was meant to minister, and not to mar,
Imperial Pleasure, queen of human hearts.
    Lorenzo! thou, her majesty's renown'd,
Though uncoift, counsel, learned in the world!
Who think'st thyself a Murray,[1] with disdain 602
May'st look on me. Yet, my Demosthenes!
Canst thou plead Pleasure's cause as well as I?
Know'st thou her nature, purpose, parentage?
Attend my song, and thou shalt know them all;
And know thyself; and know thyself to be
(Strange truth!) the most abstemious man alive.
Tell not Calista; she will laugh thee dead;
Or send thee to her hermitage with L——. 610
Absurd presumption! Thou who never knew'st
A serious thought! shalt thou dare dream of joy?
No man e'er found a happy life by chance;
Or yawn'd it into being with a wish;
Or, with the snout of grovelling appetite,
E'er smelt it out, and grubb'd it from the dirt.
An art it is, and must be learn'd; and learn'd
With unremitting effort, or be lost;
And leaves us perfect blockheads, in our bliss.
The clouds may drop down titles and estates; 620
Wealth may seek us; but Wisdom must be sought;
Sought before all; but (how unlike all else
We seek on earth!) 'tis never sought in vain.
    First, Pleasure's birth, rise, strength, and grandeur, see.
Brought forth by Wisdom, nursed by Discipline,

[1] 'Murray:' Lord Mansfield.

By Patience taught, by Perseverance crown'd,
She rears her head majestic; round her throne,   627
Erected in the bosom of the just,
Each virtue, listed, forms her manly guard.
For what are virtues? (formidable name!)
What, but the fountain, or defence, of joy?
Why, then, commanded? Need mankind commands,
At once to merit, and to make, their bliss?—
Great Legislator! scarce so great, as kind!   634
If men are rational, and love delight,
Thy gracious law but flatters human choice;
In the transgression lies the penalty;
And they the most indulge, who most obey.
    Of Pleasure, next, the final cause explore;
Its mighty purpose, its important end.   640
Not to turn human brutal, but to build
Divine on human, Pleasure came from heaven.
In aid to Reason was the goddess sent;
To call up all its strength by such a charm.
Pleasure, first, succours Virtue; in return,
Virtue gives Pleasure an eternal reign.
What, but the pleasure of food, friendship, faith,
Supports life natural, civil, and divine?
'Tis from the pleasure of repast, we live;
'Tis from the pleasure of applause, we please;   650
'Tis from the pleasure of belief, we pray
(All prayer would cease, if unbelieved the prize):
It serves ourselves, our species, and our God;
And to serve more, is past the sphere of man.
Glide, then, for ever, pleasure's sacred stream!
Through Eden, as Euphrates ran, it runs,
And fosters every growth of happy life;
Makes a new Eden where it flows;—but such
As must be lost, Lorenzo! by thy fall.
    "What mean I by thy fall?"—Thou'lt shortly see,
While Pleasure's nature is at large display'd;   661
Already sung her origin, and ends.
Those glorious ends, by kind, or by degree,
When Pleasure violates, 'tis then a vice,
A vengeance too; it hastens into pain.
From due refreshment, life, health, reason, joy;
From wild excess, pain, grief, distraction, death;
Heaven's justice this proclaims, and that her love.
What greater evil can I wish my foe,
Than his full draught of pleasure, from a cask   670
Unbroach'd by just authority, ungauged

By temperance, by reason unrefined?
A thousand demons lurk within the lee.
Heaven, others, and ourselves! uninjured these,
Drink deep; the deeper, then, the more divine;
Angels are angels, from indulgence there;
'Tis unrepenting pleasure makes a god.
  Dost think thyself a god from other joys?
A victim rather! shortly sure to bleed.
The wrong must mourn: can Heaven's appointments fail?
Can man outwit Omnipotence? strike out   681
A self-wrought happiness unmeant by Him
Who made us, and the world we would enjoy?
Who forms an instrument, ordains from whence
Its dissonance, or harmony, shall rise.
Heaven bid the soul this mortal frame inspire!
Bid virtue's ray divine inspire the soul
With unprecarious flows of vital joy;
And, without breathing, man as well might hope
For life, as, without piety, for peace.   690
  "Is virtue, then, and piety the same?"—
No; piety is more; 'tis virtue's source;
Mother of every worth, as that of joy.
Men of the world this doctrine ill digest;
They smile at piety; yet boast aloud   695
Good will to men; nor know they strive to part
What Nature joins; and thus confute themselves.
With piety begins all good on earth;
'Tis the first-born of rationality.
Conscience, her first law broken, wounded lies;
Enfeebled, lifeless, impotent to good;
A feign'd affection bounds her utmost power.   702
Some we can't love, but for th' Almighty's sake;
A foe to God was ne'er true friend to man;
Some sinister intent taints all he does;
And, in his kindest actions, he's unkind.
  On piety, humanity is built;
And, on humanity, much happiness;
And yet still more on piety itself.
A soul in commerce with her God, is heaven;   710
Feels not the tumults and the shocks of life;
The whirls of passions, and the strokes of heart.
A Deity believed, is joy begun;
A Deity adored, is joy advanced;
A Deity beloved, is joy matured.
Each branch of piety delight inspires;
Faith builds a bridge from this world to the next,

O'er death's dark gulf, and all its horror hides;
Praise, the sweet exhalation of our joy,
That joy exalts, and makes it sweeter still;   720
Prayer ardent opens heaven, lets down a stream
Of glory on the consecrated hour
Of man, in audience with the Deity.
Who worships the great God, that instant joins
The first in heaven, and sets his foot on hell.
    Lorenzo! when wast thou at church before?
Thou think'st the service long: but is it just?
Though just, unwelcome: thou hadst rather tread
Unhallow'd ground; the Muse, to win thine ear,   729
Must take an air less solemn. She complies.
Good conscience! at the sound the world retires;
Verse disaffects it, and Lorenzo smiles:
Yet has she her seraglio full of charms;
And such as age shall heighten, not impair.
Art thou dejected? Is thy mind o'ercast?
Amid her fair ones, thou there fairest choose,
To chase thy gloom.—"Go, fix some weighty truth;
Chain down some passion; do some generous good;
Teach ignorance to see, or grief to smile;
Correct thy friend; befriend thy greatest foe;   740
Or with warm heart, and confidence divine,
Spring up, and lay strong hold on Him who made thee."
Thy gloom is scatter'd, sprightly spirits flow;
Though wither'd is thy vine, and harp unstrung.
    Dost call the bowl, the viol, and the dance,
Loud mirth, mad laughter? Wretched comforters!
Physicians! more than half of thy disease.
Laughter, though never censured yet as sin
(Pardon a thought that only seems severe),
Is half immoral: Is it much indulged?   750
By venting spleen, or dissipating thought,
It shows a scorner, or it makes a fool;
And sins, as hurting others, or ourselves.
'Tis pride, or emptiness, applies the straw,
That tickles little minds to mirth effuse;
Of grief approaching, the portentous sign!
The house of laughter makes a house of woe.
A man triumphant is a monstrous sight;
A man dejected is a sight as mean.
What cause for triumph, where such ills abound?   760
What for dejection, where presides a Power,
Who call'd us into being to be bless'd?
So grieve, as conscious, grief may rise to joy;   763

So joy, as conscious, joy to grief may fall.
Most true, a wise man never will be sad;
But neither will sonorous, bubbling mirth,
A shallow stream of happiness betray:
Too happy to be sportive, he's serene.
     Yet would'st thou laugh (but at thy own expense),
This counsel strange should I presume to give—   770
"Retire, and read thy Bible, to be gay."
There truths abound of sovereign aid to peace;
Ah! do not prize them less, because inspired,
As thou, and thine, are apt and proud to do.
If not inspired, that pregnant page had stood,
Time's treasure, and the wonder of the wise!
Thou think'st, perhaps, thy soul alone at stake;
Alas!—should men mistake thee for a fool;—
What man of taste for genius, wisdom, truth,
Though tender of thy fame, could interpose?   780
Believe me, sense here acts a double part,
And the true critic is a Christian too.
     But these, thou think'st, are gloomy paths to joy.—
True joy in sunshine ne'er was found at first;
They, first, themselves offend, who greatly please;
And travel only gives us sound repose.
Heaven sells all pleasure; effort is the price;
The joys of conquest, are the joys of man;
And glory the victorious laurel spreads
O'er pleasure's pure, perpetual, placid stream.   790
     There is a time, when toil must be preferr'd,
Or joy, by mistimed fondness, is undone.
A man of pleasure, is a man of pains.
Thou wilt not take the trouble to be blest.
False joys, indeed, are born from want of thought;
From thoughts full bent, and energy, the true;
And that demands a mind in equal poise,   797
Remote from gloomy grief, and glaring joy.
Much joy not only speaks small happiness,
But happiness that shortly must expire.
Can joy, unbottom'd in reflection, stand?
And, in a tempest, can reflection live?
Can joy, like thine, secure itself an hour?
Can joy, like thine, meet accident unshock'd?   804
Or ope the door to honest poverty?
Or talk with threatening death, and not turn pale?
In such a world, and such a nature, these
Are needful fundamentals of delight:
These fundamentals give delight indeed;

Delight, pure, delicate, and durable;   810
Delight, unshaken, masculine, divine;
A constant, and a sound, but serious joy.
      Is joy the daughter of severity?
It is:—yet far my doctrine from severe.
"Rejoice for ever:" it becomes a man;
Exalts, and sets him nearer to the gods.
"Rejoice for ever!" Nature cries, "Rejoice!"
And drinks to man, in her nectareous cup,
Mix'd up of delicates for every sense;
To the great Founder of the bounteous feast,   820
Drinks glory, gratitude, eternal praise;
And he that will not pledge her, is a churl.
Ill firmly to support, good fully taste,
Is the whole science of felicity:
Yet sparing pledge: her bowl is not the best
Mankind can boast.—"A rational repast;
Exertion, vigilance, a mind in arms,
A military discipline of thought,
To foil temptation in the doubtful field;
And ever-waking ardour for the right."   830
'Tis these, first give, then guard, a cheerful heart.   831
Nought that is right, think little; well aware,
What reason bids, God bids; by His command
How aggrandized, the smallest thing we do!
Thus, nothing is insipid to the wise;
To thee, insipid all, but what is mad;
Joys season'd high, and tasting strong of guilt.
"Mad! (thou reply'st, with indignation fired);
Of ancient sages proud to tread the steps,
I follow Nature."—Follow Nature still,   840
But look it be thine own: is Conscience, then,
No part of nature? Is she not supreme?
Thou regicide! Oh, raise her from the dead!
Then, follow Nature; and resemble God.
      When, spite of Conscience, pleasure is pursued,
Man's nature is unnaturally pleased:
And what's unnatural, is painful too
At intervals, and must disgust even thee!
The fact thou know'st; but not, perhaps, the cause.
Virtue's foundations with the world's were laid;   850
Heaven mix'd her with our make, and twisted close
Her sacred interests with the strings of life.
Who breaks her awful mandate, shocks himself,
His better self: and is it greater pain,
Our soul should murmur, or our dust repine?

And one, in their eternal war, must bleed.
    If one must suffer, which should least be spared?
The pains of mind surpass the pains of sense:
Ask, then, the gout, what torment is in guilt.
The joys of sense to mental joys are mean: 860
Sense on the present only feeds; the soul
On past, and future, forages for joy.
'Tis hers, by retrospect, through time to range;
And forward time's great sequel to survey.
Could human courts take vengeance on the mind,   865
Axes might rust, and racks and gibbets fall:
Guard, then, thy mind, and leave the rest to fate.
    Lorenzo! wilt thou never be a man?
The man is dead, who for the body lives,
Lured, by the beating of his pulse, to list
With every lust, that wars against his peace;
And sets him quite at variance with himself.   872
Thyself, first, know; then love: a self there is
Of Virtue fond, that kindles at her charms.
A self there is, as fond of every vice,
While every virtue wounds it to the heart:
Humility degrades it, Justice robs,
Bless'd Bounty beggars it, fair Truth betrays,
And godlike Magnanimity destroys.
This self, when rival to the former, scorn;   880
When not in competition, kindly treat,
Defend it, feed it:—but when Virtue bids,
Toss it, or to the fowls, or to the flames.
And why? 'Tis love of pleasure bids thee bleed;
Comply, or own self-love extinct, or blind.
    For what is vice? self-love in a mistake:
A poor blind merchant buying joys too dear.
And virtue, what? 'tis self-love in her wits,
Quite skilful in the market of delight.
Self-love's good sense is love of that dread Power,   890
From whom herself, and all she can enjoy.
Other self-love is but disguised self-hate;
More mortal than the malice of our foes;
A self-hate, now, scarce felt; then felt full sore,
When being, cursed; extinction, loud implored;
And every thing preferr'd to what we are.
    Yet this self-love Lorenzo makes his choice;
And, in this choice triumphant, boasts of joy.
How is his want of happiness betray'd,   899
By disaffection to the present hour!
Imagination wanders far afield:

The future pleases: why? the present pains.—
"But that's a secret." Yes, which all men know;
And know from thee, discover'd unawares.
Thy ceaseless agitation, restless roll
From cheat to cheat, impatient of a pause;
What is it?—'tis the cradle of the soul,
From Instinct sent, to rock her in disease,
Which her physician, Reason, will not cure.
A poor expedient! yet thy best; and while   910
It mitigates thy pain, it owns it too.
  Such are Lorenzo's wretched remedies!
The weak have remedies; the wise have joys.
Superior wisdom is superior bliss.
And what sure mark distinguishes the wise?
Consistent wisdom ever wills the same;
Thy fickle wish is ever on the wing.
Sick of herself, is Folly's character,
As Wisdom's is, a modest self-applause.
A change of evils is thy good supreme;   920
Nor, but in motion, canst thou find thy rest.
Man's greatest strength is shown in standing still.
The first sure symptom of a mind in health,
Is rest of heart, and pleasure felt at home.
False pleasure from abroad her joys imports;
Rich from within, and self-sustain'd, the true.
The true is fix'd, and solid as a rock;
Slippery the false, and tossing, as the wave.
This, a wild wanderer on earth, like Cain;
That, like the fabled, self-enamour'd boy, [1]   930
Home-contemplation her supreme delight;
She dreads an interruption from without,   932
Smit with her own condition; and the more
Intense she gazes, still it charms the more.
  No man is happy, till he thinks, on earth
There breathes not a more happy than himself:
Then envy dies, and love o'erflows on all;
And love o'erflowing makes an angel here.
Such angels, all, entitled to repose
On Him who governs fate. Though tempest frowns,   940
Though nature shakes, how soft to lean on Heaven!
To lean on Him, on whom archangels lean!
With inward eyes, and silent as the grave,
They stand, collecting every beam of thought,
Till their hearts kindle with divine delight:

---

[1] 'Fabled boy:' Narcissus.

For all their thoughts, like angels, seen of old
In Israel's dream, come from, and go to, heaven.
Hence are they studious of sequester'd scenes;
While noise, and dissipation, comfort thee.
      Were all men happy, revellings would cease,   950
That opiate for inquietude within.
Lorenzo! never man was truly blest,
But it composed, and gave him such a cast,
As folly might mistake for want of joy.
A cast, unlike the triumph of the proud;
A modest aspect, and a smile at heart.
O for a joy from thy Philander's spring!
A spring perennial, rising in the breast,
And permanent, as pure! no turbid stream
Of rapturous exultation, swelling high;   960
Which, like land floods, impetuous pour a while,
Then sink at once, and leave us in the mire.
What does the man, who transient joy prefers?
What, but prefer the bubbles to the stream?
      Vain are all sudden sallies of delight;
Convulsions of a weak, distemper'd joy.   966
Joy's a fix'd state; a tenure, not a start.
Bliss there is none, but unprecarious bliss:
That is the gem: sell all, and purchase that.
Why go a-begging to contingencies,
Not gain'd with ease, nor safely loved, if gain'd?
At good fortuitous, draw back, and pause;
Suspect it; what thou canst insure, enjoy;   973
And nought but what thou givest thyself, is sure.
Reason perpetuates joy that Reason gives,
And makes it as immortal as herself:
To mortals, nought immortal, but their worth.
      Worth, conscious worth! should absolutely reign;
And other joys ask leave for their approach;
Nor, unexamined, ever leave obtain.   980
Thou art all anarchy; a mob of joys
Wage war, and perish in intestine broils;
Not the least promise of internal peace!
No bosom-comfort, or unborrow'd bliss!
Thy thoughts are vagabonds; all outward-bound,
'Mid sands, and rocks, and storms, to cruise for pleasure;
If gain'd, dear-bought; and better miss'd than gain'd.
Much pain must expiate, what much pain procured.
Fancy, and Sense, from an infected shore,
Thy cargo bring; and pestilence the prize.   990
Then, such thy thirst (insatiable thirst!

By fond indulgence but inflamed the more!),
Fancy still cruises, when poor Sense is tired.
    Imagination is the Paphian shop,
Where feeble happiness, like Vulcan, lame,
Bids foul ideas, in their dark recess,
And hot as hell (which kindled the black fires),
With wanton art, those fatal arrows form,
Which murder all thy time, health, wealth, and fame.
Would'st thou receive them, other thoughts there are,
On angel-wing, descending from above,   1001
Which these, with art divine, would counterwork,
And form celestial armour for thy peace.
    In this is seen Imagination's guilt;
But who can count her follies? She betrays thee,
To think in grandeur there is something great.
For works of curious art, and ancient fame,
Thy genius hungers, elegantly pain'd;
And foreign climes must cater for thy taste.
Hence, what disaster!—Though the price was paid,   1010
That persecuting priest, the Turk of Rome,
Whose foot (ye gods!) though cloven, must be kiss'd,
Detain'd thy dinner on the Latian shore;
(Such is the fate of honest Protestants!)
And poor Magnificence is starved to death.
Hence just resentment, indignation, ire!—
Be pacified: if outward things are great,
'Tis magnanimity great things to scorn;
Pompous expenses, and parades august,
And courts, that insalubrious soil to peace.   1020
True happiness ne'er enter'd at an eye;
True happiness resides in things unseen.
No smiles of Fortune ever bless'd the bad,
Nor can her frowns rob Innocence of joys;
That jewel wanting, triple crowns are poor:
So tell his Holiness, and be revenged.
    Pleasure, we both agree, is man's chief good;
Our only contest, what deserves the name.
Give Pleasure's name to nought, but what has pass'd
Th' authentic seal of Reason (which like Yorke,[1]   1030
Demurs on what it passes), and defies
The tooth of time; when past, a pleasure still;
Dearer on trial, lovelier for its age,   1033
And doubly to be prized, as it promotes
Our future, while it forms our present, joy.

---

[1] 'Yorke:' Lord Chancellor Hardwick.

Some joys the future overcast; and some
Throw all their beams that way, and gild the tomb.
Some joys endear eternity; some give
Abhorr'd annihilation dreadful charms.
Are rival joys contending for thy choice?   1040
Consult thy whole existence, and be safe;
That oracle will put all doubt to flight.
Short is the lesson, though my lecture long;
Be good—and let Heaven answer for the rest.
        Yet, with a sigh o'er all mankind, I grant
In this our day of proof, our land of hope,
The good man has his clouds that intervene;
Clouds, that obscure his sublunary day,
But never conquer: even the best must own,
Patience, and resignation, are the pillars   1050
Of human peace on earth. The pillars, these:
But those of Seth not more remote from thee,
Till this heroic lesson thou hast learn'd;
To frown at pleasure, and to smile in pain.
Fired at the prospect of unclouded bliss,
Heaven in reversion, like the sun, as yet
Beneath th' horizon, cheers us in this world;
It sheds, on souls susceptible of light,
The glorious dawn of our eternal day.
        "This (says Lorenzo) is a fair harangue: 1060
But can harangues blow back strong nature's stream;
Or stem the tide Heaven pushes through our veins,
Which sweeps away man's impotent resolves,
And lays his labour level with the world?"
        Themselves men make their comment on mankind;
And think nought is, but what they find at home:
Thus, weakness to chimera turns the truth.   1067
Nothing romantic has the Muse prescribed.
Above,[1] Lorenzo saw the man of earth,
The mortal man; and wretched was the sight.
To balance that, to comfort, and exalt,
Now see the man immortal: him, I mean,
Who lives as such; whose heart, full bent on heaven,
Leans all that way, his bias to the stars.
The world's dark shades, in contrast set, shall raise
His lustre more; though bright, without a foil:
Observe his awful portrait, and admire;
Nor stop at wonder; imitate, and live.
        Some angel guide my pencil, while I draw,

---

[1] 'Above:' in a former Night.

What nothing less than angel can exceed! 1080
A man on earth devoted to the skies;
Like ships in sea, while in, above the world.
    With aspect mild, and elevated eye,
Behold him seated on a mount serene,
Above the fogs of sense, and passion's storm;
All the black cares, and tumults, of this life,
Like harmless thunders, breaking at his feet,
Excite his pity, not impair his peace.
Earth's genuine sons, the sceptred, and the slave,
A mingled mob! a wandering herd! he sees, 1090
Bewilder'd in the vale; in all unlike!
His full reverse in all! What higher praise?
What stronger demonstration of the right?
    The present all their care; the future, his.
When public welfare calls, or private want,
They give to fame; his bounty he conceals.
Their virtues varnish nature; his exalt.
Mankind's esteem they court; and he, his own.
Theirs, the wild chase of false felicities;
His, the composed possession of the true. 1100
Alike throughout is his consistent peace,
All of one colour, and an even thread;
While party-colour'd shreds of happiness,
With hideous gaps between, patch up for them
A madman's robe; each puff of Fortune blows
The tatters by, and shows their nakedness.
    He sees with other eyes than theirs: where they
Behold a sun, he spies a Deity;
What makes them only smile, makes him adore.
Where they see mountains, he but atoms sees; 1110
An empire, in his balance, weighs a grain.
They things terrestrial worship, as divine:
His hopes immortal blow them by, as dust,
That dims his sight, and shortens his survey,
Which longs, in infinite, to lose all bound.
Titles and honours (if they prove his fate)
He lays aside to find his dignity;
No dignity they find in aught besides.
They triumph in externals (which conceal
Man's real glory), proud of an eclipse. 1120
Himself too much he prizes to be proud,
And nothing thinks so great in man, as man.
Too dear he holds his interest, to neglect
Another's welfare, or his right invade;
Their interest, like a lion, lives on prey.

They kindle at the shadow of a wrong:
Wrong he sustains with temper, looks on heaven,
Nor stoops to think his injurer his foe;
Nought, but what wounds his virtue, wounds his peace.
A cover'd heart their character defends;   1130
A cover'd heart denies him half his praise.
With nakedness his innocence agrees;
While their broad foliage testifies their fall:
Their no joys end, where his full feast begins;   1134
His joys create, theirs murder, future bliss.
To triumph in existence, his alone;
And his alone, triumphantly to think
His true existence is not yet begun.
His glorious course was, yesterday, complete;
Death, then, was welcome; yet life still is sweet.
    But nothing charms Lorenzo, like the firm,
Undaunted breast—and whose is that high praise?   1142
They yield to pleasure, though they danger brave,
And show no fortitude, but in the field;
If there they show it, 'tis for glory shown;
Nor will that cordial always man their hearts.
A cordial his sustains, that cannot fail;
By pleasure unsubdued, unbroke by pain,
He shares in that Omnipotence he trusts.
All-bearing, all-attempting, till he falls;   1150
And when he falls, writes VICI on his shield.
From magnanimity, all fear above;
From nobler recompence, above applause;
Which owes to man's short outlook all its charms.
    Backward to credit what he never felt,
Lorenzo cries,—"Where shines this miracle?
From what root rises this immortal man?"
A root that grows not in Lorenzo's ground;
The root dissect, nor wonder at the flower.
He follows nature (not like thee) and shows us   1160
An uninverted system of a man.
His appetite wears Reason's golden chain,
And finds, in due restraint, its luxury.
His passion, like an eagle well reclaim'd,
Is taught to fly at nought, but infinite.
Patient his hope, unanxious is his care,
His caution fearless, and his grief (if grief
The gods ordain) a stranger to despair.   1168
And why?—because affection, more than meet,
His wisdom leaves not disengaged from heaven.
Those secondary goods that smile on earth,

He, loving in proportion, loves in peace.
They most the world enjoy, who least admire.
His understanding 'scapes the common cloud
Of fumes, arising from a boiling breast.
His head is clear, because his heart is cool,
By worldly competitions uninflamed.
The moderate movements of his soul admit
Distinct ideas, and matured debate,
An eye impartial, and an even scale;   1180
Whence judgment sound, and unrepenting choice.
Thus, in a double sense, the good are wise;
On its own dunghill, wiser than the world.
What, then, the world? It must be doubly weak;
Strange truth! as soon would they believe their creed.
    Yet thus it is; nor otherwise can be;
So far from aught romantic, what I sing.
Bliss has no being, virtue has no strength,
But from the prospect of immortal life.
Who think earth all, or (what weighs just the same)   1190
Who care no farther, must prize what it yields;
Fond of its fancies, proud of its parades.
Who thinks earth nothing, can't its charms admire;
He can't a foe, though most malignant, hate,
Because that hate would prove his greater foe.
'Tis hard for them (yet who so loudly boast
Good-will to men?) to love their dearest friend;
For may not he invade their good supreme,
Where the least jealousy turns love to gall?
All shines to them, that for a season shines.   1200
Each act, each thought, he questions, "What its weight,
Its colour what, a thousand ages hence?"—   1202
And what it there appears, he deems it now.
Hence, pure are the recesses of his soul.
The godlike man has nothing to conceal.
His virtue, constitutionally deep,
Has habit's firmness, and affection's flame;
Angels, allied, descend to feed the fire;
And Death, which others slays, makes him a god.
    And now, Lorenzo! bigot of this world!   1210
Wont to disdain poor bigots caught by Heaven!
Stand by thy scorn, and be reduced to nought:
For what art thou?—Thou boaster! while thy glare,
Thy gaudy grandeur, and mere worldly worth,
Like a broad mist, at distance, strikes us most;
And, like a mist, is nothing when at hand;
His merit, like a mountain, on approach,

Swells more, and rises nearer to the skies,
By promise now, and, by possession, soon,
(Too soon, too much, it cannot be) his own.   1220
    From this thy just annihilation rise,
Lorenzo! rise to something, by reply.
The world, thy client, listens, and expects;
And longs to crown thee with immortal praise.
Canst thou be silent? No; for Wit is thine;
And Wit talks most, when least she has to say,
And Reason interrupts not her career.
She'll say—that mists above the mountains rise;
And, with a thousand pleasantries, amuse;
She'll sparkle, puzzle, flutter, raise a dust,   1230
And fly conviction, in the dust she raised.
    Wit, how delicious to man's dainty taste!
'Tis precious, as the vehicle of sense;
But, as its substitute, a dire disease.
Pernicious talent! flatter'd by the world,
By the blind world, which thinks the talent rare.   1236
Wisdom is rare, Lorenzo! wit abounds;
Passion can give it; sometimes wine inspires
The lucky flash; and madness rarely fails.
Whatever cause the spirit strongly stirs,
Confers the bays, and rivals thy renown.
For thy renown, 'twere well was this the worst;
Chance often hits it; and, to pique thee more,   1243
See Dulness, blundering on vivacities,
Shakes her sage head at the calamity,
Which has exposed, and let her down to thee.
But Wisdom, awful Wisdom! which inspects,
Discerns, compares, weighs, separates, infers,
Seizes the right, and holds it to the last;
How rare! In senates, synods, sought in vain;   1250
Or if there found, 'tis sacred to the few;
While a lewd prostitute to multitudes,
Frequent, as fatal, Wit: in civil life,
Wit makes an enterpriser; Sense, a man.
Wit hates authority; commotion loves,
And thinks herself the lightning of the storm.
In states, 'tis dangerous; in religion, death:
Shall Wit turn Christian, when the dull believe?
Sense is our helmet, wit is but the plume;
The plume exposes, 'tis our helmet saves.   1260
Sense is the diamond, weighty, solid, sound;
When cut by wit, it casts a brighter beam;
Yet, wit apart, it is a diamond still.

Wit, widow'd of good sense, is worse than nought;
It hoists more sail to run against a rock.
Thus, a half-Chesterfield is quite a fool;
Whom dull fools scorn, and bless their want of wit.
    How ruinous the rock I warn thee shun,
Where syrens sit, to sing thee to thy fate!
A joy, in which our reason bears no part,   1270
Is but a sorrow, tickling, ere it stings.
Let not the cooings of the world allure thee;
Which of her lovers ever found her true?
Happy! of this bad world who little know?—
And yet, we much must know her, to be safe;
To know the world, not love her, is thy point;
She gives but little, nor that little, long.
There is, I grant, a triumph of the pulse;
A dance of spirits, a mere froth of joy,
Our thoughtless agitation's idle child,   1280
That mantles high, that sparkles, and expires,
Leaving the soul more vapid than before.
An animal ovation! such as holds
No commerce with our reason, but subsists
On juices, through the well-toned tubes, well strain'd;
A nice machine! scarce ever tuned aright;
And when it jars—thy syrens sing no more,
Thy dance is done; the demi-god is thrown
(Short apotheosis!) beneath the man,
In coward gloom immersed, or fell despair.   1290
    Art thou yet dull enough despair to dread,
And startle at destruction? If thou art,
Accept a buckler, take it to the field;
(A field of battle is this mortal life!)
When danger threatens, lay it on thy heart;
A single sentence, proof against the world:
"Soul, body, fortune!—every good pertains
To one of these; but prize not all alike;
The goods of fortune to thy body's health,
Body to soul, and soul submit to God."   1300
Would'st thou build lasting happiness? do this;
Th' inverted pyramid can never stand.
    Is this truth doubtful? It outshines the sun;
Nay, the sun shines not, but to show us this,   1304
The single lesson of mankind on earth.
And yet—yet, what? No news! Mankind is mad;
Such mighty numbers list against the right,
(And what can't numbers, when bewitch'd, achieve!)
They talk themselves to something like belief,

That all earth's joys are theirs: as Athens' fool
Grinn'd from the port, on every sail his own.
      They grin; but wherefore? and how long the laugh?
Half ignorance, their mirth; and half, a lie;   1313
To cheat the world, and cheat themselves, they smile.
Hard either task! The most abandon'd own,
That others, if abandon'd, are undone:
Then, for themselves, the moment Reason wakes
(And Providence denies it long repose),
O how laborious is their gaiety!
They scarce can swallow their ebullient spleen,   1320
Scarce muster patience to support the farce,
And pump sad laughter till the curtain falls.
Scarce, did I say? Some cannot sit it out;
Oft their own daring hands the curtain draw,
And show us what their joy, by their despair.
      The clotted hair! gored breast! blaspheming eye!
Its impious fury still alive in death!
Shut, shut the shocking scene.—But Heaven denies
A cover to such guilt; and so should man.
Look round, Lorenzo! see the reeking blade,   1330
Th' envenom'd phial, and the fatal ball;
The strangling cord, and suffocating stream;
The loathsome rottenness, and foul decays
From raging riot (slower suicides!)
And pride in these, more execrable still!
How horrid all to thought!—but horrors, these,
That vouch the truth; and aid my feeble song.
      From vice, sense, fancy, no man can be blest: 1338
Bliss is too great, to lodge within an hour:
When an immortal being aims at bliss,
Duration is essential to the name.
O for a joy from reason! joy from that,
Which makes man Man; and, exercised aright,
Will make him more: a bounteous joy! that gives
And promises; that weaves, with art divine,
The richest prospect into present peace:
A joy ambitious! joy in common held
With thrones ethereal, and their greater far;
A joy high privileged from chance, time, death!
A joy, which death shall double, judgment crown!   1350
Crown'd higher, and still higher, at each stage,
Through bless'd eternity's long day; yet still,
Not more remote from sorrow, than from Him,
Whose lavish hand, whose love stupendous, pours
So much of Deity on guilty dust.

There, O my Lucia! may I meet thee there,
Where not thy presence can improve my bliss!
    Affects not this the sages of the world?
Can nought affect them, but what fools them too?
Eternity, depending on an hour,   1360
Makes serious thought man's wisdom, joy, and praise,
Nor need you blush (though sometimes your designs
May shun the light) at your designs on heaven:
Sole point! where over-bashful is your blame.
Are you not wise?—You know you are: yet hear
One truth, amid your numerous schemes, mislaid,
Or overlook'd, or thrown aside, if seen;
"Our schemes to plan by this world, or the next,
Is the sole difference between wise and fool."
All worthy men will weigh you in this scale;   1370
What wonder then, if they pronounce you light?   1371
Is their esteem alone not worth your care?
Accept my simple scheme of common sense:
Thus, save your fame, and make two worlds your own.
    The world replies not;—but the world persists;
And puts the cause off to the longest day,
Planning evasions for the day of doom.
So far, at that re-hearing, from redress,
They then turn witnesses against themselves;
Hear that, Lorenzo! nor be wise to-morrow.   1380
Haste, haste! a man, by nature, is in haste;
For who shall answer for another hour?
'Tis highly prudent, to make one sure friend;
And that thou canst not do, this side the skies.
    Ye sons of earth! (nor willing to be more!)
Since verse you think from priestcraft somewhat free,
Thus, in an age so gay, the Muse plain truths
(Truths, which, at church, you might have heard in prose)
Has ventured into light; well pleased the verse
Should be forgot, if you the truths retain;   1390
And crown her with your welfare, not your praise.
But praise she need not fear: I see my fate;
And headlong leap, like Curtius, down the gulf.
Since many an ample volume, mighty tome,
Must die; and die unwept; O thou minute
Devoted page! go forth among thy foes;
Go, nobly proud of martyrdom for truth,
And die a double death: mankind incensed,
Denies thee long to live: nor shalt thou rest,
When thou art dead; in Stygian shades arraign'd   1400
By Lucifer, as traitor to his throne;

And bold blasphemer of his friend,—the World;
The World, whose legions cost him slender pay,
And volunteers around his banner swarm;   1404
Prudent, as Prussia,[1] in her zeal for Gaul.
    "Are all, then, fools?" Lorenzo cries.—Yes, all,
But such as hold this doctrine (new to thee);
"The mother of true wisdom is the will;"
The noblest intellect, a fool without it.
World-wisdom much has done, and more may do,   1410
In arts and sciences, in wars, and peace:
But art and science, like thy wealth, will leave thee,
And make thee twice a beggar at thy death.
This is the most indulgence can afford;—
"Thy wisdom all can do, but—make thee wise."
Nor think this censure is severe on thee;
Satan, thy master, I dare call a dunce.   1417

---

[1] 'Prussia:' under Frederick the Great.

NIGHT NINTH.

THE CONSOLATION:

CONTAINING, AMONG OTHER THINGS,

I. A MORAL SURVEY OF THE NOCTURNAL HEAVENS.
II. A NIGHT ADDRESS TO THE DEITY.

HUMBLY INSCRIBED TO HIS GRACE THE DUKE OF NEWCASTLE, ONE OF HIS
MAJESTY'S PRINCIPAL SECRETARIES OF STATE.

Fatis contraria fata rependens.—VIRG.

As when a traveller, a long day past
In painful search of what he cannot find,
At night's approach, content with the next cot,
There ruminates, a while, his labour lost;
Then cheers his heart with what his fate affords,
And chants his sonnet to deceive the time,
Till the due season calls him to repose:
Thus I, long-travell'd in the ways of men,
And dancing, with the rest, the giddy maze,
Where Disappointment smiles at Hope's career;   10
Warn'd by the languor of life's evening ray,
At length have housed me in an humble shed;
Where, future wandering banish'd from my thought,
And waiting, patient, the sweet hour of rest,
I chase the moments with a serious song.
Song soothes our pains; and age has pains to soothe.
    When age, care, crime, and friends embraced at heart,
Torn from my bleeding breast, and death's dark shade,
Which hovers o'er me, quench th' ethereal fire;
Canst thou, O Night! indulge one labour more?   20
One labour more indulge! then sleep, my strain!   21
Till, haply, waked by Raphael's golden lyre,
Where night, death, age, care, crime, and sorrow, cease;
To bear a part in everlasting lays;
Though far, far higher set, in aim, I trust,
Symphonious to this humble prelude here.
    Has not the Muse asserted pleasures pure,
Like those above; exploding other joys?
Weigh what was urged, Lorenzo! fairly weigh;

And tell me, hast thou cause to triumph still?   30
I think, thou wilt forbear a boast so bold.
But if, beneath the favour of mistake,
Thy smile's sincere; not more sincere can be
Lorenzo's smile, than my compassion for him.
The sick in body call for aid; the sick
In mind are covetous of more disease;
And when at worst, they dream themselves quite well.
To know ourselves diseased, is half our cure.
When Nature's blush by Custom is wiped off,
And Conscience, deaden'd by repeated strokes,   40
Has into manners naturalized our crimes;
The curse of curses is, our curse to love;
To triumph in the blackness of our guilt
(As Indians glory in the deepest jet),
And throw aside our senses with our peace.
     But grant no guilt, no shame, no least alloy;
Grant joy and glory quite unsullied shone;
Yet, still, it ill deserves Lorenzo's heart.
No joy, no glory, glitters in thy sight,
But, through the thin partition of an hour,   50
I see its sables wove by destiny;
And that in sorrow buried; this, in shame;
While howling furies wring the doleful knell;
And Conscience, now so soft thou scarce canst hear   54
Her whisper, echoes her eternal peal.
     Where, the prime actors of the last year's scene;
Their port so proud, their buskin, and their plume?
How many sleep, who kept the world awake
With lustre, and with noise! has Death proclaim'd
A truce, and hung his sated lance on high?
'Tis brandish'd still; nor shall the present year
Be more tenacious of her human leaf,   62
Or spread of feeble life a thinner fall.
     But needless monuments to wake the thought;
Life's gayest scenes speak man's mortality;
Though in a style more florid, full as plain,
As mausoleums, pyramids, and tombs.
What are our noblest ornaments, but deaths
Turn'd flatterers of life, in paint, or marble,
The well-stain'd canvas, or the featured stone?   70
Our fathers grace, or rather haunt, the scene.
Joy peoples her pavilion from the dead.
     "Profess'd diversions! cannot these escape?"
Far from it: these present us with a shroud;
And talk of death, like garlands o'er a grave.

As some bold plunderers, for buried wealth,
We ransack tombs for pastime; from the dust
Call up the sleeping hero; bid him tread
The scene for our amusement: how like gods
We sit; and, wrapt in immortality,   80
Shed generous tears on wretches born to die;
Their fate deploring, to forget our own!
    What all the pomps and triumphs of our lives,
But legacies in blossom? Our lean soil,
Luxuriant grown, and rank in vanities,
From friends interr'd beneath; a rich manure!
Like other worms, we banquet on the dead;
Like other worms, shall we crawl on, nor know   88
Our present frailties, or approaching fate?
    Lorenzo! such the glories of the world!
What is the world itself? thy world—a grave.
Where is the dust that has not been alive?
The spade, the plough, disturb our ancestors;
From human mould we reap our daily bread.
The globe around earth's hollow surface shakes,
And is the ceiling of her sleeping sons.
O'er devastation we blind revels keep;
Whole buried towns support the dancer's heel.
The moist of human frame the sun exhales;
Winds scatter through the mighty void the dry;   100
Earth repossesses part of what she gave,
And the freed spirit mounts on wings of fire;
Each element partakes our scatter'd spoils;
As nature, wide, our ruins spread: man's death
Inhabits all things, but the thought of man.
    Nor man alone; his breathing bust expires,
His tomb is mortal; empires die: where, now,
The Roman? Greek? They stalk, an empty name!
Yet few regard them in this useful light;
Though half our learning is their epitaph.   110
When down thy vale, unlock'd by midnight thought,
That loves to wander in thy sunless realms,
O Death! I stretch my view: what visions rise!
What triumphs! toils imperial! arts divine!
In wither'd laurels glide before my sight!
What lengths of far-famed ages, billow'd high
With human agitation, roll along
In unsubstantial images of air!
The melancholy ghosts of dead renown,
Whispering faint echoes of the world's applause,   120
With penitential aspect, as they pass,

All point at earth, and hiss at human pride,   122
The wisdom of the wise, and prancings of the great.
     But, O Lorenzo! far the rest above,
Of ghastly nature, and enormous size,
One form assaults my sight, and chills my blood,
And shakes my frame. Of one departed world[1]
I see the mighty shadow: oozy wreath
And dismal seaweed crown her; o'er her urn
Reclined, she weeps her desolated realms,   130
And bloated sons; and, weeping, prophesies
Another's dissolution, soon, in flames.
But, like Cassandra, prophesies in vain;
In vain, to many; not, I trust, to thee.
     For, know'st thou not, or art thou loath to know,
The great decree, the counsel of the skies?
Deluge and conflagration, dreadful powers!
Prime ministers of vengeance! chain'd in caves
Distinct, apart the giant furies roar;
Apart; or, such their horrid rage for ruin,   140
In mutual conflict would they rise, and wage
Eternal war, till one was quite devour'd.
But not for this, ordain'd their boundless rage;
When Heaven's inferior instruments of wrath,
War, famine, pestilence, are found too weak
To scourge a world for her enormous crimes,
These are let loose, alternate: down they rush,
Swift and tempestuous, from th' eternal throne,
With irresistible commission arm'd,
The world, in vain corrected, to destroy,   150
And ease creation of the shocking scene.
     Seest thou, Lorenzo! what depends on man?
The fate of Nature; as for man, her birth.
Earth's actors change earth's transitory scenes,
And make creation groan with human guilt.   155
How must it groan, in a new deluge whelm'd,
But not of waters! At the destined hour,
By the loud trumpet summon'd to the charge,
See, all the formidable sons of fire,
Eruptions, earthquakes, comets, lightnings, play
Their various engines; all at once disgorge
Their blazing magazines; and take, by storm,   162
This poor terrestrial citadel of man.
     Amazing period! when each mountain-height
Outburns Vesuvius; rocks eternal pour

---

[1] 'One departed world:' the world before the flood.

193

Their melted mass, as rivers once they pour'd;
Stars rush; and final Ruin fiercely drives
Her ploughshare o'er creation!—while aloft,
More than astonishment! if more can be!
Far other firmament than e'er was seen,   170
Than e'er was thought by man! far other stars!
Stars animate, that govern these of fire;
Far other sun!—A sun, O how unlike
The Babe at Bethlehem! how unlike the Man,
That groan'd on Calvary!—Yet He it is;
That Man of Sorrows! O how changed! what pomp!
In grandeur terrible, all heaven descends!
And gods, ambitious, triumph in his train.
A swift archangel, with his golden wing,
As blots and clouds, that darken and disgrace   180
The scene divine, sweeps stars and suns aside.
And now, all dross removed, heaven's own pure day,
Full on the confines of our ether, flames:
While (dreadful contrast!) far, how far beneath!
Hell, bursting, belches forth her blazing seas,
And storms sulphureous; her voracious jaws
Expanding wide, and roaring for her prey.

    Lorenzo! welcome to this scene; the last
In nature's course; the first in wisdom's thought.   189
This strikes, if aught can strike thee; this awakes
The most supine; this snatches man from death.
Rouse, rouse, Lorenzo, then, and follow me,
Where truth, the most momentous man can hear,
Loud calls my soul, and ardour wings her flight.
I find my inspiration in my theme:
The grandeur of my subject is my Muse.

    At midnight, when mankind is wrapt in peace,
And worldly fancy feeds on golden dreams;
To give more dread to man's most dreadful hour.
At midnight, 'tis presumed, this pomp will burst   200
From tenfold darkness; sudden as the spark
From smitten steel; from nitrous grain, the blaze.
Man, starting from his couch, shall sleep no more!
The day is broke, which never more shall close!
Above, around, beneath, amazement all!
Terror and glory join'd in their extremes!
Our God in grandeur, and our world on fire!
All nature struggling in the pangs of death!
Dost thou not hear her? Dost thou not deplore
Her strong convulsions, and her final groan?   210
Where are we now? Ah me! the ground is gone,

On which we stood; Lorenzo! while thou may'st,
Provide more firm support, or sink for ever!
Where? how? from whence? Vain hope! it is too late!
Where, where, for shelter, shall the guilty fly,
When consternation turns the good man pale?

    Great day! for which all other days were made;
For which earth rose from chaos, man from earth;
And an eternity, the date of gods,
Descended on poor earth-created man!   220
Great day of dread, decision, and despair!
At thought of thee, each sublunary wish
Lets go its eager grasp, and drops the world;   223
And catches at each reed of hope in heaven.
At thought of thee!—And art thou absent then?
Lorenzo! no; 'tis here; it is begun;—
Already is begun the grand assize,
In thee, in all: deputed Conscience scales
The dread tribunal, and forestalls our doom;
Forestalls; and, by forestalling, proves it sure.   230
Why on himself should man void judgment pass?
Is idle Nature laughing at her sons?
Who Conscience sent, her sentence will support,
And God above assert that God in man.

    Thrice happy they that enter now the court
Heaven opens in their bosoms! but, how rare,
Ah me! that magnanimity, how rare!
What hero, like the man who stands himself;
Who dares to meet his naked heart alone;
Who bears, intrepid, the full charge it brings,   240
Resolved to silence future murmurs there?
The coward flies; and, flying, is undone.
(Art thou a coward? No.) The coward flies;
Thinks, but thinks slightly; asks, but fears to know;
Asks, "What is truth?" with Pilate; and retires;
Dissolves the court, and mingles with the throng;
Asylum sad! from reason, hope, and heaven!

    Shall all, but man look out with ardent eye,
For that great day, which was ordain'd for man?
O day of consummation! mark supreme   250
(If men are wise) of human thought! nor least,
Or in the sight of angels, or their King!
Angels, whose radiant circles, height o'er height,
Order o'er order, rising, blaze o'er blaze,
As in a theatre, surround this scene,
Intent on man, and anxious for his fate.
Angels look out for thee; for thee, their Lord,   257

To vindicate his glory; and for thee,
Creation universal calls aloud,
To disinvolve the moral world, and give
To Nature's renovation brighter charms.
     Shall man alone, whose fate, whose final fate
Hangs on that hour, exclude it from his thought?
I think of nothing else; I see! I feel it!
All nature, like an earthquake, trembling round!
All deities, like summer's swarms, on wing!
All basking in the full meridian blaze!
I see the Judge enthroned! the flaming guard!
The volume open'd! open'd every heart!
A sunbeam pointing out each secret thought!   270
No patron! intercessor none! now past
The sweet, the clement, mediatorial hour!
For guilt no plea! to pain, no pause! no bound!
Inexorable, all! and all, extreme!
     Nor man alone; the Foe of God and man,
From his dark den, blaspheming, drags his chain,
And rears his brazen front, with thunder scarr'd:
Receives his sentence, and begins his hell.
All vengeance past, now, seems abundant grace:
Like meteors in a stormy sky, how roll   280
His baleful eyes! he curses whom he dreads;
And deems it the first moment of his fall.
'Tis present to my thought!—and yet where is it?
Angels can't tell me; angels cannot guess
The period; from created beings lock'd
In darkness. But the process, and the place,
Are less obscure; for these may man inquire.
Say, thou great close of human hopes and fears!
Great key of hearts! great finisher of fates!
Great end! and great beginning! say, Where art thou?
Art thou in time, or in eternity?   291
Nor in eternity, nor time, I find thee.
These, as two monarchs, on their borders meet,
(Monarchs of all elapsed, or unarrived!)
As in debate, how best their powers allied,
May swell the grandeur, or discharge the wrath,
Of Him, whom both their monarchies obey.
     Time, this vast fabric for him built (and doom'd
With him to fall), now bursting o'er his head;
His lamp, the sun, extinguish'd; from beneath   300
The frown of hideous darkness, calls his sons
From their long slumber; from earth's heaving womb,
To second birth! contemporary throng!

Roused at one call, upstarted from one bed,
Press'd in one crowd, appall'd with one amaze,
He turns them o'er, Eternity! to thee.
Then (as a king deposed disdains to live)
He falls on his own scythe; nor falls alone:
His greatest foe falls with him; Time, and he
Who murder'd all Time's offspring, Death, expire.   310
 Time was! Eternity now reigns alone:
Awful eternity! offended queen!
And her resentment to mankind, how just!
With kind intent, soliciting access,
How often has she knock'd at human hearts!
Rich to repay their hospitality;
How often call'd! and with the voice of God!
Yet bore repulse, excluded as a cheat!
A dream! while foulest foes found welcome there!
A dream, a cheat, now, all things, but her smile.   320
 For, lo! her twice ten thousand gates thrown wide,
As thrice from Indus to the frozen pole,
With banners streaming as the comet's blaze,
And clarions, louder than the deep in storms,
Sonorous as immortal breath can blow,   325
Pour forth their myriads, potentates, and powers,
Of light, of darkness; in a middle field,
Wide, as creation! populous, as wide!
A neutral region! there to mark th' event
Of that great drama, whose preceding scenes
Detain'd them close spectators, through a length
Of ages, ripening to this grand result;   332
Ages, as yet unnumber'd, but by God;
Who now, pronouncing sentence, vindicates
The rights of Virtue, and his own renown.
 Eternity, the various sentence past,
Assigns the sever'd throng distinct abodes,
Sulphureous, or ambrosial. What ensues?
The deed predominant! the deed of deeds!
Which makes a hell of hell, a heaven of heaven.   340
The goddess, with determined aspect, turns
Her adamantine key's enormous size
Through destiny's inextricable wards,
Deep driving every bolt, on both their fates.
Then, from the crystal battlements of heaven,
Down, down, she hurls it through the dark profound,
Ten thousand thousand fathom; there to rust,
And ne'er unlock her resolution more.
The deep resounds; and hell, through all her glooms,

Returns, in groans, the melancholy roar.   350
    O how unlike the chorus of the skies!
O how unlike those shouts of joy, that shake
The whole ethereal! how the concave rings!
Nor strange! when deities their voice exalt;
And louder far, than when creation rose,
To see creation's godlike aim, and end,
So well accomplish'd! so divinely closed!
To see the mighty dramatist's last act,
(As meet), in glory rising o'er the rest.   359
No fancied god, a God indeed, descends,
To solve all knots; to strike the moral home;
To throw full day on darkest scenes of time;
To clear, commend, exalt, and crown the whole.
Hence, in one peal of loud, eternal praise,
The charm'd spectators thunder their applause;
And the vast void beyond, applause resounds.
    What then am I?—
                        Amidst applauding worlds,
And worlds celestial, is there found on earth,
A peevish, dissonant, rebellious string,   370
Which jars in the grand chorus, and complains?
Censure on thee, Lorenzo! I suspend,
And turn it on myself; how greatly due!
All, all is right; by God ordain'd or done;
And who, but God, resumed the friends He gave?
And have I been complaining, then, so long?
Complaining of his favours; pain, and death?
Who, without Pain's advice, would e'er be good?
Who, without Death, but would be good in vain?
Pain is to save from pain; all punishment,   380
To make for peace; and death, to save from Death;
And second death, to guard immortal life;
To rouse the careless, the presumptuous awe,
And turn the tide of souls another way;
By the same tenderness divine ordain'd,
That planted Eden, and high bloom'd for man,
A fairer Eden, endless, in the skies.
    Heaven gives us friends to bless the present scene;
Resumes them, to prepare us for the next.
All evils natural are moral goods;   390
All discipline, indulgence, on the whole.
None are unhappy: all have cause to smile,
But such as to themselves that cause deny.   393
Our faults are at the bottom of our pains;
Error, in act, or judgment, is the source

Of endless sighs: we sin, or we mistake;
And Nature tax, when false opinion stings.
Let impious grief be banish'd, joy indulged;
But chiefly then, when Grief puts in her claim.
Joy from the joyous, frequently betrays,   400
Oft lives in vanity, and dies in woe.
Joy, amidst ills, corroborates, exalts;
'Tis joy and conquest; joy, and virtue too.
A noble fortitude in ills, delights
Heaven, earth, ourselves; 'tis duty, glory, peace.
Affliction is the good man's shining scene;
Prosperity conceals his brightest ray;
As night to stars, woe lustre gives to man.
Heroes in battle, pilots in the storm,
And virtue in calamities, admire.   410
The crown of manhood is a winter-joy;
An evergreen, that stands the northern blast,
And blossoms in the rigour of our fate.
    'Tis a prime part of happiness, to know
How much unhappiness must prove our lot;
A part which few possess! I'll pay life's tax,
Without one rebel murmur, from this hour,
Nor think it misery to be a man;
Who thinks it is, shall never be a god.
Some ills we wish for, when we wish to live.   420
    What spoke proud Passion?—"Wish my being lost?"[1]
Presumptuous! blasphemous! absurd! and false!
The triumph of my soul is,—that I am;
And therefore that I may be—what? Lorenzo!
Look inward, and look deep; and deeper still;
Unfathomably deep our treasure runs   426
In golden veins, through all eternity!
Ages, and ages, and succeeding still
New ages, where the phantom of an hour,
Which courts each night, dull slumber, for repair,
Shall wake, and wonder, and exult, and praise,
And fly through infinite, and all unlock;
And (if deserved) by Heaven's redundant love,   433
Made half adorable itself, adore;
And find, in adoration, endless joy!
Where thou, not master of a moment here,
Frail as the flower, and fleeting as the gale,
May'st boast a whole eternity, enrich'd
With all a kind Omnipotence can pour.

[1] 'Being lost:' referring to the First Night.

Since Adam fell, no mortal, uninspired,   440
Has ever yet conceived, or ever shall,
How kind is God, how great (if good) is Man.
No man too largely from Heaven's love can hope,
If what is hoped he labours to secure.
Ills?—there are none: All-gracious! none from thee;
     From man full many! numerous is the race
Of blackest ills, and those immortal too,
Begot by Madness, on fair Liberty;
Heaven's daughter, hell-debauch'd! her hand alone
Unlocks destruction to the sons of men,   450
First barr'd by thine: high-wall'd with adamant,
Guarded with terrors reaching to this world,
And cover'd with the thunders of thy law;
Whose threats are mercies, whose injunctions, guides,
Assisting, not restraining, Reason's choice;
Whose sanctions, unavoidable results
From nature's course, indulgently reveal'd;
If unreveal'd, more dangerous, nor less sure.
Thus, an indulgent father warns his sons,
"Do this; fly that"—nor always tells the cause;   460
Pleased to reward, as duty to his will,
A conduct needful to their own repose.
     Great God of wonders! (if, thy love survey'd,
Aught else the name of wonderful retains),
What rocks are these, on which to build our trust!
Thy ways admit no blemish; none I find;
Or this alone—"That none is to be found."
Not one, to soften Censure's hardy crime;
Not one, to palliate peevish Grief's Complaint,
Who, like a demon, murmuring from the dust,   470
Dares into judgment call her Judge.—Supreme!
For all I bless thee; most, for the severe;
Her[1] death—my own at hand—the fiery gulf,
That flaming bound of wrath omnipotent!
It thunders;—but it thunders to preserve;
It strengthens what it strikes; its wholesome dread
Averts the dreaded pain; its hideous groans
Join heaven's sweet hallelujahs in thy praise,
Great Source of good alone! how kind in all!
In vengeance kind! Pain, Death, Gehenna, save.   480
     Thus, in thy world material, Mighty Mind!
Not that alone which solaces, and shines,
The rough and gloomy, challenges our praise.

---

[1] 'Her:' Lucia.

The winter is as needful as the spring;
The thunder, as the sun; a stagnate mass
Of vapours breeds a pestilential air:
Nor more propitious the Favonian breeze
To nature's health, than purifying storms;
The dread volcano ministers to good.
Its smother'd flames might undermine the world.   490
Loud Etnas fulminate in love to man;
Comets good omens are, when duly scann'd;   492
And, in their use, eclipses learn to shine.
    Man is responsible for ills received;
Those we call wretched are a chosen band,
Compell'd to refuge in the right, for peace.
Amid my list of blessings infinite,
Stands this the foremost, "That my heart has bled."
'Tis Heaven's last effort of good-will to man;
When Pain can't bless, Heaven quits us in despair.   500
Who fails to grieve, when just occasion calls,
Or grieves too much, deserves not to be blest;
Inhuman, or effeminate, his heart;
Reason absolves the grief, which reason ends.
May Heaven ne'er trust my friend with happiness,
Till it has taught him how to bear it well,
By previous pain; and made it safe to smile!
Such smiles are mine, and such may they remain;
Nor hazard their extinction, from excess.
My change of heart a change of style demands;   510
The Consolation cancels the Complaint,
And makes a convert of my guilty song.
    As when o'er-labour'd, and inclined to breathe,
A panting traveller, some rising ground,
Some small ascent, has gain'd, he turns him round,
And measures with his eye the various vales,
The fields, woods, meads, and rivers, he has pass'd;
And, satiate of his journey, thinks of home,
Endear'd by distance, nor affects more toil;
Thus I, though small, indeed, is that ascent   520
The Muse has gain'd, review the paths she trod;
Various, extensive, beaten but by view;
And, conscious of her prudence in repose,
Pause; and with pleasure meditate an end,
Though still remote; so fruitful is my theme.
Through many a field of moral, and divine,   526
The Muse has stray'd; and much of sorrow seen
In human ways; and much of false and vain;
Which none, who travel this bad road, can miss.

O'er friends deceased full heartily she wept;
Of love divine the wonders she display'd;
Proved man immortal; show'd the source of joy
The grand tribunal raised; assign'd the bounds
Of human grief: in few, to close the whole,
The moral Muse has shadow'd out a sketch,
Though not in form, nor with a Raphael-stroke,
Of most our weakness needs believe, or do,
In this our land of travel, and of hope,
For peace on earth, or prospect of the skies.   539
        What then remains? much! much! a mighty debt
To be discharged: these thoughts, O Night! are thine;
From thee they came, like lovers' secret sighs,
While others slept. So, Cynthia (poets feign),
In shadows veil'd, soft-sliding from her sphere,
Her shepherd cheer'd; of her enamour'd less,
Than I of thee.—And art thou still unsung,
Beneath whose brow, and by whose aid, I sing?
Immortal silence! where shall I begin?
Where end? or how steal music from the spheres,
To soothe their goddess?   550
                        O majestic Night!
Nature's great ancestor! Day's elder-born!
And fated to survive the transient sun!
By mortals, and immortals, seen with awe!
A starry crown thy raven brow adorns,
An azure zone thy waist; clouds, in heaven's loom
Wrought through varieties of shape and shade,
In ample folds of drapery divine,
Thy flowing mantle form; and, heaven throughout,
Voluminously pour thy pompous train.   560
Thy gloomy grandeurs (nature's most august,
Inspiring aspect!) claim a grateful verse;
And, like a sable curtain starr'd with gold,
Drawn o'er my labours past, shall close the scene.
        And what, O man! so worthy to be sung?
What more prepares us for the songs of heaven?
Creation, of archangels is the theme!
What, to be sung, so needful? What so well
Celestial joys prepare us to sustain?
The soul of man, His face design'd to see,   570
Who gave these wonders to be seen by man,
Has here a previous scene of objects great,
On which to dwell; to stretch to that expanse
Of thought, to rise to that exalted height
Of admiration, to contract that awe,

202

And give her whole capacities that strength,
Which best may qualify for final joy.
The more our spirits are enlarged on earth,
The deeper draught shall they receive of heaven.
    Heaven's King! whose face unveil'd consummates bliss;
Redundant bliss! which fills that mighty void,   581
The whole creation leaves in human hearts!
Thou, who didst touch the lip of Jesse's son,
Rapt in sweet contemplation of these fires,
And set his harp in concert with the spheres;
While of thy works material the supreme
I dare attempt, assist my daring song.
Loose me from earth's enclosure, from the sun's
Contracted circle set my heart at large;
Eliminate my spirit, give it range   590
Through provinces of thought yet unexplored;
Teach me, by this stupendous scaffolding,
Creation's golden steps, to climb to Thee.
Teach me with Art great Nature to control,   594
And spread a lustre o'er the shades of Night.
Feel I thy kind assent? and shall the sun
Be seen at midnight, rising in my song?
    Lorenzo! come, and warm thee: thou, whose heart,
Whose little heart, is moor'd within a nook
Of this obscure terrestrial, anchor weigh.
Another ocean calls, a nobler port;
I am thy pilot, I thy prosperous gale.   602
Gainful thy voyage through yon azure main;
Main, without tempest, pirate, rock, or shore;
And whence thou may'st import eternal wealth;
And leave to beggar'd minds the pearl and gold.
Thy travels dost thou boast o'er foreign realms?
Thou stranger to the world! thy tour begin;
Thy tour through Nature's universal orb.
Nature delineates her whole chart at large,   610
On soaring souls, that sail among the spheres;
And man how purblind, if unknown the whole!
Who circles spacious earth, then travels here,
Shall own, he never was from home before!
Come, my Prometheus,[1] from thy pointed rock
Of false ambition; if unchain'd, we'll mount;
We'll, innocently, steal celestial fire,
And kindle our devotion at the stars;
A theft, that shall not chain, but set thee free.

---

[1] 'Prometheus:' Night Eighth.

Above our atmosphere's intestine wars,   620
Rain's fountain-head, the magazine of hail;
Above the northern nests of feather'd snows,
The brew of thunders, and the flaming forge
That forms the crooked lightning; 'bove the caves
Where infant tempests wait their growing wings,
And tune their tender voices to that roar,
Which soon, perhaps, shall shake a guilty world;   627
Above misconstrued omens of the sky,
Far-travell'd comets' calculated blaze;
Elance thy thought, and think of more than man.
Thy soul, till now, contracted, wither'd, shrunk,
Blighted by blasts of earth's unwholesome air,
Will blossom here; spread all her faculties
To these bright ardours; every power unfold,
And rise into sublimities of thought.
Stars teach, as well as shine. At Nature's birth,
Thus their commission ran—"Be kind to Man."
Where art thou, poor benighted traveller?
The stars will light thee, though the moon should fail.
Where art thou, more benighted! more astray!   640
In ways immoral? The stars call thee back;
And, if obey'd their counsel, set thee right.
    This prospect vast, what is it?—Weigh'd aright,
'Tis Nature's system of divinity,
And every student of the Night inspires.
'Tis elder Scripture, writ by God's own hand:
Scripture authentic! uncorrupt by man.
Lorenzo! with my radius (the rich gift
Of thought nocturnal!) I'll point out to thee
Its various lessons; some that may surprise   650
An un-adept in mysteries of Night;
Little, perhaps, expected in her school,
Nor thought to grow on planet, or on star.
Bulls, lions, scorpions, monsters here we feign;
Ourselves more monstrous, not to see what here
Exists indeed;—a lecture to mankind.
    What read we here?—Th' existence of a God?
Yes; and of other beings, man above;
Natives of ether! sons of higher climes!
And, what may move Lorenzo's wonder more,   660
Eternity is written in the skies.   661
And whose eternity?—Lorenzo! thine
Mankind's eternity. Nor Faith alone,
Virtue grows here; here springs the sovereign cure
Of almost every vice; but chiefly thine;

Wrath, Pride, Ambition, and impure Desire.
    Lorenzo! thou canst wake at midnight too,
Though not on morals bent: Ambition, Pleasure!
Those tyrants I for thee so lately fought,[1]
Afford their harass'd slaves but slender rest.   670
Thou, to whom midnight is immoral noon,
And the sun's noontide blaze, prime dawn of day;
Not by thy climate, but capricious crime,
Commencing one of our antipodes!
In thy nocturnal rove, one moment halt,
'Twixt stage and stage, of riot, and cabal;
And lift thine eye (if bold an eye to lift,
If bold to meet the face of injured Heaven)
To yonder stars: for other ends they shine,
Than to light revellers from shame to shame,   680
And, thus, be made accomplices in guilt.
    Why from yon arch, that infinite of space,
With infinite of lucid orbs replete,
Which set the living firmament on fire,
At the first glance, in such an overwhelm
Of wonderful, on man's astonish'd sight,
Rushes Omnipotence—To curb our pride;
Our reason rouse, and lead it to that Power,
Whose love lets down these silver chains of light;
To draw up man's ambition to Himself,   690
And bind our chaste affections to His throne.
Thus the three virtues, least alive on earth,
And welcomed on heaven's coast with most applause,
An humble, pure, and heavenly-minded heart,   694
Are here inspired:—and canst thou gaze too long?
    Nor stands thy wrath deprived of its reproof,
Or un-upbraided by this radiant choir.
The planets of each system represent
Kind neighbours; mutual amity prevails;
Sweet interchange of rays, received, return'd;
Enlightening, and enlighten'd! all, at once,
Attracting, and attracted! Patriot like,   702
None sins against the welfare of the whole;
But their reciprocal, unselfish aid,
Affords an emblem of millennial love.
Nothing in nature, much less conscious being,
Was e'er created solely for itself:
Thus man his sovereign duty learns in this
Material picture of benevolence.

[1] 'Lately fought:' Night Eighth.

And know, of all our supercilious race, 710
Thou most inflammable! thou wasp of men!
Man's angry heart, inspected, would be found
As rightly set, as are the starry spheres;
'Tis Nature's structure, broke by stubborn will,
Breeds all that uncelestial discord there.
Wilt thou not feel the bias Nature gave?
Canst thou descend from converse with the skies,
And seize thy brother's throat?—For what—a clod,
An inch of earth? The planets cry, "Forbear!"
They chase our double darkness; Nature's gloom, 720
And (kinder still!) our intellectual night.

And see, Day's amiable sister sends
Her invitation, in the softest rays
Of mitigated lustre; courts thy sight,
Which suffers from her tyrant brother's blaze.
Night grants thee the full freedom of the skies,
Nor rudely reprimands thy lifted eye;
With gain, and joy, she bribes thee to be wise. 728
Night opes the noblest scenes, and sheds an awe,
Which gives those venerable scenes full weight,
And deep reception, in th' intender'd heart;
While light peeps through the darkness, like a spy;
And darkness shows its grandeur by the light.
Nor is the profit greater than the joy,
If human hearts at glorious objects glow,
And admiration can inspire delight.

What speak I more, than I, this moment, feel?
With pleasing stupor first the soul is struck
(Stupor ordain'd to make her truly wise!):
Then into transport starting from her trance, 740
With love, and admiration, how she glows!
This gorgeous apparatus! this display!
This ostentation of creative power!
This theatre!—what eye can take it in?
By what divine enchantment was it raised,
For minds of the first magnitude to launch
In endless speculation, and adore?
One sun by day, by night ten thousand shine;
And light us deep into the Deity;
How boundless in magnificence and might! 750
O what a confluence of ethereal fires,
Form urns unnumber'd, down the steep of heaven,
Streams to a point, and centres in my sight!
Nor tarries there; I feel it at my heart.
My heart, at once, it humbles, and exalts;

Lays it in dust, and calls it to the skies.
Who sees it unexalted? or unawed?
Who sees it, and can stop at what is seen?
Material offspring of Omnipotence!
Inanimate, all-animating birth!   760
Work worthy Him who made it! worthy praise!
All praise! praise more than human! nor denied   762
Thy praise divine!—But though man, drown'd in sleep,
Withholds his homage, not alone I wake;
Bright legions swarm unseen, and sing, unheard
By mortal ear, the glorious Architect,
In this His universal temple hung
With lustres, with innumerable lights,
That shed religion on the soul; at once,
The temple, and the preacher! O how loud   770
It calls devotion! genuine growth of Night!
     Devotion! daughter of Astronomy!
An undevout astronomer is mad.
True; all things speak a God; but in the small,
Men trace out Him; in great, He seizes man;
Seizes, and elevates, and wraps, and fills
With new inquiries, 'mid associates new.
Tell me, ye stars! ye planets! tell me, all
Ye starr'd, and planeted, inhabitants! what is it?
What are these sons of wonder? say, proud arch   780
(Within those azure palaces they dwell),
Built with divine ambition! in disdain
Of limit built! built in the taste of heaven!
Vast concave! ample dome! wast thou design'd
A meet apartment for the Deity?—
Not so; that thought alone thy state impairs,
Thy lofty sinks, and shallows thy profound,
And straitens thy diffusive; dwarfs the whole,
And makes a universe an orrery.
     But when I drop mine eye, and look on man,   790
Thy right regain'd, thy grandeur is restored,
O Nature! wide flies off th' expanding round.
As when whole magazines, at once, are fired,
The smitten air is hollow'd by the blow;
The vast displosion dissipates the clouds;
Shock'd ether's billows dash the distant skies;   796
Thus (but far more) th' expanding round flies off,
And leaves a mighty void, a spacious womb,
Might teem with new creation; reinflamed
Thy luminaries triumph, and assume
Divinity themselves. Nor was it strange,

Matter high-wrought to such surprising pomp,
Such godlike glory, stole the style of gods,   803
From ages dark, obtuse, and steep'd in sense;
For, sure, to sense, they truly are divine,
And half absolved idolatry from guilt;
Nay, turn'd it into virtue. Such it was
In those, who put forth all they had of man
Unlost, to lift their thought, nor mounted higher;
But, weak of wing, on planets perch'd; and thought   810
What was their highest, must be their adored.
    But they how weak, who could no higher mount?
And are there, then, Lorenzo! those, to whom
Unseen, and unexistent, are the same?
And if incomprehensible is join'd,
Who dare pronounce it madness, to believe?
Why has the mighty Builder thrown aside
All measure in His work; stretch'd out His line
So far, and spread amazement o'er the whole?
Then (as he took delight in wide extremes),   820
Deep in the bosom of His universe,
Dropp'd down that reasoning mite, that insect, Man,
To crawl, and gaze, and wonder at the scene?—
That man might ne'er presume to plead amazement
For disbelief of wonders in himself.
Shall God be less miraculous, than what
His hand has form'd? Shall mysteries descend
From unmysterious? things more elevate,
Be more familiar? uncreated lie
More obvious than created, to the grasp   830
Of human thought? The more of wonderful
Is heard in Him, the more we should assent.
Could we conceive Him, God He could not be;
Or He not God, or we could not be men.
A God alone can comprehend a God;
Man's distance how immense! On such a theme,
Know this, Lorenzo! (seem it ne'er so strange)
Nothing can satisfy, but what confounds;
Nothing, but what astonishes, is true.
The scene thou seest, attests the truth I sing,   840
And every star sheds light upon thy creed.
These stars, this furniture, this cost of heaven,
If but reported, thou hadst ne'er believed;
But thine eye tells thee, the romance is true.
The grand of nature is th' Almighty's oath,
In Reason's court, to silence Unbelief.
    How my mind, opening at this scene, imbibes

The moral emanations of the skies,
While nought, perhaps, Lorenzo less admires!
Has the Great Sovereign sent ten thousand worlds   850
To tells us, He resides above them all,
In glory's unapproachable recess?
And dare earth's bold inhabitants deny
The sumptuous, the magnific embassy
A moment's audience? Turn we, nor will hear
From whom they come, or what they would impart
For man's emolument; sole cause that stoops
Their grandeur to man's eye? Lorenzo! rouse;
Let thought, awaken'd, take the lightning's wing,
And glance from east to west, from pole to pole.   860
Who sees, but is confounded, or convinced?
Renounces reason, or a God adores?
Mankind was sent into the world to see:
Sight gives the science needful to their peace;   864
That obvious science asks small learning's aid.
Would'st thou on metaphysic pinions soar?
Or wound thy patience amid logic thorns?
Or travel history's enormous round?
Nature no such hard task enjoins: she gave
A make to man directive of his thought;
A make set upright, pointing to the stars,
As who shall say, "Read thy chief lesson there."   872
Too late to read this manuscript of heaven,
When, like a parchment scroll, shrunk up by flames,
It folds Lorenzo's lesson from his sight.
     Lesson how various! Not the God alone,
I see His ministers; I see, diffused
In radiant orders, essences sublime,
Of various offices, of various plume,
In heavenly liveries, distinctly clad,   880
Azure, green, purple, pearl, or downy gold,
Or all commix'd; they stand, with wings outspread,
Listening to catch the Master's least command,
And fly through nature, ere the moment ends;
Numbers innumerable!—well conceived
By Pagan, and by Christian! O'er each sphere
Presides an angel, to direct its course,
And feed, or fan, its flames; or to discharge
Other high trusts unknown. For who can see
Such pomp of matter, and imagine, Mind,   890
For which alone Inanimate was made,
More sparingly dispensed? that nobler son,
Far liker the great Sire!—'Tis thus the skies

Inform us of superiors numberless,
As much, in excellence, above mankind,
As above earth, in magnitude, the spheres.
These, as a cloud of witnesses, hang o'er us;
In a throng'd theatre are all our deeds;   898
Perhaps, a thousand demigods descend
On every beam we see, to walk with men.
Awful reflection! Strong restraint from ill!
      Yet, here, our virtue finds still stronger aid
From these ethereal glories sense surveys.
Something, like magic, strikes from this blue vault;
With just attention is it view'd? We feel
A sudden succour, unimplored, unthought;
Nature herself does half the work of Man.
Seas, rivers, mountains, forests, deserts, rocks,
The promontory's height, the depth profound
Of subterranean, excavated grots,   910
Black brow'd, and vaulted high, and yawning wide
From Nature's structure, or the scoop of Time;
If ample of dimension, vast of size,
Even these an aggrandizing impulse give;
Of solemn thought enthusiastic heights
Even these infuse.—But what of vast in these?
Nothing;—or we must own the skies forgot.
Much less in art.—Vain art! Thou pigmy power!
How dost thou swell and strut, with human pride,
To show thy littleness! What childish toys,   920
Thy watery columns squirted to the clouds!
Thy basin'd rivers, and imprison'd seas!
Thy mountains moulded into forms of men!
Thy hundred-gated capitals! or those
Where three days' travel left us much to ride;
Gazing on miracles by mortals wrought,
Arches triumphal, theatres immense,
Or nodding gardens pendent in mid-air!
Or temples proud to meet their gods half-way!
Yet these affect us in no common kind.   930
What then the force of such superior scenes?
Enter a temple, it will strike an awe: 932
What awe from this the Deity has built!
A good man seen, though silent, counsel gives:
The touch'd spectator wishes to be wise:
In a bright mirror His own hands have made,
Here we see something like the face of God.
Seems it not then enough, to say, Lorenzo!
To man abandon'd, "Hast thou seen the skies?"

And yet, so thwarted Nature's kind design   940
By daring man, he makes her sacred awe
(That guard from ill) his shelter, his temptation
To more than common guilt, and quite inverts
Celestial art's intent. The trembling stars
See crimes gigantic, stalking through the gloom
With front erect, that hide their head by day,
And making night still darker by their deeds.
Slumbering in covert, till the shades descend,
Rapine and Murder, link'd, now prowl for prey.
The miser earths his treasure; and the thief,   950
Watching the mole, half beggars him ere morn.
Now plots, and foul conspiracies, awake;
And, muffling up their horrors from the moon,
Havoc and devastation they prepare,
And kingdoms tottering in the field of blood.
Now sons of riot in mid-revel rage.
What shall I do?—suppress it? or proclaim?—
Why sleeps the thunder? Now, Lorenzo! now,
His best friend's couch the rank adulterer
Ascends secure; and laughs at gods and men.   960
Preposterous madmen, void of fear or shame,
Lay their crimes bare to these chaste eyes of Heaven;
Yet shrink, and shudder, at a mortal's sight.
Were moon, and stars, for villains only made?
To guide, yet screen them, with tenebrious light?
No; they were made to fashion the sublime   966
Of human hearts, and wiser make the wise.
    Those ends were answer'd once; when mortals lived
Of stronger wing, of aquiline ascent
In theory sublime. O how unlike
Those vermin of the night, this moment sung,
Who crawl on earth, and on her venom feed!   972
Those ancient sages, human stars! They met
Their brothers of the skies, at midnight hour;
Their counsel ask'd; and, what they ask'd, obey'd.
The Stagirite, and Plato, he who drank[1]
The poison'd bowl, and he of Tusculum,[2]
With him of Corduba,[3] (immortal names!)
In these unbounded, and Elysian, walks,
An area fit for gods, and godlike men,   980
They took their nightly round, through radiant paths

---

[1] 'He who drank:' Socrates.

[2] 'He of Tusculum:' Cicero.

[3] 'Him of Corduba:' Seneca.

By seraphs trod; instructed, chiefly, thus,
To tread in their bright footsteps here below;
To walk in worth still brighter than the skies.
There they contracted their contempt of earth;
Of hopes eternal kindled, there, the fire;
There, as in near approach, they glow'd, and grew
(Great visitants!) more intimate with God,
More worth to men, more joyous to themselves.
Through various virtues, they, with ardour, ran   990
The zodiac of their learn'd, illustrious lives.
    In Christian hearts, O for a Pagan zeal!
A needful, but opprobrious prayer! As much
Our ardour less, as greater is our light.
How monstrous this in morals! Scarce more strange
Would this phenomenon in nature strike,
A sun, that froze her, or a star, that warm'd.
What taught these heroes of the moral world?   998
To these thou givest thy praise, give credit too.
These doctors ne'er were pension'd to deceive thee;
And Pagan tutors are thy taste.—They taught,
That, narrow views betray to misery:
That, wise it is to comprehend the whole:
That, virtue, rose from nature, ponder'd well,
The single base of virtue built to heaven:
That God, and nature, our attention claim:
That nature is the glass reflecting God,
As, by the sea, reflected is the sun,
Too glorious to be gazed on in his sphere:
That, mind immortal loves immortal aims: 1010
That, boundless mind affects a boundless space:
That vast surveys, and the sublime of things,
The soul assimilate, and make her great:
That, therefore, heaven her glories, as a fund
Of inspiration, thus spreads out to man.
Such are their doctrines; such the Night inspired.
    And what more true? what truth of greater weight?
The soul of man was made to walk the skies;
Delightful outlet of her prison here!
There, disencumber'd from her chains, the ties   1020
Of toys terrestrial, she can rove at large;
There, freely can respire, dilate, extend,
In full proportion let loose all her powers;
And, undeluded, grasp at something great.
Nor, as a stranger, does she wander there;
But, wonderful herself, through wonder strays;
Contemplating their grandeur, finds her own;

Dives deep in their economy divine,
Sits high in judgment on their various laws,
And, like a master, judges not amiss.   1030
Hence greatly pleased, and justly proud, the soul
Grows conscious of her birth celestial; breathes   1032
More life, more vigour, in her native air;
And feels herself at home amongst the stars;
And, feeling, emulates her country's praise.
      What call we, then, the firmament, Lorenzo?—
As earth the body, since the skies sustain
The soul with food, that gives immortal life,
Call it, the noble pasture of the mind;
Which there expatiates, strengthens, and exults,   1040
And riots through the luxuries of thought.
Call it, the garden of the Deity,
Blossom'd with stars, redundant in the growth
Of fruit ambrosial; moral fruit to man.
Call it, the breastplate of the true High Priest,
Ardent with gems oracular, that give,
In points of highest moment, right response;
And ill neglected, if we prize our peace.
      Thus, have we found a true astrology;
Thus, have we found a new, and noble sense,   1050
In which alone stars govern human fates.
O that the stars (as some have feign'd) let fall
Bloodshed, and havoc, on embattled realms,
And rescued monarchs from so black a guilt!
Bourbon! this wish how generous in a foe!
Would'st thou be great, would'st thou become a god,
And stick thy deathless name among the stars,
For mighty conquests on a needle's point?
Instead of forging chains for foreigners,
Bastile thy tutor: grandeur all thy aim?   1060
As yet thou know'st not what it is: how great,
How glorious, then, appears the mind of man,
When in it all the stars, and planets, roll!
And what it seems, it is: great objects make
Great minds, enlarging as their views enlarge;   1065
Those still more godlike, as these more divine.
      And more divine than these, thou canst not see.
Dazzled, o'erpower'd, with the delicious draught
Of miscellaneous splendours, how I reel
From thought to thought, inebriate, without end!
An Eden, this! a Paradise unlost!
I meet the Deity in every view,   1072
And tremble at my nakedness before him!

O that I could but reach the tree of life!
For here it grows, unguarded from our taste;
No flaming sword denies our entrance here;
Would man but gather, he might live for ever.
        Lorenzo! much of moral hast thou seen.
Of curious arts art thou more fond? Then mark
The mathematic glories of the skies,   1080
In number, weight, and measure, all ordain'd.
Lorenzo's boasted builders, Chance, and Fate,
Are left to finish his aërial towers;
Wisdom and choice, their well-known characters
Here deep impress; and claim it for their own.
Though splendid all, no splendour void of use;
Use rivals beauty; art contends with power;
No wanton waste, amid effuse expense;
The great Economist adjusting all
To prudent pomp, magnificently wise.   1090
How rich the prospect! and for ever new!
And newest to the man that views it most;
For newer still in infinite succeeds.
Then, these aërial racers, O how swift!
How the shaft loiters from the strongest string!
Spirit alone can distance the career.
Orb above orb ascending without end!
Circle in circle, without end, enclosed!
Wheel, within wheel; Ezekiel! like to thine!   1099
Like thine, it seems a vision or a dream;
Though seen, we labour to believe it true!
What involution! what extent! what swarms
Of worlds, that laugh at earth! immensely great!
Immensely distant from each other's spheres!
What, then, the wondrous space through which they roll?
At once it quite engulfs all human thought;
'Tis comprehension's absolute defeat.
        Nor think thou seest a wild disorder here;
Through this illustrious chaos to the sight,
Arrangement neat, and chastest order, reign.   1110
The path prescribed, inviolably kept,
Upbraids the lawless sallies of mankind.
Worlds, ever thwarting, never interfere;
What knots are tied! how soon are they dissolved,
And set the seeming married planets free!
They rove for ever, without error rove;
Confusion unconfused! nor less admire
This tumult untumultuous; all on wing!
In motion, all! yet what profound repose!

What fervid action, yet no noise! as awed   1120
To silence, by the presence of their Lord;
Or hush'd by His command, in love to man,
And bid let fall soft beams on human rest,
Restless themselves. On yon cerulean plain,
In exultation to their God, and thine,
They dance, they sing eternal jubilee,
Eternal celebration of His praise.
But, since their song arrives not at our ear,
Their dance perplex'd exhibits to the sight
Fair hieroglyphic of His peerless power.   1130
Mark how the labyrinthian turns they take,
The circles intricate, and mystic maze,
Weave the grand cipher of Omnipotence;   1133
To gods, how great! how legible to man!
        Leaves so much wonder greater wonder still?
Where are the pillars that support the skies?
What more than Atlantean shoulder props
Th' incumbent load? What magic, what strange art,
In fluid air these ponderous orbs sustains?
Who would not think them hung in golden chains?—   1140
And so they are; in the high will of heaven,
Which fixes all; makes adamant of air,
Or air of adamant; makes all of nought,
Or nought of all; if such the dread decree.
        Imagine from their deep foundations torn
The most gigantic sons of earth, the broad
And towering Alps, all toss'd into the sea;
And, light as down, or volatile as air,
Their bulks enormous, dancing on the waves,
In time, and measure, exquisite; while all   1150
The winds, in emulation of the spheres,
Tune their sonorous instruments aloft;
The concert swell, and animate the ball.
Would this appear amazing? What, then, worlds,
In a far thinner element sustain'd,
And acting the same part, with greater skill,
More rapid movement, and for noblest ends?
        More obvious ends to pass, are not these stars
The seats majestic, proud imperial thrones,
On which angelic delegates of heaven,   1160
At certain periods, as the Sovereign nods,
Discharge high trusts of vengeance, or of love;
To clothe, in outward grandeur, grand design,
And acts most solemn still more solemnize?
Ye citizens of air! what ardent thanks,

What full effusion of the grateful heart,
Is due from man indulged in such a sight! 1167
A sight so noble! and a sight so kind!
It drops new truths at every new survey!
Feels not Lorenzo something stir within,
That sweeps away all period? As these spheres
Measure duration, they no less inspire
The godlike hope of ages without end.
The boundless space, through which these rovers take
Their restless roam, suggests the sister thought
Of boundless time. Thus, by kind Nature's skill,
To man unlabour'd, that important guest,
Eternity, finds entrance at the sight:
And an eternity, for man ordain'd,
Or these his destined midnight counsellors, 1180
The stars, had never whisper'd it to man.
Nature informs, but ne'er insults, her sons.
Could she then kindle the most ardent wish
To disappoint it?—That is blasphemy.
Thus, of thy creed a second article,
Momentous, as th' existence of a God,
Is found (as I conceive) where rarely sought;
And thou may'st read thy soul immortal, here.
      Here, then, Lorenzo! on these glories dwell;
Nor want the gilt, illuminated, roof, 1190
That calls the wretched gay to dark delights.
Assemblies?—This is one divinely bright;
Here, unendanger'd in health, wealth, or fame,
Range through the fairest, and the Sultan scorn;
He, wise as thou, no crescent holds so fair,
As that, which on his turban awes a world;
And thinks the moon is proud to copy him.
Look on her, and gain more than worlds can give,
A mind superior to the charms of power.
Thou muffled in delusions of this life! 1200
Can yonder moon turn ocean in his bed, 1201
From side to side, in constant ebb, and flow,
And purify from stench his watery realms?
And fails her moral influence? wants she power
To turn Lorenzo's stubborn tide of thought
From stagnating on earth's infected shore,
And purge from nuisance his corrupted heart?
Fails her attraction when it draws to heaven?
Nay, and to what thou valuest more, earth's joy?
Minds elevate, and panting for unseen, 1210
And defecate from sense, alone obtain

Full relish of existence undeflower'd,
The life of life, the zest of worldly bliss:
All else on earth amounts—to what? to this:
"Bad to be suffer'd; blessings to be left:"
Earth's richest inventory boasts no more.

    Of higher scenes be, then, the call obey'd.
O let me gaze!—Of gazing there's no end.
O let me think!—Thought too is wilder'd here;
In midway flight imagination tires;   1220
Yet soon reprunes her wing to soar anew,
Her point unable to forbear, or gain;
So great the pleasure, so profound the plan!
A banquet, this, where men, and angels, meet,
Eat the same manna, mingle earth and heaven.
How distant some of these nocturnal suns!
So distant (says the sage), 'twere not absurd
To doubt, if beams, set out at Nature's birth,
Are yet arrived at this so foreign world;
Though nothing half so rapid as their flight.   1230
An eye of awe and wonder let me roll,
And roll for ever: who can satiate sight
In such a scene? in such an ocean wide
Of deep astonishment? where depth, height, breadth,
Are lost in their extremes; and where to count   1235
The thick-sown glories in this field of fire,
Perhaps a seraph's computation fails.
Now, go, Ambition! boast thy boundless might
In conquest, o'er the tenth part of a grain.
    And yet Lorenzo calls for miracles,
To give his tottering faith a solid base.
Why call for less than is already thine?   1242
Thou art no novice in theology;
What is a miracle?—'Tis a reproach,
'Tis an implicit satire, on mankind;
And while it satisfies, it censures too.
To common sense, great Nature's course proclaims
A Deity: when mankind falls asleep,
A miracle is sent, as an alarm;
To wake the world, and prove Him o'er again,   1250
By recent argument, but not more strong.
Say, which imports more plenitude of power,
Or nature's laws to fix, or to repeal?
To make a sun, or stop his mid career?
To countermand his orders, and send back
The flaming courier to the frighted east,
Warm'd, and astonish'd, at his evening ray?

Or bid the moon, as with her journey tired,
In Ajalon's soft, flowery vale repose?
Great things are these; still greater, to create.   1260
From Adam's bower look down through the whole train
Of miracles;—resistless is their power?
They do not, can not, more amaze the mind,
Than this, call'd unmiraculous survey,
If duly weigh'd, if rationally seen,
If seen with human eyes. The brute, indeed,
Sees nought but spangles here; the fool, no more.
Say'st thou, "The course of nature governs all?"
The course of Nature is the art of God.   1269
The miracles thou call'st for, this attest;
For say, could Nature Nature's course control?
    But, miracles apart, who sees Him not,
Nature's controller, author, guide, and end?
Who turns his eye on Nature's midnight face,
But must inquire—"What hand behind the scene,
What arm almighty, put these wheeling globes
In motion, and wound up the vast machine?
Who rounded in his palm these spacious orbs?
Who bowl'd them flaming through the dark profound,
Numerous as glittering gems of morning dew,   1280
Or sparks from populous cities in a blaze,
And set the bosom of old Night on fire?
Peopled her desert, and made horror smile?"
Or, if the military style delights thee
(For stars have fought their battles, leagued with man),
"Who marshals this bright host? enrols their names?
Appoints their posts, their marches, and returns,
Punctual, at stated periods? who disbands
These veteran troops, their final duty done,
If e'er disbanded?"—He, whose potent word,   1290
Like the loud trumpet, levied first their powers
In Night's inglorious empire, where they slept
In beds of darkness: arm'd them with fierce flames,
Arranged, and disciplined, and clothed in gold;
And call'd them out of chaos to the field,
Where now they war with vice and unbelief.
O let us join this army! joining these,
Will give us hearts intrepid, at that hour,
When brighter flames shall cut a darker night;
When these strong demonstrations of a God   1300
Shall hide their heads, or tumble from their spheres,
And one eternal curtain cover all!
    Struck at that thought, as new awaked, I lift   1303

A more enlighten'd eye, and read the stars
To man still more propitious; and their aid
(Though guiltless of idolatry) implore;
Nor longer rob them of their noblest name.
O ye dividers of my time! ye bright
Accountants of my days, and months, and years,
In your fair calendar distinctly mark'd!   1310
Since that authentic, radiant register,
Though man inspects it not, stands good against him;
Since you, and years, roll on, though man stands still;
Teach me my days to number, and apply
My trembling heart to wisdom; now beyond
All shadow of excuse for fooling on.
Age smooths our path to prudence; sweeps aside
The snares keen appetite and passion spread
To catch stray souls; and woe to that grey head,
Whose folly would undo, what age has done!   1320
Aid then, aid, all ye stars!—Much rather, Thou,
Great Artist! Thou, whose finger set aright
This exquisite machine, with all its wheels,
Though intervolved, exact; and pointing out
Life's rapid, and irrevocable flight,
With such an index fair, as none can miss,
Who lifts an eye, nor sleeps till it is closed.
Open mine eye, dread Deity! to read
The tacit doctrine of thy works; to see
Things as they are, unalter'd through the glass   1330
Of worldly wishes. Time, eternity!
('Tis these, mismeasured, ruin all mankind)
Set them before me; let me lay them both
In equal scale, and learn their various weight.
Let time appear a moment, as it is;
And let eternity's full orb, at once,
Turn on my soul, and strike it into heaven.   1337
When shall I see far more than charms me now?
Gaze on creation's model in thy breast
Unveil'd, nor wonder at the transcript more?
When this vile, foreign, dust, which smothers all
That travel earth's deep vale, shall I shake off?
When shall my soul her incarnation quit,
And, readopted to thy bless'd embrace,
Obtain her apotheosis in Thee?

    Dost think, Lorenzo, this is wandering wide?
No, 'tis directly striking at the mark;
To wake thy dead devotion was my point;
And how I bless Night's consecrating shades,

Which to a temple turn an universe; 1350
Fill us with great ideas, full of heaven,
And antidote the pestilential earth!
In every storm, that either frowns, or falls,
What an asylum has the soul in prayer!
And what a fane is this, in which to pray!
And what a God must dwell in such a fane!
Oh, what a genius must inform the skies!
And is Lorenzo's salamander heart
Cold, and untouch'd, amid these sacred fires?
O ye nocturnal sparks! ye glowing embers, 1360
On heaven's broad hearth! who burn, or burn no more,
Who blaze, or die, as Great Jehovah's breath
Or blows you, or forbears; assist my song;
Pour your whole influence; exorcise his heart,
So long possess'd; and bring him back to man.
        And is Lorenzo a demurrer still?
Pride in thy parts provokes thee to contest
Truths, which, contested, put thy parts to shame.
Nor shame they more Lorenzo's head than heart,
A faithless heart, how despicably small! 1370
Too strait, aught great or generous to receive! 1371
Fill'd with an atom! fill'd, and foul'd, with self!
And self mistaken! self, that lasts an hour!
Instincts and passions, of the nobler kind,
Lie suffocated there; or they alone,
Reason apart, would wake high hope; and open,
To ravish'd thought, that intellectual sphere,
Where order, wisdom, goodness, providence,
Their endless miracles of love display,
And promise all the truly great desire. 1380
The mind that would be happy, must be great;
Great, in its wishes; great, in its surveys.
Extended views a narrow mind extend;
Push out its corrugate, expansive make,
Which, ere long, more than planets shall embrace.
A man of compass makes a man of worth;
Divine contemplate, and become divine.
        As man was made for glory, and for bliss,
All littleness is in approach to woe;
Open thy bosom, set thy wishes wide, 1390
And let in manhood; let in happiness;
Admit the boundless theatre of thought
From nothing, up to God; which makes a man.
Take God from nature, nothing great is left;
Man's mind is in a pit, and nothing sees;

Man's heart is in a jakes, and loves the mire.
Emerge from thy profound; erect thine eye;
See thy distress! how close art thou besieged!
Besieged by Nature, the proud sceptic's foe!
Enclosed by these innumerable worlds,   1400
Sparkling conviction on the darkest mind,
As in a golden net of Providence.
How art thou caught, sure captive of belief!
From this thy bless'd captivity, what art,
What blasphemy to reason, sets thee free!   1405
This scene is heaven's indulgent violence:
Canst thou bear up against this tide of glory?
What is earth bosom'd in these ambient orbs,
But, faith in God imposed, and press'd on man?
Darest thou still litigate thy desperate cause,
Spite of these numerous, awful, witnesses,
And doubt the deposition of the skies?   1412
O how laborious is thy way to ruin!
    Laborious! 'tis impracticable quite;
To sink beyond a doubt, in this debate,
With all his weight of wisdom and of will,
And crime flagitious, I defy a fool.
Some wish they did; but no man disbelieves.
God is a spirit; spirit cannot strike
These gross, material organs; God by man   1420
As much is seen, as man a God can see,
In these astonishing exploits of power.
What order, beauty, motion, distance, size!
Concertion of design, how exquisite!
How complicate, in their divine police!
Apt means! great ends! consent to general good!—
Each attribute of these material gods,
So long (and that with specious pleas) adored,
A separate conquest gains o'er rebel thought;
And leads in triumph the whole mind of man.   1430
    Lorenzo! this may seem harangue to thee;
Such all is apt to seem, that thwarts our will.
And dost thou, then, demand a simple proof
Of this great master moral of the skies,
Unskill'd, or disinclined, to read it there?
Since 'tis the basis, and all drops without it,
Take it, in one compact, unbroken chain.
Such proof insists on an attentive ear;
'Twill not make one amid a mob of thoughts,   1439
And, for thy notice, struggle with the world.
Retire;—the world shut out;—thy thoughts call home;—

Imagination's airy wing repress;—
Lock up thy senses;—let no passion stir;—
Wake all to Reason;—let her reign alone;—
Then, in thy soul's deep silence, and the depth
Of Nature's silence, midnight, thus inquire,
As I have done; and shall inquire no more.
In nature's channel, thus the questions run:
    "What am I? and from whence?—I nothing know,
But that I am; and, since I am, conclude   1450
Something eternal: had there e'er been nought,
Nought still had been: eternal there must be.—
But what eternal?—Why not human race?
And Adam's ancestors without an end?—
That's hard to be conceived; since every link
Of that long-chain'd succession is so frail;
Can every part depend, and not the whole?
Yet grant it true; new difficulties rise;
I'm still quite out at sea; nor see the shore.
Whence earth, and these bright orbs?—eternal too?
Grant matter was eternal; still these orbs   1461
Would want some other father;—much design
Is seen in all their motions, all their makes;
Design implies intelligence, and art;
That can't be from themselves—or man; that art
Man scarce can comprehend, could man bestow?
And nothing greater yet allow'd than man.—
Who, motion, foreign to the smallest grain,
Shot through vast masses of enormous weight?
Who bid brute matter's restive lump assume   1470
Such various forms, and gave it wings to fly?
Has matter innate motion? then each atom,
Asserting its indisputable right   1473
To dance, would form an universe of dust:
Has matter none? Then whence these glorious forms
And boundless flights, from shapeless, and reposed?
Has matter more than motion? Has it thought,
Judgment, and genius? Is it deeply learn'd
In mathematics? Has it framed such laws,
Which but to guess, a Newton made immortal?—   1480
If so, how each sage atom laughs at me,
Who think a clod inferior to a man!
If art, to form; and counsel, to conduct;
And that with greater far than human skill;
Resides not in each block;—a Godhead reigns.—
Grant, then, invisible, eternal, Mind;
That granted, all is solved.—But, granting that,

Draw I not o'er me a still darker cloud?
Grant I not that which I can ne'er conceive?
A being without origin, or end!—   1490
Hail, human liberty! There is no God—
Yet, why? On either scheme that knot subsists;
Subsist it must, in God, or human race;
If in the last, how many knots beside,
Indissoluble all?—Why choose it there,
Where, chosen, still subsist ten thousand more?
Reject it, where, that chosen, all the rest
Dispersed, leave reason's whole horizon clear?
This is not reason's dictate; Reason says,
Close with the side where one grain turns the scale;—   1500
What vast preponderance is here! can reason
With louder voice exclaim—Believe a God?
And reason heard, is the sole mark of man.
What things impossible must man think true,
On any other system! and how strange
To disbelieve, through mere credulity!"

    If, in this chain, Lorenzo finds no flaw,   1507
Let it for ever bind him to belief.
And where the link, in which a flaw he finds?
And, if a God there is, that God how great!
How great that Power, whose providential care
Through these bright orbs' dark centres darts a ray!
Of nature universal threads the whole!
And hangs creation, like a precious gem,
Though little, on the footstool of his throne!

    That little gem, how large! A weight let fall
From a fix'd star, in ages can it reach
This distant earth! Say, then, Lorenzo! where,
Where, ends this mighty building? where, begin
The suburbs of creation? where, the wall   1520
Whose battlements look o'er into the vale
Of non-existence! Nothing's strange abode!
Say, at what point of space Jehovah dropp'd
His slacken'd line, and laid his balance by;
Weigh'd worlds, and measured infinite, no more?
Where, rears His terminating pillar high
Its extra-mundane head? and says, to gods,
In characters illustrious as the sun,—

    "I stand, the plan's proud period; I pronounce
The work accomplish'd; the creation closed: 1530
Shout, all ye gods! nor shout ye gods alone;
Of all that lives, or, if devoid of life,
That rests, or rolls, ye heights, and depths, resound!

Resound! resound! ye depths, and heights, resound!"

Hard are those questions!—answer harder still.
Is this the sole exploit, the single birth,
The solitary son of power divine?
Or has th' Almighty Father, with a breath,
Impregnated the womb of distant space?   1539
Has He not bid, in various provinces,
Brother-creations the dark bowels burst
Of night primeval; barren, now, no more?
And He the central sun, transpiercing all
Those giant generations, which disport
And dance, as motes, in his meridian ray;
That ray withdrawn, benighted, or absorb'd,
In that abyss of horror, whence they sprung;
While Chaos triumphs, repossess'd of all
Rival Creation ravish'd from his throne?
Chaos! of Nature both the womb, and grave!   1550
     Think'st thou my scheme, Lorenzo, spreads too wide?
Is this extravagant?—No; this is just;
Just, in conjecture, though 'twere false in fact.
If 'tis an error, 'tis an error sprung
From noble root, high thought of the Most High.
But wherefore error? who can prove it such?—
He that can set Omnipotence a bound.
Can man conceive beyond what God can do?
Nothing, but quite impossible is hard.
He summons into being, with like ease,   1560
A whole creation, and a single grain.
Speaks he the word? a thousand worlds are born!
A thousand worlds? there's space for millions more:
And in what space can his great fiat fail?
Condemn me not, cold critic! but indulge
The warm imagination: why condemn?
Why not indulge such thoughts, as swell our hearts
With fuller admiration of that Power,
Who gives our hearts with such high thoughts to swell?
Why not indulge in His augmented praise?   1570
Darts not His glory a still brighter ray,
The less is left to Chaos, and the realms
Of hideous Night, where Fancy strays aghast;   1573
And, though most talkative, makes no report?
     Still seems my thought enormous? Think again;—
Experience' self shall aid thy lame belief.
Glasses (that revelation to the sight!)
Have they not led us in the deep disclose
Of fine-spun nature, exquisitely small,

And, though demonstrated, still ill-conceived?   1580
If, then, on the reverse, the mind would mount
In magnitude, what mind can mount too far,
To keep the balance, and creation poise?
Defect alone can err on such a theme;
What is too great, if we the cause survey?
Stupendous Architect! Thou, Thou art all!
My soul flies up and down in thoughts of Thee,
And finds herself but at the centre still!
I AM, thy name! Existence, all thine own!
Creation's nothing; flatter'd much, if styled   1590
"The thin, the fleeting atmosphere of God."
        O for the voice—of what? of whom?—What voice
Can answer to my wants, in such ascent,
As dares to deem one universe too small?
Tell me, Lorenzo! (for now fancy glows;
Fired in the vortex of almighty power)
Is not this home creation, in the map
Of universal nature, as a speck,
Like fair Britannia in our little ball;
Exceeding fair, and glorious, for its size,   1600
But, elsewhere, far outmeasured, far outshone?
In fancy (for the fact beyond us lies)
Canst thou not figure it, an isle, almost
Too small for notice, in the vast of being;
Sever'd by mighty seas of unbuilt space
From other realms; from ample continents
Of higher life, where nobler natives dwell;   1607
Less northern, less remote from Deity,
Glowing beneath the line of the Supreme;
Where souls in excellence make haste, put forth
Luxuriant growths; nor the late autumn wait
Of human worth, but ripen soon to gods?
        Yet why drown fancy in such depths as these?
Return, presumptuous rover! and confess
The bounds of man; nor blame them, as too small.
Enjoy we not full scope in what is seen?
Pull ample the dominions of the sun!
Full glorious to behold! How far, how wide,
The matchless monarch, from his flaming throne,   1619
Lavish of lustre, throws his beams about him,
Farther, and faster, than a thought can fly,
And feeds his planets with eternal fires!
This Heliopolis,[1] by greater far,

---

[1] 'Heliopolis:' meaning the *City of the Sun.*

Than the proud tyrant of the Nile, was built;
And He alone, who built it, can destroy.
Beyond this city, why strays human thought?
One wonderful, enough for man to know!
One infinite! enough for man to range!
One firmament, enough for man to read!
O what voluminous instruction here!   1630
What page of wisdom is denied him? None;
If learning his chief lesson makes him wise.
Nor is instruction, here, our only gain;
There dwells a noble pathos in the skies,
Which warms our passions, proselytes our hearts.
How eloquently shines the glowing pole!
With what authority it gives its charge,
Remonstrating great truths in style sublime,
Though silent, loud! heard earth around; above
The planets heard; and not unheard in hell;   1640
Hell has her wonder, though too proud to praise.
Is earth, then, more infernal? Has she those,
Who neither praise (Lorenzo!) nor admire?
      Lorenzo's admiration, pre-engaged,
Ne'er ask'd the moon one question; never held
Least correspondence with a single star;
Ne'er rear'd an altar to the Queen of Heaven
Walking in brightness; or her train adored.
Their sublunary rivals have long since
Engross'd his whole devotion; stars malign,   1650
Which made the fond astronomer run mad;
Darken his intellect, corrupt his heart;
Cause him to sacrifice his fame and peace
To momentary madness, call'd delight.
Idolater, more gross than ever kiss'd
The lifted hand to Luna, or pour'd out
The blood to Jove!—O Thou, to whom belongs
All sacrifice! O Thou Great Jove unfeign'd!
Divine Instructor! Thy first volume, this,
For man's perusal; all in capitals!   1660
In moon, and stars (heaven's golden alphabet!)
Emblazed to seize the sight; who runs, may read;
Who reads, can understand. 'Tis unconfined
To Christian land, or Jewry; fairly writ,
In language universal, to mankind:
A language, lofty to the learn'd: yet plain
To those that feed the flock, or guide the plough,
Or, from his husk, strike out the bounding grain.
A language, worthy the Great Mind, that speaks!

Preface, and comment, to the sacred page! 1670
Which oft refers its reader to the skies,
As presupposing his first lesson there,
And Scripture self a fragment, that unread.
Stupendous book of wisdom, to the wise! 1674
Stupendous book! and open'd, Night! by thee.
     By thee much open'd, I confess, O Night!
Yet more I wish; but how shall I prevail?
Say, gentle Night! whose modest, maiden beams
Give us a new creation, and present
The world's great picture soften'd to the sight;
Nay, kinder far, far more indulgent still,
Say, thou, whose mild dominion's silver key 1682
Unlocks our hemisphere, and sets to view
Worlds beyond number; worlds conceal'd by day
Behind the proud and envious star of noon!
Canst thou not draw a deeper scene?—and show
The mighty Potentate, to whom belong
These rich regalia pompously display'd
To kindle that high hope? Like him of Uz,[1]
I gaze around; I search on every side— 1690
O for a glimpse of Him my soul adores!
As the chased hart, amid the desert waste,
Pants for the living stream; for Him who made her,
So pants the thirsty soul, amid the blank
Of sublunary joys. Say, goddess! where?
Where blazes His bright court? where burns His throne?
Thou know'st; for thou art near Him; by thee, round
His grand pavilion, sacred fame reports
The sable curtain drawn. If not, can none
Of thy fair daughter train, so swift of wing, 1700
Who travel far, discover where He dwells?
A star His dwelling pointed out below.
Ye Pleiades! Arcturus! Mazaroth!
And thou, Orion! of still keener eye!
Say ye, who guide the wilder'd in the waves,
And bring them out of tempest into port! 1706
On which hand must I bend my course to find Him?
These courtiers keep the secret of their King;
I wake whole nights, in vain, to steal it from them.
     I wake; and, waking, climb Night's radiant scale,
From sphere to sphere; the steps by nature set
For man's ascent; at once to tempt and aid;

---

[1] 'Him of Uz:' referring to Job's language, 'Oh that I knew where I might find him!'
&c.

227

To tempt his eye, and aid his towering thought;   1713
Till it arrives at the great goal of all.
    In ardent Contemplation's rapid car,
From earth, as from my barrier, I set out.
How swift I mount! Diminish'd earth recedes;
I pass the moon; and, from her farther side,
Pierce heaven's blue curtain; strike into remote;
Where, with his lifted tube, the subtle sage   1720
His artificial, airy journey takes,
And to celestial lengthens human sight.
I pause at every planet on my road,
And ask for Him who gives their orbs to roll,
Their foreheads fair to shine. From Saturn's ring,
In which, of earths an army might be lost,
With the bold comet, take my bolder flight,
Amid those sovereign glories of the skies,
Of independent, native lustre, proud;
The souls of systems! and the lords of life,   1730
Through their wide empires!—What behold I now?
A wilderness of wonder burning round;
Where larger suns inhabit higher spheres;
Perhaps the villas of descending gods;
Nor halt I here; my toil is but begun;
'Tis but the threshold of the Deity;
Or, far beneath it, I am grovelling still.
Nor is it strange; I built on a mistake;
The grandeur of his works, whence folly sought
For aid, to reason sets his glory higher;   1740
Who built thus high for worms (mere worms to Him),
Oh, where, Lorenzo! must the Builder dwell?
    Pause, then; and, for a moment, here respire—
If human thought can keep its station here.
Where am I?—Where is earth?—Nay, where art thou,
O sun?—Is the sun turn'd recluse?—and are
His boasted expeditions short to mine?—
To mine, how short! On nature's Alps I stand,
And see a thousand firmaments beneath!
A thousand systems! as a thousand grains!   1750
So much a stranger, and so late arrived,
How can man's curious spirit not inquire,
What are the natives of this world sublime,
Of this so foreign, unterrestrial sphere,
Where mortal, untranslated, never stray'd?
    "O ye, as distant from my little home,
As swiftest sunbeams in an age can fly!
Far from my native element I roam,

In quest of new, and wonderful, to man.
What province this, of His immense domain, 1760
Whom all obeys? Or mortals here, or gods?
Ye borderers on the coasts of bliss! what are you?
A colony from heaven? or, only raised,
By frequent visit from heaven's neighbouring realms,
To secondary gods, and half divine?—
Whate'er your nature, this is past dispute,
Far other life you live, far other tongue
You talk, far other thought, perhaps, you think,
Than man. How various are the works of God?
But say, what thought? Is Reason here enthroned, 1770
And absolute? or Sense in arms against her?
Have you two lights? Or need you no reveal'd?
Enjoy your happy realms their golden age?
And had your Eden an abstemious Eve? 1774
Our Eve's fair daughters prove their pedigree,
And ask their Adams—'Who would not be wise?'
Or, if your mother fell, are you redeem'd?
And if redeem'd—is your Redeemer scorn'd?
Is this your final residence? If not,
Change you your scene, translated? or by death?
And if by death; what death?—Know you disease?
Or horrid war?—With war, this fatal hour, 1782
Europa groans (so call we a small field,
Where kings run mad). In our world, Death deputes
Intemperance to do the work of Age;
And hanging up the quiver Nature gave him,
As slow of execution, for despatch
Sends forth imperial butchers; bids them slay
Their sheep (the silly sheep they fleeced before),
And toss him twice ten thousand at a meal. 1790
Sit all your executioners on thrones?
With you, can rage for plunder make a god?
And bloodshed wash out every other stain?—
But you, perhaps, can't bleed: from matter gross
Your spirits clean, are delicately clad
In fine-spun ether, privileged to soar,
Unloaded, uninfected; how unlike
The lot of man! how few of human race
By their own mud unmurder'd! how we wage
Self-war eternal!—Is your painful day 1800
Of hardy conflict o'er? or, are you still
Raw candidates at school? and have you those
Who disaffect reversions, as with us?—
But what are we? You never heard of man;

Or earth, the bedlam of the universe!
Where Reason (undiseased with you) runs mad,
And nurses Folly's children as her own;
Fond of the foulest. In the sacred mount   1808
Of holiness, where Reason is pronounced
Infallible; and thunders, like a god;
Even there, by saints, the demons are outdone;
What these think wrong, our saints refine to right;
And kindly teach dull hell her own black arts;
Satan, instructed, o'er their morals smiles.—
But this, how strange to you, who know not man!
Has the least rumour of our race arrived?
Call'd here Elijah in his flaming car?
Pass'd by you the good Enoch, on his road
To those fair fields, whence Lucifer was hurl'd;
Who brush'd, perhaps, your sphere in his descent,   1820
Stain'd your pure crystal ether, or let fall
A short eclipse from his portentous shade?
O that the fiend had lodged on some broad orb
Athwart his way; nor reach'd his present home,
Then blacken'd earth with footsteps foul'd in hell,
Nor wash'd in ocean, as from Rome he pass'd
To Britain's isle; too, too, conspicuous there!"
    But this is all digression: where is He,
That o'er heaven's battlements the felon hurl'd
To groans, and chains, and darkness? Where is He,   1830
Who sees creation's summit in a vale?
He, whom, while man is man, he can't but seek;
And if he finds, commences more than man?
O for a telescope His throne to reach!
Tell me, ye learn'd on earth! or blest above!
Ye searching, ye Newtonian angels! tell.
Where, your Great Master's orb? His planets, where?
Those conscious satellites, those morning stars,
First-born of Deity! from central love,
By veneration most profound, thrown off;   1840
By sweet attraction, no less strongly drawn;
Awed, and yet raptured; raptured, yet serene;   1842
Past thought illustrious, but with borrow'd beams;
In still approaching circles, still remote,
Revolving round the sun's eternal Sire?
Or sent, in lines direct, on embassies
To nations—in what latitude?—Beyond
Terrestrial thought's horizon!—And on what
High errands sent?—Here human effort ends;
And leaves me still a stranger to His throne.   1850

Full well it might! I quite mistook my road.
Born in an age more curious than devout;
More fond to fix the place of heaven, or hell,
Than studious this to shun, or that secure.
'Tis not the curious, but the pious path,
That leads me to my point: Lorenzo! know,
Without or star, or angel, for their guide,
Who worship God, shall find him. Humble Love,
And not proud Reason, keeps the door of heaven;
Love finds admission, where proud Science fails.   1860
Man's science is the culture of his heart;
And not to lose his plummet in the depths
Of nature, or the more profound of God.
Either to know, is an attempt that sets
The wisest on a level with the fool.
To fathom nature (ill attempted here!)
Past doubt is deep philosophy above;
Higher degrees in bliss archangels take,
As deeper learn'd; the deepest, learning still.
For, what a thunder of omnipotence   1870
(So might I dare to speak) is seen in all!
In man! in earth! in more amazing skies!
Teaching this lesson, Pride is loath to learn—
"Not deeply to discern, not much to know,
Mankind was born to wonder, and adore."

　　　And is there cause for higher wonder still,   1876
Than that which struck us from our past surveys?
Yes; and for deeper adoration too.
From my late airy travel unconfined,
Have I learn'd nothing?—Yes, Lorenzo! this:
Each of these stars is a religious house;
I saw their altars smoke, their incense rise;
And heard hosannas ring through every sphere,   1883
A seminary fraught with future gods.
Nature all o'er is consecrated ground,
Teeming with growths immortal, and divine.
The Great Proprietor's all-bounteous hand
Leaves nothing waste; but sows these fiery fields
With seeds of reason, which to virtues rise
Beneath His genial ray; and, if escaped   1890
The pestilential blasts of stubborn will,
When grown mature, are gather'd for the skies.
And is devotion thought too much on earth,
When beings, so superior, homage boast,
And triumph in prostrations to the Throne?
　　　But wherefore more of planets, or of stars?

Ethereal journeys, and, discover'd there,
Ten thousand worlds, ten thousand ways devout,
All nature sending incense to the Throne,
Except the bold Lorenzos of our sphere?   1900
Opening the solemn sources of my soul,
Since I have pour'd, like feign'd Eridanus,[1]
My flowing numbers o'er the flaming skies,
Nor see, of fancy, or of fact, what more
Invites the Muse.—Here turn we, and review
Our past nocturnal landscape wide:—then say,
Say, then, Lorenzo! with what burst of heart,
The whole, at once, revolving in his thought,
Must man exclaim, adoring, and aghast?   1909
"Oh, what a root! Oh, what a branch, is here!
Oh, what a Father! what a family!
Worlds! systems! and creations!—and creations,
In one agglomerated cluster, hung,
Great Vine![2] on Thee, on Thee the cluster hangs;
The filial cluster! infinitely spread
In glowing globes, with various being fraught;
And drinks (nectareous draught!) immortal life.
Or, shall I say (for who can say enough?)
A constellation of ten thousand gems,
(And, oh! of what dimension! of what weight!)   1920
Set in one signet, flames on the right hand
Of Majesty Divine! The blazing seal,
That deeply stamps, on all created mind,
Indelible, His sovereign attributes,
Omnipotence, and love! that, passing bound:
And this, surpassing that. Nor stop we here,
For want of power in God, but thought in man.
Even this acknowledged, leaves us still in debt:
If greater aught, that greater all is Thine,
Dread Sire!—Accept this miniature of Thee;   1930
And pardon an attempt from mortal thought,
In which archangels might have fail'd, unblamed."
        How such ideas of th' Almighty's power,
And such ideas of th' Almighty's plan
(Ideas not absurd), distend the thought
Of feeble mortals! Nor of them alone!
The fulness of the Deity breaks forth
In inconceivables to men, and gods.
Think, then, oh, think; nor ever drop the thought;

---

[1] 'Eridanus,' or Phaeton: famous for his fall from the chariot of the sun.
[2] 'Great Vine:' John xv. 1.

How low must man descend, when gods adore! 1940
Have I not, then, accomplish'd my proud boast?
Did I not tell thee, "We would mount, Lorenzo! 1942
And kindle our devotion at the stars"?
    And have I fail'd? and did I flatter thee?
And art all adamant? and dost confute
All urged, with one irrefragable smile?
Lorenzo! mirth how miserable here!
Swear by the stars, by Him who made them, swear,
Thy heart, henceforth, shall be as pure as they:
Then thou, like them, shalt shine; like them, shalt rise
From low to lofty; from obscure to bright; 1951
By due gradation, Nature's sacred law.
The stars, from whence?—Ask Chaos—he can tell.
These bright temptations to idolatry,
From darkness, and confusion, took their birth;
Sons of deformity! from fluid dregs
Tartarean, first they rose to masses rude;
And then, to spheres opaque; then dimly shone;
Then brighten'd; then blazed out in perfect day.
Nature delights in progress; in advance 1960
From worse to better: but, when minds ascend,
Progress, in part, depends upon themselves.
Heaven aids exertion; greater makes the great;
The voluntary little lessens more.
Oh, be a man! and thou shalt be a god!
And half self-made!—Ambition how divine!
    O thou, ambitious of disgrace alone!
Still undevout? unkindled?—Though high-taught,
School'd by the skies, and pupil of the stars;
Rank coward to the fashionable world! 1970
Art thou ashamed to bend thy knee to heaven?
Cursed fume of pride, exhaled from deepest hell!
Pride in religion is man's highest praise.
Bent on destruction! and in love with death!
Not all these luminaries, quench'd at once,
Were half so sad, as one benighted mind, 1976
Which gropes for happiness, and meets despair.
How, like a widow in her weeds, the Night,
Amid her glimmering tapers, silent sits!
How sorrowful, how desolate, she weeps
Perpetual dews, and saddens nature's scene!
A scene more sad sin makes the darken'd soul,
All comfort kills, nor leaves one spark alive. 1983
    Though blind of heart, still open is thine eye:
Why such magnificence in all thou seest?

Of matter's grandeur, know, one end is this,
To tell the rational, who gazes on it—
"Though that immensely great, still greater He,
Whose breast, capacious, can embrace, and lodge,
Unburden'd, nature's universal scheme;   1990
Can grasp creation with a single thought;
Creation grasp; and not exclude its Sire"—
To tell him farther—"It behoves him much
To guard th' important, yet depending, fate
Of being, brighter than a thousand suns:
One single ray of thought outshines them all."—
And if man hears obedient, soon he'll soar
Superior heights, and on his purple wing,
His purple wing bedropp'd with eyes of gold,
Rising, where thought is now denied to rise,   2000
Look down triumphant on these dazzling spheres.
      Why then persist?—No mortal ever lived
But, dying, he pronounced (when words are true)
The whole that charms thee, absolutely vain;
Vain, and far worse!—Think thou, with dying men;
Oh, condescend to think as angels think!
Oh, tolerate a chance for happiness!
Our nature such, ill choice ensures ill fate;
And hell had been, though there had been no God.
Dost thou not know, my new astronomer!   2010
Earth, turning from the sun, brings night to man?
Man, turning from his God, brings endless night;
Where thou canst read no morals, find no friend,
Amend no manners, and expect no peace.
How deep the darkness! and the groan, how loud!
And far, how far, from lambent are the flames!—
Such is Lorenzo's purchase! such his praise!
The proud, the politic, Lorenzo's praise!
Though in his ear, and levell'd at his heart,
I've half read o'er the volume of the skies.   2020
      For think not thou hast heard all this from me;
My song but echoes what great Nature speaks.
What has she spoken? Thus the goddess spoke,
Thus speaks for ever:—"Place, at nature's head,
A sovereign, which o'er all things rolls his eye,
Extends his wing, promulgates his commands,
But, above all, diffuses endless good;
To whom, for sure redress, the wrong'd may fly;
The vile, for mercy; and the pain'd, for peace;
By whom, the various tenants of these spheres,   2030
Diversified in fortunes, place, and powers,

Raised in enjoyment, as in worth they rise,
Arrive at length (if worthy such approach)
At that bless'd fountain-head, from which they stream;
Where conflict past redoubles present joy;
And present joy looks forward on increase;
And that, on more; no period! every step
A double boon! a promise, and a bliss."
How easy sits this scheme on human hearts!
It suits their make; it soothes their vast desires;   2040
Passion is pleased; and Reason asks no more;
'Tis rational! 'tis great!—But what is thine?
It darkens! shocks! excruciates! and confounds!
Leaves us quite naked, both of help, and hope,   2044
Sinking from bad to worse; few years, the sport
Of Fortune; then the morsel of Despair.
     Say, then, Lorenzo! (for thou know'st it well)
What's vice?—Mere want of compass in our thought.
Religion, what?—The proof of common sense.
How art thou hooted, where the least prevails!
Is it my fault, if these truths call thee fool?
And thou shalt never be miscall'd by me.   2052
Can neither shame, nor terror, stand thy friend;
And art thou still an insect in the mire?
How, like thy guardian angel, have I flown;
Snatch'd thee from earth; escorted thee through all
Th' ethereal armies; walk'd thee, like a god,
Through splendours of first magnitude, arranged
On either hand; clouds thrown beneath thy feet;
Close cruised on the bright paradise of God;   2060
And almost introduced thee to the Throne!
And art thou still carousing, for delight,
Rank poison; first, fermenting to mere froth,
And then subsiding into final gall?
To beings of sublime, immortal make,
How shocking is all joy, whose end is sure!
Such joy, more shocking still, the more it charms!
And dost thou choose what ends ere well begun;
And infamous, as short? And dost thou choose
(Thou, to whose palate glory is so sweet)   2070
To wade into perdition, through contempt,
Not of poor bigots only, but thy own?
For I have peep'd into thy cover'd heart,
And seen it blush beneath a boastful brow;
For, by strong guilt's most violent assault,
Conscience is but disabled, not destroy'd.
     O thou most awful being, and most vain!

Thy will, how frail! how glorious is thy power!   2078
Though dread eternity has sown her seeds
Of bliss, and woe, in thy despotic breast;
Though heaven, and hell, depend upon thy choice;
A butterfly comes cross, and both are fled.
Is this the picture of a rational?
This horrid image, shall it be most just?
Lorenzo! no: it cannot,—shall not, be,
If there is force in reason; or, in sounds
Chanted beneath the glimpses of the moon,
A magic, at this planetary hour,
When slumber locks the general lip, and dreams
Through senseless mazes hunt souls uninspired.   2090
Attend—the sacred mysteries begin—
My solemn night-born adjuration hear;
Hear, and I'll raise thy spirit from the dust;
While the stars gaze on this enchantment new;
Enchantment, not infernal, but divine!
    "By silence, Death's peculiar attribute;
By darkness, Guilt's inevitable doom;
By Darkness, and by Silence, sisters dread!
That draw the curtain round Night's ebon throne,
And raise ideas, solemn as the scene!   2100
By Night, and all of awful, Night presents
To thought, or sense (of awful much, to both,
The goddess brings)! By these her trembling fires,
Like Vesta's, ever burning; and, like hers,
Sacred to thoughts immaculate, and pure!
By these bright orators, that prove, and praise,
And press thee to revere, the Deity;
Perhaps, too, aid thee, when revered a while,
To reach his throne; as stages of the soul,
Through which, at different periods, she shall pass,   2110
Refining gradual, for her final height,
And purging off some dross at every sphere!   2112
By this dark pall thrown o'er the silent world!
By the world's kings, and kingdoms, most renown'd,
From short ambition's zenith set for ever;
Sad presage to vain boasters, now in bloom!
By the long list of swift mortality,
From Adam downward to this evening knell,
Which midnight waves in Fancy's startled eye;
And shocks her with an hundred centuries,   2120
Round Death's black banner throng'd, in human thought!
By thousands, now, resigning their last breath,
And calling thee—wert thou so wise to hear!

By tombs o'er tombs arising; human earth
Ejected, to make room for—human earth;
The monarch's terror! and the sexton's trade!
By pompous obsequies that shun the day,
The torch funereal, and the nodding plume,
Which makes poor man's humiliation proud;
Boast of our ruin! triumph of our dust!   2130
By the damp vault that weeps o'er royal bones;
And the pale lamp that shows the ghastly dead,
More ghastly, through the thick incumbent gloom!
By visits (if there are) from darker scenes,
The gliding spectre! and the groaning grave!
By groans, and graves, and miseries that groan
For the grave's shelter! By desponding men,
Senseless to pains of death, from pangs of guilt!
By guilt's last audit! By yon moon in blood,
The rocking firmament, the falling stars,   2140
And thunder's last discharge, great nature's knell!
By second chaos; and eternal night"—
Be wise—nor let Philander blame my charm;
But own not ill discharged my double debt,
Love to the living; duty to the dead.

    For know I'm but executor; he left   2146
This moral legacy; I make it o'er
By his command; Philander hear in me;
And Heaven in both.—If deaf to these, oh! hear
Florello's tender voice; his weal depends
On thy resolve; it trembles at thy choice;
For his sake—love thyself. Example strikes
All human hearts; a bad example more;   2153
More still a father's; that ensures his ruin.
As parent of his being, would'st thou prove
Th' unnatural parent of his miseries,
And make him curse the being which thou gavest?
Is this the blessing of so fond a father?
If careless of Lorenzo! spare, oh! spare
Florello's father, and Philander's friend!   2160
Florello's father ruin'd, ruins him;
And from Philander's friend the world expects
A conduct, no dishonour to the dead.
Let passion do, what nobler motive should;
Let love, and emulation, rise in aid
To reason; and persuade thee to be—blest.

    This seems not a request to be denied;
Yet (such th' infatuation of mankind!)
'Tis the most hopeless, man can make to man.

Shall I then rise, in argument, and warmth?   2170
And urge Philander's posthumous advice,
From topics yet unbroach'd?——
But, oh! I faint! my spirits fail!—Nor strange!
So long on wing, and in no middle clime!
To which my great Creator's glory call'd:
And calls—but, now, in vain. Sleep's dewy wand
Has stroked my drooping lips, and promises
My long arrear of rest; the downy god
(Wont to return with our returning peace)
Will pay, ere long, and bless me with repose.   2180
Haste, haste, sweet stranger! from the peasant's cot,
The shipboy's hammock, or the soldier's straw,
Whence sorrow never chased thee; with thee bring,
Not hideous visions, as of late; but draughts
Delicious of well-tasted, cordial, rest;
Man's rich restorative; his balmy bath,
That supples, lubricates, and keeps in play
The various movements of this nice machine,
Which asks such frequent periods of repair.
When tired with vain rotations of the day,   2190
Sleep winds us up for the succeeding dawn;
Fresh we spin on, till sickness clogs our wheels,
Or death quite breaks the spring, and motion ends.
When will it end with me?
                              ——"Thou only know'st,
Thou, whose broad eye the future, and the past,
Joins to the present; making one of three
To moral thought! Thou know'st, and Thou alone,
All-knowing!—all unknown!—and yet well known!
Near, though remote! and, though unfathom'd, felt!   2200
And, though invisible, for ever seen!
And seen in all! the great and the minute:
Each globe above, with its gigantic race,
Each flower, each leaf, with its small people swarm'd,
(Those puny vouchers of Omnipotence!)
To the first thought, that asks, 'From whence?' declare
Their common source. Thou Fountain, running o'er
In rivers of communicated joy!
Who gavest us speech for far, far humbler themes!
Say, by what name shall I presume to call   2210
Him I see burning in these countless suns,
As Moses, in the bush? Illustrious Mind!
The whole creation, less, far less, to Thee,
Than that to the creation's ample round.   2214
How shall I name Thee?—How my labouring soul

Heaves underneath the thought, too big for birth!
　"Great System of perfections! Mighty Cause
Of causes mighty! Cause uncaused! sole Root
Of nature, that luxuriant growth of God!
First Father of effects! that progeny
Of endless series; where the golden chain's
Last link admits a period, who can tell?　　　　　　　2222
Father of all that is or heard, or hears!
Father of all that is or seen, or sees!
Father of all that is, or shall arise!
Father of this immeasurable mass
Of matter multiform; or dense, or rare;
Opaque, or lucid; rapid, or at rest;
Minute, or passing bound! in each extreme
Of like amaze, and mystery, to man.　　　　　　　　2230
Father of these bright millions of the night!
Of which the least full godhead had proclaim'd,
And thrown the gazer on his knee—or, say,
Is appellation higher still, Thy choice?
Father of matter's temporary lords!
Father of spirits! nobler offspring! sparks
Of high paternal glory; rich endow'd
With various measures, and with various modes
Of instinct, reason, intuition; beams
More pale, or bright from day divine, to break　　　2240
The dark of matter organized (the ware
Of all created spirit); beams, that rise
Each over other in superior light,
Till the last ripens into lustre strong,
Of next approach to Godhead. Father fond
(Far fonder than e'er bore that name on earth)
Of intellectual beings! beings bless'd
With powers to please Thee; not of passive ply　　2248
To laws they know not; beings lodged in seats
Of well-adapted joys, in different domes
Of this imperial palace for thy sons;
Of this proud, populous, well policied,
Though boundless habitation, plann'd by Thee:
Whose several clans their several climates suit;
And transposition, doubtless, would destroy.
Or, oh! indulge, immortal King, indulge
A title, less august indeed, but more
Endearing; ah! how sweet in human ears!
Sweet in our ears, and triumph in our hearts!
Father of immortality to man!　　　　　　　　　　2260

A theme that lately¹ set my soul on fire.—
And Thou the next! yet equal! Thou, by whom
That blessing was convey'd; far more! was bought;
Ineffable the price! by whom all worlds
Were made; and one redeem'd! illustrious Light
From Light illustrious! Thou, whose regal power,
Finite in time, but infinite in space,
On more than adamantine basis fix'd,
O'er more, far more, than diadems, and thrones,
Inviolably reigns; the dread of gods!   2270
And oh! the friend of man! beneath whose foot,
And by the mandate of whose awful nod,
All regions, revolutions, fortunes, fates,
Of high, of low, of mind, and matter, roll
Through the short channels of expiring time,
Or shoreless ocean of eternity,
Calm, or tempestuous (as thy Spirit breathes),
In absolute subjection!—And, O Thou
The glorious Third! distinct, not separate!
Beaming from both! with both incorporate;   2280
And (strange to tell!) incorporate with dust!   2281
By condescension, as Thy glory, great,
Enshrined in man! Of human hearts, if pure,
Divine inhabitant! The tie divine
Of heaven with distant earth! by whom, I trust
(If not inspired), uncensured this address
To Thee, to Them—to whom?—Mysterious Power!
Reveal'd—yet unreveal'd! darkness in light;
Number in unity! our joy! our dread!
The triple bolt that lays all wrong in ruin!   2290
That animates all right, the triple sun!
Sun of the soul! her never-setting sun!
Triune, unutterable, unconceived,
Absconding, yet demonstrable, Great God!
Greater than greatest! better than the best!
Kinder than kindest! with soft pity's eye,
Or (stronger still to speak it) with Thine own,
From Thy bright home, from that high firmament,
Where Thou, from all eternity, hast dwelt;
Beyond archangels' unassisted ken;   2300
From far above what mortals highest call;
From elevation's pinnacle; look down,
Through—what? Confounding interval! through all
And more than labouring Fancy can conceive;

¹ 'Lately:' Nights Sixth and Seventh.

Through radiant ranks of essences unknown;
Through hierarchies from hierarchies detach'd
Round various banners of Omnipotence,
With endless change of rapturous duties fired;
Through wondrous being's interposing swarms,
All clustering at the call, to dwell in Thee;   2310
Through this wide waste of worlds! this vista vast,
All sanded o'er with suns; suns turn'd to night
Before thy feeblest beam—Look down—down—down,
On a poor breathing particle in dust,
Or, lower, an immortal in his crimes.   2315
His crimes forgive! forgive his virtues, too!
Those smaller faults, half converts to the right.
Nor let me close these eyes, which never more
May see the sun (though night's descending scale
Now weighs up morn), unpitied, and unblest!
In Thy displeasure dwells eternal pain;
Pain, our aversion; pain, which strikes me now;
And, since all pain is terrible to man,   2323
Though transient, terrible; at Thy good hour,
Gently, ah, gently, lay me in my bed,
My clay-cold bed! by nature, now, so near;
By nature, near; still nearer by disease!
Till then, be this an emblem of my grave:
Let it out-preach the preacher; every night
Let it out-cry the boy at Philip's ear;[1]   2330
That tongue of death! that herald of the tomb!
And when (the shelter of Thy wing implored)
My senses, soothed, shall sink in soft repose,
Oh, sink this truth still deeper in my soul,
Suggested by my pillow, sign'd by fate,
First, in Fate's volume, at the page of man—
Man's sickly soul, though turn'd and toss'd for ever,
From side to side, can rest on nought but Thee:
Here, in full trust, hereafter, in full joy;
On Thee, the promised, sure, eternal down   2340
Of spirits, toil'd in travel through this vale.
Nor of that pillow shall my soul despond;
For—Love almighty! Love almighty! (sing,
Exult, creation!) Love almighty, reigns!
That death of Death! that cordial of despair!
And loud Eternity's triumphant song!
      "Of whom, no more:—For, O thou Patron-God!
Thou God and mortal! thence more God to man!   2348

---

[1] 'Philip's ear:' 'Remember, Philip, thou art mortal.'

Man's theme eternal! man's eternal theme!
Thou canst not 'scape uninjured from our praise.
Uninjured from our praise can He escape,
Who, disembosom'd from the Father, bows
The heaven of heavens, to kiss the distant earth!
Breathes out in agonies a sinless soul!
Against the cross, Death's iron sceptre breaks!
From famish'd Ruin plucks her human prey!
Throws wide the gates celestial to his foes!
Their gratitude, for such a boundless debt,
Deputes their suffering brothers to receive!
And, if deep human guilt in payment fails;   2360
As deeper guilt prohibits our despair!
Enjoins it, as our duty, to rejoice!
And (to close all) omnipotently kind,
Takes his delights among the sons of men."[1]
        What words are these—and did they come from heaven?
And were they spoke to man? to guilty man?
What are all mysteries to love like this?
The songs of angels, all the melodies
Of choral gods, are wafted in the sound;
Heal and exhilarate the broken heart;   2370
Though plunged, before, in horrors dark as night.
Rich prelibation of consummate joy!
Nor wait we dissolution to be blest.
        This final effort of the moral Muse,
How justly titled![2] Nor for me alone:
For all that read; what spirit of support,
What heights of Consolation, crown my song!
        Then, farewell Night! of darkness, now, no more:
Joy breaks, shines, triumphs; 'tis eternal day.
Shall that which rises out of nought complain   2380
Of a few evils, paid with endless joys?   2381
My soul! henceforth, in sweetest union join
The two supports of human happiness,
Which some, erroneous, think can never meet;
True taste of life, and constant thought of death!
The thought of death, sole victor of its dread!
Hope, be thy joy; and probity thy skill;
Thy patron He, whose diadem has dropp'd
Yon gems of heaven; eternity, thy prize:
And leave the racers of the world their own,   2390
Their feather, and their froth, for endless toils:

---

[1] Prov. viii. 31.
[2] 'Titled:' The Consolation.

They part with all for that which is not bread;
They mortify, they starve, on wealth, fame, power;
And laugh to scorn the fools that aim at more.
How must a spirit, late escaped from earth,—
Suppose Philander's, Lucia's, or Narcissa's,—
The truth of things new-blazing in its eye,
Look back, astonish'd, on the ways of men,
Whose lives' whole drift is to forget their graves!
And when our present privilege is past,   2400
To scourge us with due sense of its abuse,
The same astonishment will seize us all.
What then must pain us, would preserve us now.
Lorenzo! 'tis not yet too late; Lorenzo!
Seize Wisdom, ere 'tis torment to be wise;
That is, seize Wisdom, ere she seizes thee.
For what, my small philosopher! is hell?
'Tis nothing but full knowledge of the truth,
When Truth, resisted long, is sworn our foe;
And calls Eternity to do her right.   2410
        Thus, darkness aiding intellectual light,
And sacred silence whispering truths divine,
And truths divine converting pain to peace,
My song the midnight raven has outwing'd,
And shot, ambitious of unbounded scenes,   2415
Beyond the flaming limits of the world,
Her gloomy flight. But what avails the flight
Of fancy, when our hearts remain below?
Virtue abounds in flatterers, and foes;
'Tis pride, to praise her; penance, to perform.
To more than words, to more than worth of tongue,
Lorenzo! rise, at this auspicious hour;
An hour, when Heaven's most intimate with man;
When, like a fallen star, the ray divine
Glides swift into the bosom of the just;   2425
And just are all, determined to reclaim;
Which sets that title high within thy reach.
Awake, then; thy Philander calls: awake!
Thou, who shalt wake, when the creation sleeps;
When, like a taper, all these suns expire;
When Time, like him of Gaza[1] in his wrath,
Plucking the pillars that support the world,
In Nature's ample ruins lies entomb'd;
And Midnight, universal Midnight! reigns.   2434

---

[1] 'Him of Gaza:' Samson.

Made in the USA
Monee, IL
09 November 2020